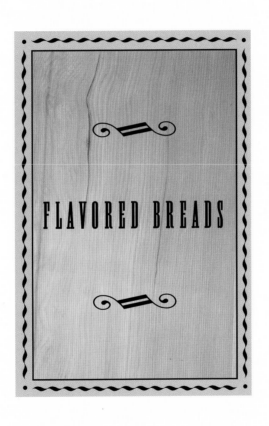

FLAVORED BREADS

FLAVORED BREADS

RECIPES FROM MARK MILLER'S COYOTE CAFE

**MARK MILLER
AND ANDREW MACLAUCHLAN
WITH JOHN HARRISSON**

Photography by Judith Vejvoda and Scott Vlaun

Ten Speed Press
Berkeley, California

Ten Speed Press
Box 7123
Berkeley, California 94707

Distributed in Australia by E. J. Dwyer Pty. Ltd., in Canada by Publishers Group West, in
New Zealand by Tandem Press, in South Africa by Real Books, and in the United King-
dom and Europe by Airlift Books.

Cover and text design by Morla Design, San Francisco.
Cover and text design implemented by Jaime Robles.
Photographs on pages 30, 55, and 72 by JudithVejvoda.
Photograph on page13 by Scott Vlaun.
All other photographs by Judith Vejvoda and Scott Vlaun.

Liberty Ale, used in Liberty Ale Rye on page 71, is a registered trademark of the Anchor
Brewing Company, San Francisco.
Sonoma Jack cheese, used in Sonoma Jack Bread on page 134, is a registered trademark
of the Sonoma Cheese Factory, Sonoma, CA.

Library of Congress Cataloging-in-Publication Data

Miller, Mark, Charles, 1949–
Flavored breads : recipes from Mark Miller's
Coyote Cafe / Mark Miller and Andrew
MacLauchlan with John Harrisson : photography by Judith
Vejvoda and Scott Vlaun.
p.   cm.
Includes bibliographical references and index.
ISBN 0-89815-862-1 (paper : alk. paper).
ISBN 0-89815-889-3 (cloth : alk. paper)
1. Bread. 2. Cookery, American—Southwestern style. 3. Cookery, American—Western
style.
 4. Coyote Cafe (Santa Fe, N.M.)
I. MacLauchlan, Andrew. II. Harrisson, John. III. Title.
TX769.M555 1996
641. 8
15—dc20   96-32861
                            CIP

Printed in China

First printing, 1996

1 2 3 4 5 6 7 8 9 10 — 00 99 98 97 96

For Mother Earth,
who gives us grains
in abundance

CONTENTS

Please see page 204 for a very important note about altitude

There is nothing more positive than bread.

— **Fyodor Dostoyevsky**

BREAD IN ANCIENT TIMES & CONTEMPORARY LIFE

Times are changing. In today's age of virtual reality, we are demanding more *real* foods. Nothing is more real than great bread, with its complex flavor, yeasty aroma, and crunchy crust. After decades of being supplanted by tasteless mass-produced loaves, real bread is enjoying a revival, finally appreciated for the wholesome, nourishing food that it is. It's become more than a convenient filler to dabble with until the main meal arrives or two forgettable white slabs sandwiching peanut butter and anchovies.

Bread enjoys one of the longest and most interesting histories of any food. Bread has paralleled the development of humankind, and its significance is only truly understood when considered in a historical context.While the ancient Egyptians are credited with developing leavened bread, flatbreads and hearth cakes have been part of the human diet for millennia. Over 10,000 years ago, small communities on different continents were established in areas where the most productive wild grasses grew. Over time, these grasses were domesticated and developed into the cereal staples we recognize today—wheat, corn, rye, barley, oats, rice, and millet, to name just a few of the most important. These early grains were made into the first breads—flatbreads. The grains were harvested, toasted, and ground into flour, mixed with water, and cooked on hot rocks. Contemporary flatbreads, such as tortillas, corn pone, chapatis, lavash, focacce, and Chinese pancakes, all evolved from this practice, and are still used every day in most of the world's cuisines.

Between 4,000 and 5,000 BC Egyptians in the Nile Valley refined methods of farming wheat, which would become the basic cereal crop of western civilization. In Turkey, Persia, and other parts of the Middle East (and even in parts of Europe) wheat was cultivated as early as 7,500 BC.

We know from hieroglyphics in the pyramids and other archeological sites that Egyptians attached great importance to harvesting grain and bread making. These pictorial histories also show that grain and bread were considered sacred gifts from the gods and used as ceremonial offerings (wheat grains were one of the foods typically buried with the pharaohs in the pyramids), and bakers belonged to a sacred order who enjoyed the same status as priests. Hieroglyphics also suggest that the Egyptians made the first leavened breads by using the sourdough method, deriving a fermented starter from a previous batch of dough. Simultaneously, yeast was used to create beer, which the Egyptians also developed.

It was the Egyptians who invented ovens to bake leavened breads, and although these oven-baked, refined breads were consumed by the affluent, simpler forms of bread were the primary food for the rest of the population. In fact, bread was so significant that the administrative system was based on it; even wealth was measured by "numbers of breads," and wages were paid, in part, in bread (this is probably the origin of our slang usage of the word "bread," or similarly "dough," meaning "money"). Other ancient peoples referred to the Egyptians (sometimes disparagingly) as "the bread eaters." Egyptians were almost certainly the first to flavor their breads; among the ingredients they used were honey, herbs, sesame seeds, anise, poppy seeds, and camphor. They also shaped their breads and created intriguing designs. One popular form was a molded, pyramid-shaped bread. Ancient writings describe more than fifty types of bread made and consumed by early Egyptians.

Wheat was the most valuable crop of the ancient world. It was made into bread, porridge or mush, and hearth cakes and was a staple for ancient Greeks and Romans. Both cultures were sustained by enormous quantities of imported wheat and were driven to expand by the need to secure and establish new sources of wheat to feed their growing populations. Whole fleets and navies were built with the prime objective of transporting (mostly from Egypt) and protecting the grain, and the decline in supply by the cutting of these trade routes ultimately contributed to the demise of both empires. In Rome, the complimentary wheat Roman emperors often received was distributed free to the poorer citizens, hence the exaggeration coined by the satirical writer Juvenal that society at large was ruled, and satisfied, by the provision of "bread and circuses."

The Greeks developed the earliest millstones for grinding as well as the bread oven as we know it today: a chamber that can be preheated, that has an opening at the front, and that can be closed during the baking process. The Romans refined the technology for both millstones and ovens, creating finely textured bread for the first time. The Romans even had a goddess of the oven, Fornax, and developed dried yeast from fermented sundried grapes. Roman bread was more elaborate than the Egyptians', and Roman bakers were designated as highly skilled craftsmen whose rights were guaranteed by a state-established guild. These craftsmen fashioned bread in a variety of different shapes, and the shaping of bread became an important aspect of the craft. Special designs were specifically created for certain occasions and celebrations. Modern-day pizza (and the pissaladière of southern France) are the direct descendants of a type of Roman bread called *piada*. By 500 BC at least 80 different types of bread were available in Rome. The importance of bread, and concern for its availability, is further indicated by the many references made to it in the Bible—including "Cast thy bread upon the waters," "I am the bread of life," and "Give us this day our daily bread."

The introduction of wind- and water-powered mills to early medieval Europe from the Middle East transformed bread making, and bakers accorded craftsman status worked in all the major cities from the sixth century on. However, bread was often made with grains such as barley, rye, and oats rather than wheat, which was relatively expensive, especially in northern Europe, because of high transportation costs. The production of bread played an important role in the feudal system, and (brown) bread played a disproportionately large role in the diet of the peasantry; bread of all kinds truly was the "staff of life" for all in the Middle Ages. In fact, bread was considered such an important staple in France that laws enabling the government to mandate its price were established in the seventh century and only repealed in 1981. In the eleventh century, bakers' guilds were established to standardize and control bread making, but selling underweight and adulterated bread remained common, despite harsh punishments. Until Renaissance times, a standard meal consisted of a thick slice of bread called a "trencher," on which meat, vegetables, or sauces were placed, often to feed two. (The medieval word "trencherman" refers either to someone with a hearty appetite or sharers of bread.)

The Spanish and, later, other European settlers brought wheat with them to the New World and carried corn back to Europe. However, it took a while for wheat to become an established crop in the Americas. Meanwhile, the abundance of corn saved many of the early settlements from famine. Settlers and farmers alike developed a taste for corn in many forms, including bread, but by the late 1800s, the Midwest was blanketed with wheat and the United States became the largest wheat-producing nation in the world—a status it has held ever since. During the Civil War, the Senate's quarters in the Capitol building in Washington, DC, were transformed into a bakery that supplied the Union forces with wheat bread. (As authors Evan and Judith Jones point out this may well have been the most productive period in the history of congress!) Although wheat bread became the standard once wheat flour was available, corn bread remains a popular tradition in certain parts of the United States—particularly in the South and Southwest.

The agricultural revolution that took place in Europe in the eighteenth century and the new technology that the Industrial Revolution brought changed the faces of farming and bread making. The system of crop rotation was introduced on a widespread basis both in Europe and, later, in the United States, and new high-yield strains of wheat were developed. Faster milling technology developed in the nineteenth century matched the growth in wheat production, and as a result wheat (and bread) became more widely available and affordable, literally sustaining the rapidly growing populations on both sides of the Atlantic. Increasingly, families made bread at home, either out of convenience or preference, so that by the turn of the twentieth century, almost all flour sold was used in the home. Since then, changes in lifestyle and baking habits, and the growth of baking into the largest food-processing industry in the United States, have caused this figure to decline precipitously, to about 15 percent.

The phrase "you are what you eat" has always especially applied to bread. Ever since ancient Greek and Roman times, bread has been a measure of a group's social status. "To know the color of one's bread" was a popular phrase that referred to knowing one's social station; the darker the bread, the lower one was on the class scale. The word "lord" is derived from the Anglo-Saxon word "hlaford," meaning "loaf ward," or the provider of the bread; likewise, "lady," from "hlaefdige," or "loaf maker." Leavened white bread has always been seen as a symbol of refinement and wealth because it was more processed and more costly. The pure unleavened white bread offered by the Christian church as the Eucharistic Host to represent the bread of (spiritual) life further exalted the symbolism and significance of white bread.

Conversely, brown, whole-wheat breads (as well as unleavened flatbreads of any kind) were viewed by the aristocracies of western societies as inferior and only for those who could not afford anything better. Ironically, white bread was often adulterated with powdered chalk, bone, plaster of Paris, and other additives. Nevertheless, the "purity" of refined white flour was deemed the quintessential symbol of civilization. This bias has been consistently perpetuated in virtually all societies—including our own—until the present day. Even as recently as twenty years ago, brown bread containing the germ and bran of whole wheat and, consequently, nutrition and flavor characteristics not present in white bread, was often hard to find.

The decline in home bread baking since the turn of the twentieth century is reversing, due in part to increasing awareness of the nutritional and flavor qualities inherent in bread and to the invention of home bread machines, which make the labor-intensive task of baking bread delightfully easy. More than ten million bread machines have been purchased over the last few years in the United States, and the aroma of home-baked, crusty loaves once more fills the air. Part of the pleasure we derive from making bread comes from turning raw ingredients into food of real substance—bread is truly greater than the sum of its parts. Bread was one of the first complex masterpieces in the history of cuisine, and we have come to recognize that bread baking mirrors elemental processes, symbolizing man's transformation of natural raw materials into cultural artifact.

As we knead dough in our home kitchens, it is humbling yet inspiring to acknowledge that we are reliving a creative process practiced by our ancient ancestors. Whether you use a bread machine or make these recipes the time-honored, old-fashioned way—by hand—this book celebrates the innovative potential of bread, and explores the limitless range of easy-to-make, economical styles and flavorings.

Until the last few years, during which we have seen quality bakeries spring into production all over the country, bread had become an overlooked resource in America. It was a food we took for granted. We would nonchalantly grab loaves off supermarket shelves, primarily because the range of tastes, textures, and shapes was too limited to inspire more discriminating shopping. Bread had become mass-produced and bland. Then, in the 1970s, the American bread revolution began, with individuals like Alice Waters (Chez Panisse, Berkeley), Nancy Silverton (first at Spago and now at La Brea Bakery, Los Angeles), Steve Sullivan (Acme Bakery, Berkeley), and Noel Comess (Tom Cat Bakery, New York) leading the way and putting tasty, *real* breads back on the map. They reminded us that bread is much more than just an accompaniment, that it is a food to be enjoyed for its own special qualities. As a consequence, we are now rediscovering the pleasure of bread and learning to appreciate the long and distinguished legacy of one of humankind's seminal foods.

My philosophy about breads can be summed up in three words: More is better! That's why, from the very beginning, at Coyote Cafe we chose to offer a variety of flavored breads, usually imbued with the vibrant, zesty flavors of the Southwest. These breads call attention to themselves and let you know they are not just an afterthought or to be marginalized as side dishes. They provide a medium for creativity, they deserve time and respect, and they carry on a long-standing important tradition. Best of all, they taste so good! Bread is a basic food that is good for you on many levels—just smelling and tasting it should infuse you with happiness, and the creative process of making it should fill you with satisfaction. I hope these recipes will bring excitement, adventure, and good memories to your table, just as they have to mine.

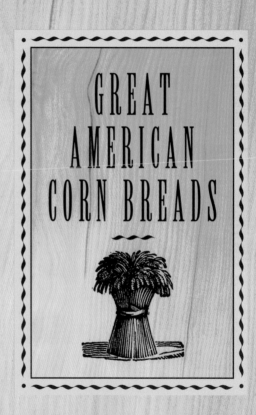

GREAT
AMERICAN
CORN BREADS

Corn is as American as apple pie and hot fudge sundaes. It has long been the most important food plant of the New World—a form of green-sheathed gold that has proved more valuable than the metal. The story of corn is a long one. For 7,000 years, it sustained the civilizations of Mesoamerica and North America, growing nowhere else on the planet. In these cultures, corn was exalted as a gift from the gods, the origin of life, a symbol of fertility and regeneration. The Mayans and Aztecs believed that mankind was directly created from corn. Among the reverential names bestowed on corn by various cultures are Sacred Mother, Giver of Life, and Seed of Seeds. These agricultural societies were far more advanced than most of their contemporaries elsewhere in the world. For example, they practiced the earliest form of genetic engineering by culturally selecting types of corn for specific characteristics such as size, color, and flavor and for its ability to prosper in different microclimates, growing seasons, terrains, and altitudes. Over the millennia they progressively developed corn from its original form—a coarse wild grass—into a complex plant with thousands of different varieties.

On November 5, 1492, Columbus, who was on his first voyage to the Caribbean, became the first European to mention corn when he recorded in his diary that "it is good-tasting and all the people in this land live on it." The early settlers who later landed on the North American mainland were astonished to learn that this enormous grain could grow in just 90 days and were equally impressed by the extent of its cultivation—the vast fields of green and yellow seemed to occupy all of the open land. Corn was brought back to Spain as a botanical curiosity and was grown only as animal fodder in Andalusia in the early 1500s. However, the Venetian republic and its traders quickly recognized the value of corn, especially for the eastern Mediterranean region, which was periodically beset by famine. Corn plantations were established on Crete and Turkey, where the plants were enthusiastically embraced. Portuguese explorers took the grain to Asia and Africa. Today, there are more than 8,000 varieties of corn, and the heritage of the genetic treasury created by Mesoamerican civilizations is still very much with us.

The Americas are by far the major producer of corn in the world. Throughout the Americas, corn continues to hold an almost sacred status, much like that of rice in Japan. The word "food" is the same as "corn" in many Indian dialects, and meals are invariably accompanied by corn tortillas. Each May, on the feast day of San Isidro, seed corn is blessed in churches across Mexico. For Native American groups of the Southwest, such as the Hopi, blue corn is a sacred symbol in ceremonies such as those for naming newborns and ritual kachina dances. Corn myths and legends abound, and the different colors of corn hold special significance. For some groups, a different color is associated with each of the four points of the compass. For the Hopi, for example, white corn, especially important in prayer ceremonies, represents the north and the strength of ancestors; yellow symbolizes the south, the season of spring and regeneration; red represents the west and long life; and blue symbolizes the east as well as wisdom and insight. For the Zuni, in contrast, white corn denotes east; yellow, north; red, south; and blue, west. In addition, multicolored corn represents the zenith point, and black the nadir.

Native Americans of the Southwest also save corn kernels for seed, then store and plant them with great care and reverence, passing them on as property of the matrilineal line. Grandmothers teach their young granddaughters to grind corn, a learning process that culminates in marriage and motherhood and perpetuates the tradition of communal corn grinding. These practices are also common in Mexico and South America. On a recent trip to Oaxaca in southern Mexico, I was fortunate to be invited to witness the role that corn played in the life of a family. I watched as three generations of women ground corn the traditional way on stone *metates* and then transformed it into the most delicate and delicious tamales, tortillas, soups, and drinks I had ever tasted. The pride and pleasure the women clearly derived from their work showed that the task was more a measure of their identity and self-worth, more a building block of their social foundation, than an act of labor. Through grinding, the women and corn come together to continue the rhythm of life.

Today, we take corn for granted in the United States. The most familiar forms are movie popcorn, buttered corn on the cob, or morning corn flakes. But corn, in the form of corn bread, was a mainstay of colonial diets, in both the North and the South, for almost two centuries. One historical report made in the Carolinas in the late 1600s describes how the main crop, "Indian Corn," makes "wholesome Bread, and good Bisket, which gives a strong, sound, and nourishing Diet." Benjamin Franklin passionately defended corn in a letter to a London newspaper in 1766: "Indian Corn…is one of the most agreeable and wholesome grains in the world…and that johny or hoecake, hot from the fire, is better than a Yorkshire muffin." Later, corn bread became a staple of the western range, where European tastes had less influence than local resources and traditions. Part of the reason for this was that corn grew far more easily in these regions than wheat. Rich, soft, and steamy corn bread has become a distinctly American bread, and many of its various forms—including those mentioned by Ben Franklin, together with hush puppies, spoon bread, corn pones, and ash cakes—are particularly associated with the South.

In Santa Fe, one of the centers of southwestern culture, corn has always been a staple. As the settlers moved northward from Mexico on the Camino Real and westward on the historic Santa Fe Trail, they took advantage of the corn cultivation and culinary uses they found. At Coyote Cafe, corn bread has always proved an essential addition to our baskets of assorted breads. The recipes in this chapter directly reflect the flavors and forms of southwestern and western range cuisines and, in many cases, they include some of our biggest "hits."

Unless otherwise specified, the recipes in this chapter use good-quality, medium-grind cornmeal. We prefer to use stone-ground cornmeal, which retains more nutrients and flavor and provides a more interesting, grainy texture than corn ground with metal rollers. Make sure the stone-ground cornmeal you buy is fresh, as it turns rancid more quickly than the standard commercially ground corn. Stone-ground cornmeal is generally available from health food and specialty stores.

Cornmeal, unlike wheat flour, contains very little texture-giving gluten, which is why most of the recipes in this chapter include flour to give the breads structure and texture.

COYOTE'S CORN BREAD

Our light and tasty rendition of the American classic is a perennial favorite. What's not to like about a moist and wonderfully seasoned corn bread that's fast and easy to make? Yogurt is a healthful alternative to whole milk or buttermilk—a principle that applies to most other recipes, too—and you can use lowfat or nonfat yogurt with equally successful results. Take care not to overmix the dry and liquid ingredients. Overmixing activates the gluten development of the flour, creating a breadlike (rather than cakelike) consistency. Serve this corn bread with stews, late-night suppers, weekend brunches, chili, or baked beans.

½ cup butter, melted

1¼ cups milk, at room temperature

1 cup buttermilk or plain yogurt

5 eggs, separated

¼ cup honey

Dry Ingredients

2¼ cups all-purpose flour

1¾ cups cornmeal

1 tablespoon baking powder

1 tablespoon salt

½ cup sugar

1 tablespoon ground cumin

1 cup fresh corn kernels, roasted (page 209)

2 teaspoons cracked black peppercorns

1. Preheat the oven to 375°.
2. Lightly coat a 12- to 14-inch rectangular (or round) baking pan with canola oil or softened butter.
3. Combine the butter, milk, and buttermilk in a mixing bowl.
4. Whisk in the egg yolks and honey until incorporated and set aside.
5. Combine the dry ingredients and sift into a separate mixing bowl.
6. Stir in the corn and peppercorns and set aside.
7. Place the egg whites in another mixing bowl and beat to stiff peaks. Set aside.
8. Fold the dry ingredients into the milk mixture until incorporated; do not overmix.
9. Gently fold in the beaten egg whites.
10. Pour the batter into the prepared pan and spread out evenly with a rubber spatula or spoon.
11. Bake in the preheated oven for 18 to 20 minutes, or until lightly browned and a paring knife or toothpick comes out clean when inserted in the center; the corn bread should spring back when pressed with your finger.
12. Place the pan on a rack to cool.
13. Cut when cool (it will crumble if cut when hot).
14. Reheat, covered, in a 250° oven and serve warm.

Yield: 20 to 30 servings

JACK CHEESE AND JALAPEÑO CORN BREAD

Chiles and cheese, like fire and ice, are partners in opposition. Chiles heat you up, and cheese dampens the flames. Jalapeños, the chiles that have defined Tex-Mex cuisine, are native, fittingly, to the Mexican Gulf state of Tabasco. With some sadness, however, I must report a recent development that will dismay all chile lovers: heatless jalapeños are now being grown in Texas for sensitive (read wimpy) palates. Heatless chiles: what's the point?

Cheese making has been a Mexican tradition since the early days of the Spanish conquest, reinforced by French Huguenot refugees who arrived in the seventeenth century. The role of dairy products in Mexican (as well as Tex-Mex and southwestern) cuisine is perhaps epitomized by the ubiquitous dollop of crema (Mexican-style sour cream) on top of many dishes. In the Southwest, cheese and chiles are a classic pairing, and jalapeño-flecked jack cheese is particularly popular. In this recipe, the richness of jack cheese and the heat of jalapeños act as a foil to the corn, resulting in a perfectly balanced bread.

1½ cups lukewarm milk
½ cup lukewarm water
2 tablespoons canola or vegetable oil
1 tablespoon active dry yeast

Dry Ingredients

4 cups all-purpose flour
1 cup cornmeal
¾ cup whole-wheat flour
4 teaspoons salt
2 teaspoons ground cumin
1 teaspoon freshly ground black pepper

½ cup chopped fresh cilantro
1 cup grated Monterey jack cheese
7 jalapeño chiles, stemmed, seeded, and minced

1. Preheat the oven to 400°.
2. Gently whisk the milk, water, and oil in a large mixing bowl.
3. Sprinkle the yeast over the milk mixture and let sit for 3 or 4 minutes.
4. Combine the dry ingredients and sift into a separate mixing bowl.
5. Add the dry ingredients to the yeast mixture and mix or knead for 6 minutes, or until the dough is smooth and elastic.
6. Add the cilantro, cheese, and jalapeños, and mix or knead until thoroughly and evenly distributed.
7. Transfer the dough to a lightly oiled bowl and cover with plastic wrap.
8. Let rise in a warm place for 20 minutes.
9. Dust a baking sheet with cornmeal or flour.
10. Divide the dough into 2 equal portions and shape into round loaves. (See photos and additional instructions on pages 206–207.)
11. Place the loaves on the prepared baking sheet and cover with plastic wrap.
12. Let rise in a warm place for 25 minutes.
13. Bake for 18 to 20 minutes, or until golden brown and a paring knife or toothpick comes out clean when inserted in the center.
14. Place the loaves on a rack to cool.
15. Cut when cool or slightly warm and serve.

Yield: two 1-pound loaves

SWEET POLENTA-ALMOND LOAF

The porridgelike polenta that has sustained Tuscan peasants for centuries—since corn was brought back from the New World—has now become highly fashionable in the United States and can be found in some of the best restaurants, where it is flavored with wild mushrooms, roasted garlic, fresh herbs, or blue cheese, among other ingredients. Coarse polenta gives this bread a unique crunchiness, which when combined with the almonds and amaretto, results in a complex and delicious bread.

Native Americans were the first to combine corn and nuts. They used pine nuts, pecans, beechnuts, and hickory nuts for flavorings as well as a source of calories and nutrients during the winter months. This corn bread is particularly enjoyable with brunch or coffee or tea. If you prefer, use Frangelico, a hazelnut liqueur, or brandy instead of the almond-flavored amaretto. Don't use almond extract; its flavor is unsuited to this recipe.

Dry Ingredients

½ cup coarse polenta

¾ cup all-purpose flour

2 tablespoons cornstarch

1 tablespoon baking powder

1 cup confectioners' sugar

1½ cups slivered or sliced almonds, toasted (page 209)

¾ cup butter, softened

4 eggs

¼ cup amaretto

Zest of 1 orange, minced

½ cup slivered or sliced almonds, lightly toasted (page 209)

1. Preheat the oven to 325°.
2. Combine the dry ingredients, sift into a mixing bowl, and set aside.
3. Place the confectioners' sugar and almonds in a food processor and process until smooth, about 30 seconds.
4. Place the butter in the bowl of an electric mixer, and cream at high speed until light colored and fluffy, about 4 to 5 minutes.
5. With the mixer running, add the almond mixture to the whipped butter, and cream until smooth.
6. Add the eggs, one at a time, and continue mixing until smooth.
7. Fold the dry ingredients into the butter mixture until just combined.
8. Stir in the amaretto and orange zest.
9. Lightly coat two 8 x 4-inch loaf pans with oil or softened butter and lightly dust with cornmeal.
10. Divide the batter between the pans and sprinkle the tops of the loaves with the slivered almonds.

11. Bake for 30 to 40 minutes, or until a paring knife or toothpick comes out clean when inserted in the center.
12. Let the bread cool in the pans for 10 minutes, or until slightly warm.
13. Turn the loaves out of the pans and transfer to a rack to finish cooling.

Yield: 2 loaves

For a nuttier, more rustic and authentic polenta flavor, use polenta entero, which contains more of the entire corn kernel and bran than other polenta grinds. It is packaged by Dean & Deluca and is available at gourmet markets or by mail (page 210).

SKILLET PIÑON CORN BREAD

Serving this corn bread in a skillet or rustic corn bread pan is a comforting, homey touch, plus the thick cast iron keeps the bread warm at the table. In pioneer days, corn bread was often made in Dutch ovens (also called bake ovens). The large cast iron cooking vessels were imported from Europe and used for cooking foods over campfires or on the hearth next to the main fireplace. As the name suggests, the Dutch oven originated in Holland in the 1600s, but it was later patented and produced in large quantities by Abraham Darby at Colebrookdale in England, one of the first major centers of the Industrial Revolution. In this recipe, the flavors of the sage and piñons, or pine nuts, give the bread a richness and earthiness that evoke the open range and hillsides of the Southwest.

¼ cup butter, melted

2 tablespoons canola oil or vegetable oil

¼ cup warm water

½ cup buttermilk

2 eggs

Dry Ingredients

1¼ cups cornmeal

¾ cup all-purpose flour

2 teaspoons baking powder

½ teaspoon salt

½ cup piñon nuts, toasted (page 209)

½ cup fresh corn kernels, roasted (page 209)

15 fresh sage leaves, chopped

1 small onion, diced

1. Preheat the oven to 400°.
2. Whisk together the butter, oil, water, buttermilk, and eggs in a mixing bowl. Set aside.
3. Combine the dry ingredients and sift into a separate mixing bowl.
4. Add the dry ingredients to the wet ingredients and mix until completely incorporated.
5. Stir in the pine nuts, corn kernels, sage, and onion until incorporated.
6. Coat a 10-inch ovenproof cast iron skillet with softened butter (about 2 tablespoons) and heat in the oven for 5 minutes.
7. Remove the hot skillet and pour the batter into it.
8. Bake for 18 to 20 minutes, or until a paring knife or toothpick comes out clean when inserted in the center.
9. Remove the skillet from the oven and let cool slightly.
10. Serve out of the skillet.

Yield: 12 to 14 servings

GREEN CHILE SPOON BREAD

Spoon bread is a traditional Southern food, so named for its light, almost puddinglike consistency, which usually requires that it be eaten with a spoon. (Thus, spoon bread is more of a side dish than a traditional bread.) In the old days, spoon breads were also known as batter breads. The story goes that a frontierswoman created spoon bread when she accidentally combined ingredients for corn bread and corn mush. This version has a fluffy consistency, like a very light polenta. The sweetness of the corn and the moderate spiciness of the chiles make a classic, pleasing pairing that complement any meal.

This easy spoon bread goes well with red and white meats, especially game, as well as fish; serve it as you would Yorkshire pudding, with a standing rib roast or prime rib. If possible, use organic, unpasteurized buttermilk, which is available from health food stores. If fresh New Mexico chiles are unavailable, use ½ cup thawed frozen green chiles (see page 210), draining any excess water. Alternatively, substitute 2 or 3 roasted, seeded, and chopped jalapeños.

1½ cups milk

2 tablespoons butter

2 tablespoons olive oil

1 cup cornmeal

1 teaspoon salt

¼ teaspoon freshly ground black pepper

¼ teaspoon ground cayenne

2 New Mexico green chiles (preferably Hatch), or Anaheim chiles, roasted, stemmed, seeded, and chopped (page 209)

¾ cup fresh corn kernels, roasted (page 209)

½ cup buttermilk

2 eggs, separated

1. Preheat the oven to 350°.
2. Coat an 8-inch square (or round) baking pan or a large (1- to 1½-quart) ovenproof bowl with about 2 teaspoons of softened butter.
3. Place the milk, butter, and olive oil in a saucepan and bring to a simmer over medium heat.
4. Stir in the cornmeal, salt, black pepper, and cayenne, and cook for about 1½ minutes, stirring as the mixture thickens. Remove from the heat.
5. Stir in the chiles, corn, and buttermilk, then stir in the egg yolks.
6. Place the egg whites in a mixing bowl and beat to soft peaks.
7. Gently fold the egg whites into the batter.
8. Pour the batter into the prepared baking pan.
9. Place the baking pan in a larger pan. Pour hot water into the larger pan so that it comes halfway up the sides of the baking pan.
10. Bake for 20 to 25 minutes, or until light golden brown and a paring knife or toothpick comes out clean when inserted in the center.
11. Serve warm out of the baking pan.

Yield: 8 to 10 servings

CARROT-CHEDDAR CORN STICKS

The unique combination and hearty flavors of Cheddar cheese, carrots, and coriander make these corn sticks something to get excited about. If you don't have corn stick pans (preferably with 6 to 8 partitions each), you can use muffin pans or a single large 10 by 8-inch (or round 9-inch) baking pan. The benefit of using corn stick pans is that you get more crust per bite while the middle remains temptingly soft. Use a good melting cheese that's not too dry. Jack, smoked Havarti, fontina, smoked provolone, or Muenster are all excellent substitutes for the Cheddar, and each type of cheese will give the bread a subtly different flavor.

¼ cup butter, melted
¾ cup milk, at room temperature
2 eggs, separated
2 tablespoons dark molasses

Dry Ingredients

1 cup all-purpose flour
½ cup plus 2 tablespoons cornmeal
1½ teaspoons baking powder
2 teaspoons salt
2 tablespoons sugar
1 teaspoon ground coriander

1 cup grated carrot
1 cup grated sharp or mild Cheddar cheese

1. Preheat the oven to 375°.
2. Thoroughly combine the butter, milk, egg yolks, and molasses in a mixing bowl. Set aside.
3. Combine the dry ingredients and sift into a separate mixing bowl.
4. Stir in the carrot and cheese and set aside.
5. Place the egg whites in a separate mixing bowl and beat to stiff peaks. Set aside.
6. Add the dry ingredients to the milk mixture and mix until completely incorporated.
7. Gently fold in the beaten egg whites.
8. Coat 2 or 3 cast iron corn stick pans with canola oil or softened butter and heat in the oven for about 8 minutes.
9. Remove the hot pans and pour the batter into them, filling each indentation up to about ⅛ inch from the top.
10. Bake for 11 to 14 minutes, or until very lightly browned and a paring knife or toothpick comes out clean when inserted in the middle.
11. Let the corn sticks cool in the pans until they are slightly warm.
12. Turn the sticks out of the pans and serve.

Yield: 12 to 14 corn sticks

MAPLE-BLUE CORN STICKS

These delicious corn sticks have an addictive quality, so be prepared. It's hard to eat just one. Blue corn is distinctively southwestern. It matches the Southwest's boundless blue skies and has been grown by the region's Native Americans for centuries, both for its nutritional qualities and for its cultural and religious significance. In pre-Columbian times, most Native Americans of the Southwest consumed blue corn every day, and corn accounted for as much as 60 percent of their total diet. Each summer, fields of corn sway gently in the breeze, golden tassels contrasting against the brick red earth, creating one of the most beautiful images of the Southwest. In this recipe, the subtle, nutty flavor of blue corn provides the perfect medium for the more assertive flavors of the pepper, cumin, and garlic seasonings. As with the previous recipe, you can use heavy muffin tins or a large baking pan instead of the corn stick pans.

3 tablespoons butter, melted
½ cup milk
1 egg, separated
1 tablespoon maple syrup

Dry Ingredients
½ cup all-purpose flour
¼ cup yellow cornmeal
¼ cup blue cornmeal
1 teaspoon baking powder
1 teaspoon salt
1 tablespoon sugar
1 teaspoon ground cumin
1 teaspoon freshly ground black pepper

1 large clove garlic, chopped
¼ cup fresh corn kernels

1. Preheat the oven to 375°.
2. Thoroughly combine the butter, milk, egg yolk, and maple syrup in a mixing bowl. Set aside.
3. Combine the dry ingredients and sift into a separate mixing bowl. Set aside.
4. Place the egg white in a small mixing bowl and beat to stiff peaks. Set aside.
5. Add the dry ingredients to the milk mixture and mix until completely incorporated.
6. Gently fold in the garlic, corn kernels, and beaten egg white.
7. Brush 2 or 3 cast iron corn stick pans with canola oil or butter and heat in the oven for about 8 minutes.
8. Remove the hot pans and pour the batter into them, filling each indentation up to about ⅛ inch from the top.
9. Bake for 11 to 14 minutes, or until very lightly browned and a paring knife or toothpick comes out clean when inserted in the middle.
10. Let the corn sticks cool in the pans until they are slightly warm.
11. Turn the corn sticks out of the pans and serve.

Yield: 10 to 12 corn sticks

OPEN-FIRE COWBOY CORN BREAD

This bread evokes the open range and the tradition of cowboys cooking bread in cast iron skillets over smoky campfires. It is truly best prepared over a real fire—if not over a campfire, then on a covered barbecue grill or on a rack in a wood-burning fireplace. However, it can be cooked in a conventional oven at 375° for 18 to 20 minutes. Either way, the smoky chipotle chiles accentuate the overall effect. You'll enjoy the picante flavors that distinguish this bread from other corn breads.

½ cup milk

½ cup buttermilk

½ cup canola or vegetable oil

2 eggs, beaten

2 tablespoons firmly packed brown sugar

1 tablespoon dark molasses

1 tablespoon Coyote's Smoky Chipotle Sauce, chipotle purée, or any good-quality smoky barbecue sauce (see Note)

Dry Ingredients

1 cup yellow or blue cornmeal

¾ cup all-purpose flour

¼ cup whole-wheat flour

4 teaspoons baking powder

1 teaspoon salt

1 tablespoon ground dried chipotle chile with seeds or other chile molido (freshly ground pure chile powder)

1. Prepare a fire, light the coals in a grill, or preheat the oven to 375°.
2. Combine the milk, buttermilk, oil, eggs, brown sugar, molasses, and chipotle sauce in a mixing bowl.
3. Combine the dry ingredients and sift into a separate mixing bowl.
4. Add the dry ingredients to the milk mixture and mix until completely incorporated.
5. Coat a 10-inch cast iron skillet with softened butter and heat over the fire or in the oven just until hot to the touch, about 5 minutes.
6. Remove the hot skillet, pour the batter into it, and cover with aluminum foil.
7. Place the skillet over the fire where it is hot but not touching the coals or place it in the oven. Do not place the skillet over the hottest part of the fire. Use a rack if necessary so that the skillet does not touch the coals or wood.
8. Bake for 18 to 20 minutes, or until a paring knife or toothpick comes out clean when inserted into the center.
9. Remove the pan from the heat and let the corn bread cool slightly.
10. Serve warm out of the skillet.

Yield: 8 to 10 servings

Note:

Coyote's Smoky Chipotle Sauce, chipotle purée, and ground chipotles are available through the mail from the Coyote Cafe General Store. See page 210 for ordering information.

CORNMEAL BISCUITS

Modern varieties of corn grown for human consumption in the United States are much sweeter and less "corny" in flavor than the traditional varieties developed over the centuries by Native Americans or those grown and enjoyed in Central and South America. This explains why the fresh corn on the cob, tortillas, and tamales in Latin America have a richer and more complex flavor than their counterparts in the States. Unfortunately, U.S. agribusiness's main criteria for hybridized corn are uniformity, yield, and storability rather than flavor characteristics. However, there are times when our most delicate varieties of sweet corn, such as Platinum Lady or Silver Queen, really shine, and these biscuits are one example of that. They are perfect for breakfast and an ideal accompaniment for stews and soups— nothing goes better with traditional New Mexican posole or a hearty green chile stew. The unusual combination of vanilla, cilantro, and corn gives the biscuits a refreshing quality.

1 tablespoon butter
1 cup sliced yellow onion

Dry Ingredients
½ cup yellow cornmeal
2 cups all-purpose flour
1 tablespoon sugar
2 teaspoons baking powder
½ teaspoon baking soda
½ teaspoon salt

6 tablespoons chilled butter, diced

1 cup buttermilk
1 egg yolk
½ teaspoon pure vanilla extract
1 cup fresh corn kernels, roasted (page 209)
1 tablespoon chopped fresh cilantro

1. Preheat the oven to 400°.
2. Melt the 1 tablespoon butter in a sauté pan.
3. Add the onion and sauté over medium-high heat for 12 to 14 minutes, stirring periodically, or until caramelized and dark golden brown. Set aside to cool.
4. Combine the dry ingredients and sift into a mixing bowl.
5. Mix the butter into the dry ingredients, preferably with your hands, until a crumbly mixture forms.
6. In a separate mixing bowl, combine the buttermilk, egg yolk, vanilla, sautéed onion, corn, and cilantro.
7. Add the dry ingredients to the buttermilk mixture and mix just until the dough is sticky. Be careful not to overmix.
8. Turn the dough out on a lightly floured work surface and roll out to a thickness of 1 inch.
9. Cut the biscuits into 2½- to 3-inch rounds and place on an ungreased baking sheet.
10. Bake for 16 to 18 minutes, or until deep brown on top.
11. Let the biscuits cool on the baking sheet, then serve warm or cold.

Yield: 10 to 12 biscuits

ZESTY BLACK PEPPER-LEMON CORN BREAD

The combination of the earthy, pungent pepper and the perfumed, clean, high tones of the lemon elevate this aromatic, zingy corn bread to a higher level. If you prefer, you can use orange or tangerine zest and juice instead of lemon, or you can experiment with other kinds of citrus. Alternatively, substitute the combination of pepper and lemon with curry powder, a dry Thai spice mixture, or ground Szechwan pepper for the zest. This bread is the ideal partner for light soups, such as those based on vegetable or chicken broth, or Mexican-style caldos.

3 cups milk, at room temperature

4 teaspoons black peppercorns, toasted and ground (page 210)

3 eggs

½ cup sugar

¾ cup butter, melted

Zest of 4 lemons

Juice of 2 lemons

Dry Ingredients

3½ cups all-purpose flour

2½ cups cornmeal

2 tablespoons baking powder

1 tablespoon salt

1½ cups fresh corn kernels, roasted (page 209)

1. Preheat the oven to 375°.
2. Place the milk and peppercorns in a saucepan and bring to a simmer.
3. Remove the pan from the heat and set aside to cool.
4. Beat the eggs and sugar in a mixing bowl to soft peaks, about 4 minutes, and set aside.
5. In a separate mixing bowl, combine the milk, butter, lemon zest, and juice. Set aside.
6. Combine the dry ingredients and sift into a separate mixing bowl. Stir in the corn.
7. Fold one-third of the dry ingredients into the milk mixture, then fold in one-third of the egg mixture. Repeat until all ingredients are thoroughly combined.
8. Grease two 9- or 10-inch square (or round) baking pans.
9. Spread the batter in the prepared pans.
10. Bake for 18 to 20 minutes, or until a paring knife or toothpick comes out clean when inserted in the center.
11. Let the corn bread cool in the pan then serve warm or cold.

Yield: 18 to 20 servings

QUICK BREADS, MUFFINS, & SCONES

Quick breads are distinguished from most other breads in that they are leavened with baking powder or baking soda rather than yeast. Consequently, because it is unnecessary to knead the dough and wait for it to rise, these breads take far less time to prepare; they are, literally, quick to make. In many cases, they can be made in less time than it takes to go down to the store and buy an inferior-tasting loaf. Unlike other breads in this book, you can make many of these recipes at the last minute—or first thing in the morning—and enjoy them for breakfast or brunch. However, quick breads cannot be made in a bread machine because all machines have cycles that are designed to activate gluten, which is not a factor in these breads. For the most part, they are also the easiest breads to make and among the most satisfying because they yield wonderful results and delicious flavors with a minimum of effort and equipment. For this reason, they are ideal for those who are building their bread-making confidence or teaching children to bake.

Baking powder, the essential ingredient for quick breads, was first commercially marketed around 1850, following its "discovery" or development earlier in the century. It is a chemical compound based on bicarbonate of soda (baking soda) and a natural crystalline acid such as cream of tartar. When baking powder is mixed with liquid and heated, it acts as a catalyst so that carbon dioxide bubbles are released, causing the dough to rise. Quick breads usually have a denser texture than other breads, partly because of the minimal leavening time, but also because the gluten in the flour is barely activated or developed since little mixing and no kneading occurs. Without yeast or a fermentation process, quick breads rely on added ingredients (mostly fruits and nuts) for flavor, so they present a wonderful opportunity for creativity; the only limiting factors are product availability and your imagination.

Muffins and scones (like doughnuts and crumpets) are popular types of quick bread that originated in the Old World, falling into the general category of tea breads or tea cakes, as they were generally accompanied by copious cups of hot, milky tea. American muffins may have the same name as their English precursor, but share little else, as they bear no resemblance whatsoever to English muffins, which are made with a yeast dough, split in half, toasted, and buttered. (Even the product marketed as English muffins in the United States faintly resembles the real thing.) Muffins became popular in eighteenth-century England, and were sold in the streets by "the muffin man" who carried them in a basket covered with a towel to keep them warm. The muffin men were armed with a bell to attract potential customers, although this accouterment was officially banned by the Parliament in the 1840s.

In *London Labor and the London Poor*, published in 1851, Victorian social chronicler Henry Mayhew recorded the words of a muffin man: "People likes them warm, sir ... to satisfy them they're fresh, and they almost always *are* fresh; but it can't matter so much about their being warm, as they have to be toasted again. I only wish butter was a sight cheaper, and that would make the muffins go. Butter's half the battle. ... My best customers is genteel houses, 'cause I sells a genteel thing. I like wet days best, 'cause there's werry respectable ladies what don't keep a servant, and they buys to save themselves going out. We're a great convenience to the ladies sir ..."

While scones are of Scottish descent (and related to Irish soda bread), there is vigorous debate about the origin of the word. Some say they are named after the place, Scone, that was the seat of the Scottish monarchy; others hold that the name is derived from the Gaelic "sgonn," meaning a large mouthful. Either way, scones have a delightful nickname in their homeland: Singing Hinnies. Scones form the centerpoint in the grand British tradition of cream teas: split in half and slathered with generous helpings of thick clotted (or Devonshire) cream and fruit jam, and served with strong, piping hot tea. Scones make equally fine partners for coffee, and their tremendous rise in popularity in the United States over the last few years mirrors the boom in coffee drinking and the resurgence of cafes, coffee bars, and coffee houses.

For the breads in this chapter as well as the breakfast breads (pages 159–183), a perfect cup of tea is an ideal and authentic accompaniment. Follow these instructions for making a real "cuppa":

Fill a kettle with purified or spring water and bring to a full boil. Carefully add some of the boiling water to a clean teapot and let it stand for a few minutes to thoroughly warm the teapot. Drain the hot water from the teapot and immediately place good-quality leaf tea of recent vintage (far preferable to tea bags) in the teapot (allow 1 teaspoon per person, plus 1 "for the pot"). Return the kettle to a boil and carefully pour the boiling water over the tea leaves in the teapot (the water must be actively boiling to extract the full flavor from the leaves). Cover the pot, preferably with an authentic "tea cosy," or a towel, and let the teapot stand for 3 to 5 minutes to allow the leaves to brew. Stir once after 2 minutes if you like even stronger tea. Meanwhile, pour a little milk into tea cups (tea without milk is a sin in the eyes of all upstanding Brits) and then strain the tea into the cups (adding milk to poured tea is likewise considered heresy). Add sugar, if desired, and sit back and think of England.

SWEET & SPICY CANDIED GINGER BREAD

Sugar-coating or candying fruit or ingredients such as ginger is a means of preserving as well as intensifying—and, of course, sweetening—the ingredients' natural flavors. The Moors traded for sugar with the Arabs, who were the first to grow it commercially. Moors were also the first to introduce candied foods to Europe. Because the ingredients used in candying items were expensive, such treats were considered a great delicacy. The sweetness and spiciness of this bread, especially when toasted, makes it perfect for midmorning or midafternoon tea or coffee. It's also a delicious simple dessert; try it garnished with a dollop of whipped cream, topped with sliced fresh apples or pears, or soaked in a little ginger liqueur.

½ cup peeled, finely minced ginger
1 tablespoon minced lemon zest
½ cup sugar

Dry Ingredients

2¾ cups all-purpose flour
1 teaspoon salt
1½ teaspoons baking powder
¼ cup confectioners' sugar

¾ cup butter, melted
2 eggs, beaten
1 cup milk

Glaze

2 tablespoons firmly packed brown sugar
1 tablespoon dark rum

1. Preheat the oven to 350°.
2. Place the ginger, lemon zest, and ½ cup sugar in a small sauté pan over medium heat.
3. As the sugar begins to melt, stir occasionally and cook for 8 to 10 minutes, or until the ginger candies and becomes translucent. Taste a little of the ginger to be sure it's sweet and no bitterness remains. Set aside.
4. Combine the dry ingredients and sift into a mixing bowl.
5. In a separate mixing bowl, whisk the butter, eggs, and milk.
6. Stir the dry ingredients into the milk mixture with a wooden spoon until combined.
7. Stir in the candied ginger.
8. Lightly coat two 7 x 4 x 3-inch loaf pans with softened butter or oil, and lightly dust with all-purpose flour.
9. Evenly divide the batter between the two loaf pans.
10. Bake for 45 to 50 minutes, or until golden brown and a paring knife or toothpick comes out clean when inserted in the center.
11. When the bread has only a few minutes left to bake, prepare the glaze. Place the sugar and rum in a saucepan over medium heat. Stir for 1 minute until the sugar dissolves.
12. Using a pastry brush, brush the glaze over the crusts of the loaves as soon as they are removed from the oven.
13. Let the loaves cool in the pans for 15 minutes.
14. Turn the loaves out of the pans and serve warm or transfer to a rack to cool completely.

Yield: 2 loaves

DATE-WALNUT BREAD

I grew up on my mother's terrific date-walnut bread, and nothing went better with it than cream cheese, but if fresh goat cheese had been available back then, I'm sure I would have liked that, too! If you want to try cream cheese with this bread, avoid brands made with xanthan gum, which makes the cheese dense and gummy; instead, buy the more flavorful and better textured product at natural food stores. While you're there, look for Bari or Medjooli dates, which are our favorites. Some of these varieties are grown on plantations around Palm Springs and they're likely to be the freshest available.

The cocoa, molasses, dates, and Kahlua combine to make this a dark, satisfying bread that's another breakfast or brunch favorite. The sweetness of the molasses and sugar is balanced by the savory flavor of the walnuts, a combination that creates an interesting bread. At the same time, the oats provide a pleasant and slightly chewy texture and body. This bread also makes a great dessert with whipped cream or fresh applesauce. Tightly wrapped in foil, it holds up well in the refrigerator. It also freezes well.

Dry Ingredients

2¾ cups all-purpose flour

1 cup whole-wheat flour

2 tablespoons cocoa powder

2 teaspoons baking soda

1 teaspoon baking powder

2 cups pitted, chopped dates

1½ cups chopped walnuts or pecans, toasted (page 209)

¾ cup rolled oats

1 cup butter, melted

¼ cup canola oil

1 cup firmly packed brown sugar

3 eggs, beaten

1½ cups milk

½ cup dark molasses

2 tablespoons Kahlua or brewed coffee (optional)

2 teaspoons pure vanilla extract

1. Preheat the oven to 350°.
2. Combine the dry ingredients in a mixing bowl.
3. Stir the dates, walnuts, and ¼ cup of the rolled oats into the dry ingredients.
4. In a separate mixing bowl, whisk the butter, oil, brown sugar, eggs, milk, molasses, Kahlua, and vanilla.
5. Stir the dry ingredients into the milk mixture with a wooden spoon until combined.
6. Lightly coat two 8 x 4-inch loaf pans with softened butter or oil and lightly dust with all-purpose flour.
7. Evenly divide the batter between the two loaf pans.
8. Sprinkle the remaining ¼ cup rolled oats over the loaves.
9. Bake for 45 to 55 minutes, or until a toothpick or a paring knife comes out clean when inserted in the center.
10. Let cool in the pans for 15 minutes.
11. Turn the loaves out of the pans and serve warm, or transfer to a rack to cool completely.

Yield: 2 loaves

DRIED-FRUIT HARVEST BREAD

With today's supermarkets carrying a wide variety of familiar and exotic fruit year-round, it's difficult to imagine that fresh fruit was once a luxury, eaten only in season by the very affluent. Dried fruit was likewise rare. Heavy, dark fruit breads, often soaked in brandy or rum, made for the winter religious holidays (particularly Christmas) are a European tradition. In addition to traditional British "fruitcakes," there are the stollens of East Germany, hutzelbrots of Bavaria, and panettones and panfortes of Italy, to name a few. They are often made weeks or months ahead, tightly wrapped, and stored in a cool place. European settlers brought this holiday tradition to the New World, and being of French-Canadian descent growing up in New England, Christmas fruitcake was a tradition for my family. In the South, blond fruitcakes are an interesting variation; they are lighter in color and texture due to the addition of flour and reduced amount of fruit.

This rich, dark, and hearty bread is ideal for breakfast Christmas morning or during the holiday season. At Coyote Cafe, we served it one New Year's Eve. It is not only a welcome change from yeast breads, it can be a pleasant reminder of the bounty of summer fruits in the middle of winter. For this recipe, I recommend using 1 cup each of the four dried fruits of your choice. Try to buy unsulphured dried fruit, available at natural food stores, as it has more flavor and none of the chemical preservatives and many people are allergic to sulphur.

This bread keeps, wrapped and refrigerated, for up to 2 weeks.

4 cups mixed dried fruit, such as cherries, raisins, apples, pears, apricots, cranberries, figs, prunes, dates, or papaya

1 cup water

Dry Ingredients

1½ cups all-purpose flour

½ cup whole-wheat flour

½ cup granulated sugar

2 teaspoons baking soda

½ tablespoon ground cinnamon

¼ teaspoon ground cloves

1 teaspoon salt

Pinch of freshly ground black pepper

¾ cup canola oil or corn oil

2 eggs, beaten

¼ cup dark molasses

½ cup firmly packed brown sugar

2 tablespoons bourbon

1½ teaspoons pure vanilla extract

1. Preheat the oven to 350°.
2. Chop the fruit into uniform pieces.
3. Heat the water in a large sauté pan or saucepan, add the dried fruit, and bring to a simmer. Remove from the heat and let sit for 10 to 15 minutes, or until soft.
4. Combine the dry ingredients and sift into a mixing bowl.
5. In a separate mixing bowl, whisk together the oil, eggs, molasses, brown sugar, bourbon, and vanilla.

(continued)

6. Stir the dry ingredients into the egg mixture with a wooden spoon until combined.

7. Drain the softened dried fruit and stir it into the batter.

8. Lightly coat two 7 x 4 x 3-inch loaf pans with softened butter or oil, and lightly dust with all-purpose flour.

9. Evenly divide the batter between the two loaf pans.

10. Bake for 45 to 55 minutes, or until a toothpick or paring knife comes out clean when inserted in the center.

11. Let the loaves cool in the pans for 15 minutes.

12. Turn the loaves out of the pans and serve warm or transfer to a rack to cool completely.

Yield: 2 loaves

SOUTH PACIFIC COCONUT-MACADAMIA BREAD

This recipe is inspired by the tropics and makes a particularly satisfying bread for cold, dark winter days. The richness of coconut and macadamia nuts evokes memories of warm places, sun-drenched beaches, and palm fronds swaying gently in the breeze. Although most people associate Hawaii with macadamias, and while the fiftieth state produces most of the world's crop, the macadamia tree is native to Australia. It was named after John MacAdam, the scientist who first cultivated it.

The best way to obtain shaved or grated coconut is to start with a fresh coconut. Pierce the "eyes" and drain the coconut water, which makes a refreshing drink. Smash the coconut by dropping it on a hard (nonbreakable) surface or hitting it with a hammer (look for the ready-grooved, easy-to-open coconuts in your market). Separate the white flesh from the shell with a spoon or blunt knife, and shave the flesh with a potato peeler or a grater. (Alternatively, use a coconut grater with rounded teeth, which are inexpensive and often available at Indian food markets and specialty cookware stores.) Toast on a baking sheet in a 325° oven for 12 to 15 minutes, or until lightly browned, stirring occasionally. If you use packaged shredded coconut, check the label to see if sugar is listed because unsweetened is far preferable. If you can only find sweetened coconut, use ¼ cup less granulated sugar.

Dry Ingredients

2 cups all-purpose flour
5 teaspoons baking powder
½ cup granulated sugar
½ teaspoon salt
½ teaspoon ground nutmeg

1 cup shaved, grated, or shredded coconut,
   toasted (see above)
2 ripe bananas, chopped into 1 x 2-inch pieces
1 cup crushed macadamia nuts

½ cup butter, melted
¼ cup firmly packed brown sugar
2 eggs, beaten
½ cup milk

1. Preheat the oven to 350°.
2. Combine the dry ingredients and sift into a mixing bowl.
3. Stir in the coconut, bananas, and macadamia nuts. Set aside.
4. In a separate mixing bowl, whisk together the butter, brown sugar, eggs, and milk.
5. Stir the dry ingredients into the milk mixture with a wooden spoon until combined.
6. Lightly coat two 4 x 3 x 7-inch loaf pans with softened butter or oil and lightly dust with all-purpose flour.
7. Evenly divide the batter between the two loaf pans.
8. Bake for 45 to 55 minutes, or until golden brown on top and a toothpick or paring knife comes out clean when inserted in the center.
9. Let cool in the pans for 15 minutes.
10. Turn the loaves out of the pans and serve warm, or transfer to a rack to cool completely.

Yield: 2 loaves

TROPICAL FOREST BREAD WITH BRAZIL NUTS & MANGO

Here's another tropical recipe, but this one is best made during the summer months when fresh mangoes and pineapples are at their best. The roasted Brazil nuts have a rich, deep flavor that contrasts and combines wonderfully with the bright tones and acidity of the mango and pineapple. Brazil nuts grow on tall trees that are native to the Amazon rain forest. I recently tasted some fresh nuts while visiting a processing factory in Bolivia—they were out of this world. While there, I learned that one reason Brazil nuts are expensive is that each must be cracked open by hand, using a special vise, to extract the kernel in one piece. This is a delicious breakfast bread, especially when spread with an exotic fruit jam such as star fruit (carambola) or guava, or one of the fruit-based recipes from the Sweet and Savory Accompaniments chapter (page 185).

1 ripe plantain

Dry Ingredients

2 cups all-purpose flour

5 teaspoons baking powder

½ cup granulated sugar

½ teaspoon salt

½ teaspoon ground nutmeg

¼ cup butter, melted

¼ cup canola oil

¼ cup firmly packed brown sugar

2 eggs, beaten

1 cup milk

1 cup shredded or grated coconut, toasted (page 31)

1 cup diced ripe mango

1 cup diced ripe pineapple

1 cup sliced or chopped Brazil nuts, lightly toasted (page 209)

1. Preheat the oven to 400°.
2. Roast the plantain in its peel in the preheated oven for 20 minutes.
3. Meanwhile, combine the dry ingredients and sift into a mixing bowl.
4. In a separate mixing bowl, whisk the butter, oil, sugar, eggs, and milk.
5. Peel the plantain, mash, and whisk into the milk mixture.
6. Lower the oven temperature to 350°.
7. Stir in the coconut, mango, pineapple, and Brazil nuts. Set aside.
8. Stir the dry ingredients into the liquid mixture with a wooden spoon until combined.
9. Lightly coat two 4 x 3 x 7-inch loaf pans with softened butter or oil and lightly dust with all-purpose flour.
10. Evenly divide the batter between the two loaf pans.
11. Bake for 45 to 55 minutes, or until golden brown and a toothpick or paring knife comes out clean when inserted in the center.
12. Let cool in the pans for 15 minutes.
13. Turn the loaves out of the pans and serve warm or transfer to a rack to cool completely.

Yield: 2 loaves

CRANBERRY-ORANGE MUFFINS

Cranberries are native to the northern United States and New England, where the early European settlers were introduced to them soon after their arrival. The Native Americans of the region ate the astringent scarlet berries raw and also cooked them with honey or maple sugar. Indigenous cranberries grow on long vines that trail along swampy areas; they are commercially cultivated in large bogs and then harvested by flooding the bog and raking berries off of the surface of the water.

The flavors of cranberry and orange are a classic combination for the holiday season, and these muffins are a wonderful addition to the Thanksgiving or Christmas dinner bread basket. The addition of cinnamon and clove rounds out the fruit flavors, and the pecans give the muffins an appealing crunchiness. The addition of whole-wheat flour improves their texture and flavor, setting them apart from the white, puffy, mushy muffins available in too many supermarkets or doughnut shops. If you wish, substitute dried cherries or cranberries for the fresh cranberries and lemon for the orange.

Dry Ingredients

3 cups all-purpose flour

½ cup whole-wheat flour

½ cup granulated sugar

½ teaspoon salt

2 teaspoons baking powder

1 teaspoon baking soda

½ teaspoon ground cinnamon

Pinch of ground cloves

1 tablespoon grated orange zest

1 orange, cut into sections and chopped

1 cup cranberries, chopped

½ cup pecans, toasted (optional, page 209)

½ cup butter, melted

¼ cup canola oil

½ cup firmly packed brown sugar

¼ cup honey

⅔ cup buttermilk

2 eggs, beaten

1. Preheat the oven to 375°.
2. Combine the dry ingredients and sift into a mixing bowl.
3. Stir in the zest, orange, cranberries, and pecans. Set aside.
4. In a separate mixing bowl, whisk the butter, oil, brown sugar, honey, buttermilk, and eggs.
5. Stir the dry ingredients into the buttermilk mixture with a wooden spoon just until combined. Do not overmix; some of the flour should still be visible.
6. Lightly coat a muffin pan with softened butter or oil, and lightly dust with all-purpose flour.
7. Spoon the batter into the muffin pan, filling each cup to the top.
8. Bake for 25 to 30 minutes, or until golden brown and a toothpick or paring knife comes out clean when inserted in one of the muffins in the middle of the pan.

9. Let cool in the pan for 5 minutes.
10. Turn the muffins out of the pan and serve warm, or transfer to a rack to cool completely.

Yield: 10 to 12 muffins

The muffin recipes in this chapter make 6 to 8 large muffins, 10 to 12 medium-sized muffins, or 18 to 20 miniature muffins, depending on the size of your muffin pan.

WHOLE-BRAN MUFFINS

The earthy, wheaty flavor of these classic muffins is the perfect way to start the day. Bran is a well-known source of fiber, as well as other vitamins, oils, and minerals; it's the outer layer of wheat (more specifically, the fine layers of skin surrounding the wheat germ) that is separated from the grain during the milling process for producing white bread. Buy bran in small amounts as its high oil content prevents it from keeping indefinitely. For maximum freshness, purchase it at a store with high turnover. The bran contributes a light and pleasantly grainy texture, and its flavor is heightened in this recipe by the tanginess of the buttermilk. For a lowfat version, replace the milk and buttermilk with 1½ cups nonfat yogurt, the eggs with 4 egg whites or ½ cup egg substitute, and the butter with canola or safflower oil.

Dry Ingredients

3 cups bran flakes
2 cups all-purpose flour
1 tablespoon baking powder
½ teaspoon salt
½ cup granulated sugar

1 cup raisins (optional)
½ cup hot water (optional)

6 tablespoons butter, melted
2 tablespoons dark molasses
¼ cup firmly packed brown sugar
⅔ cup buttermilk
¾ cup milk
2 eggs, beaten

1. Preheat the oven to 375°.
2. Toast the bran flakes in a sauté pan over medium heat for 5 minutes.
3. Transfer to a mixing bowl. Combine the remaining dry ingredients and sift into the bowl of bran.
4. Place the raisins in a bowl, add the hot water, and let them plump for 10 minutes.
5. Drain the raisins, place in a separate mixing bowl, add the butter, molasses, brown sugar, buttermilk, milk, and eggs, and whisk.
6. With a wooden spoon, stir the dry ingredients into the buttermilk mixture just until combined. Do not overmix; some of the flour should still be visible.
7. Lightly coat a muffin pan with softened butter or oil, and lightly dust with all-purpose flour.
8. Spoon the batter into the muffin pan, filling each cup to the top.
9. Bake for 25 to 30 minutes, or until golden brown and a toothpick or paring knife comes out clean when inserted into one of the muffins in the middle of the pan.
10. Let cool in the pan for 5 minutes.
11. Turn the muffins out of the pan and serve warm, or transfer to a rack to cool completely.

Yield: 10 to 12 muffins

APPLE-CINNAMON-WALNUT MUFFINS

When the apples begin to fall from the trees in the Rio Grande orchards surrounding Santa Fe, we're inclined to make these muffins before anything else. It's the best way to enjoy a fresh new crop of crisp, green Gravensteins, or rosy Jonathans or McIntosh apples. Any crunchy flavorful apple will do; if you have a favorite type, use it. These muffins are also an excellent way to use up the glut of apples that inevitably hits during the fall if you have one or more apple trees in the back yard. My mother used to bake a moist and delicious cake in a tube pan with these same ingredients, and it was one of the first cakes I ever made. Try these delicious muffins for breakfast or with tea or coffee—Coyote prefers his with a double cappuccino.

Dry Ingredients

3½ cups all-purpose flour
¼ cup whole-wheat flour
¾ cup granulated sugar
1 tablespoon baking powder
¾ teaspoon salt
1 tablespoon ground cinnamon

2 cups peeled, seeded, cored, and coarsely
    chopped apple
1 cup chopped walnuts, toasted (optional,
    page 209)

1¼ cups unfiltered apple cider or apple juice
1 cup vegetable oil
¼ cup firmly packed brown sugar
3 eggs, beaten

1. Preheat the oven to 375°.
2. Combine the dry ingredients and sift into a mixing bowl.
3. Stir in ½ cup of the apple and all of the walnuts. Set aside.
4. Combine the remaining 1½ cups apple and ¼ cup of the cider in a nonreactive saucepan.
5. Cook over medium heat, stirring occasionally, for 6 to 8 minutes, or until the apples are soft and resemble lumpy applesauce.
6. Transfer to a separate mixing bowl, add the remaining 1 cup cider and the oil, brown sugar, and eggs, and whisk.
7. With a wooden spoon, stir the dry ingredients into the apple mixture just until combined. Do not overmix; some of the flour should still be visible.
8. Lightly coat a muffin pan with softened butter or oil, and lightly dust with all-purpose flour.
9. Spoon the batter into the muffin pan, filling each cup just to the top.
10. Bake for 25 to 30 minutes, or until golden brown and a toothpick or paring knife comes out clean when inserted in one of the muffins in the middle of the pan.
11. Let cool in the pan for 5 minutes.
12. Turn the muffins out of the pan and serve warm, or transfer to a rack to cool completely.

Yield: 10 to 12 muffins

PISTACHIO-DATE MUFFINS

These muffins have a definite Middle Eastern influence. Fresh dates, native to that region but also grown in California and Arizona, are sold in the fall, but the more familiar dried dates are available year-round. Choose dried dates that are still a little syrupy and moist. The pale green pistachios are grown in California as well as their native Middle East; buy them shelled and make sure they are unsalted. Don't use pistachios that are dyed red, a carnival tradition that originated in the 1940s. Pistachios are related to cashews and were used as a thickening agent for sauces thousands of years ago by cooks in Mesopotamia, who valued the nuts' fresh, unique flavor. Pistachio trees were among those in the Hanging Gardens of Babylon, one of the famed ancient wonders of the world. Cardamom is a pungent spice related to ginger that's native to India; it's the third most expensive spice in the world, after saffron and vanilla. It's often added to curries and contributes a wonderful savory touch to these delightfully rich muffins. Buy green cardamom in pod form, and grind them fresh whenever you need them. For more about dates, see page 27.

Dry Ingredients

½ cup all-purpose flour

1 cup pistachios, lightly toasted (page 209)

¼ cup whole-wheat flour

1 tablespoon baking powder

¼ cup granulated sugar

¾ teaspoon salt

½ teaspoon ground cardamom

½ teaspoon ground ginger

2 cups pitted, chopped dates

½ cup butter, melted

½ cup firmly packed brown sugar

2 tablespoons honey

1 cup milk

2 eggs, beaten

1 cup grated carrot (optional)

1. Preheat the oven to 375°.

2. Place the flour and pistachios in a food processor and pulverize until the nuts are finely ground. Transfer to a mixing bowl.

3. Combine the remaining dry ingredients and sift into the bowl containing the flour and pistachio mixture.

4. Stir in the dates and set aside.

5. In a separate mixing bowl, whisk the butter, brown sugar, honey, milk, eggs, and carrot.

6. With a wooden spoon, stir the dry ingredients into the milk mixture just until combined. Do not overmix; some of the flour should still be visible.

7. Lightly coat a muffin pan with softened butter or oil, and lightly dust with all-purpose flour.

8. Spoon the batter into the muffin pan, filling each cup to the top.

9. Bake for 25 to 30 minutes, or until golden brown and a toothpick or paring knife comes out clean when inserted in one of the muffins in the middle of the pan.

10. Let cool in the pan for 5 minutes.

11. Turn the muffins out of the pan and serve warm, or transfer to a rack to cool completely.

Yield: 10 to 12 muffins

BANANA-PECAN MUFFINS

A steaming mug of hot chocolate and a banana muffin—there's no better way to begin a day. Many people are surprised to learn that the banana plant is the world's largest herb. Another interesting fact about bananas is that due to man's intervention in selectively breeding them as a seedless fruit, the cultivated varieties are effectively sterile and unable to propagate on their own. Whenever a recipe calls for cooking bananas, use very ripe ones, which impart the best flavor when cooked; their skin should be heavily speckled or completely brown and they should feel very soft. If necessary, you can hasten the ripening process by keeping the bananas in a brown paper bag with the top rolled down for a few days. The whole-wheat flour gives these muffins a rustic, hearty touch.

Dry Ingredients

2½ cups all-purpose flour

¼ cup whole-wheat flour

¾ cup granulated sugar

1 teaspoon baking powder

1 teaspoon baking soda

½ teaspoon salt

¼ cup rolled oats

¾ cup chocolate chips (optional)

½ cup chopped pecans, toasted (optional, page 209)

3 very ripe bananas, thoroughly puréed

¾ cup butter, melted

¾ cup milk

½ cup firmly packed brown sugar

3 eggs, beaten

1. Preheat the oven to 375°.
2. Combine the dry ingredients and sift into a mixing bowl.
3. Stir in the rolled oats, chocolate chips, and pecans. Set aside.
4. In a separate mixing bowl, whisk the bananas, butter, milk, brown sugar, and eggs.
5. With a wooden spoon, stir the dry ingredients into the banana mixture just until combined. Do not overmix; some of the flour should still be visible.
6. Lightly coat a muffin pan with softened butter or oil and lightly dust with all-purpose flour.
7. Spoon the batter into the muffin pan, filling each cup just to the top.
8. Bake for 25 to 30 minutes, or until golden brown and a toothpick or paring knife comes out clean when inserted in one of the muffins in the middle of the pan.
9. Let cool in the pan for 5 minutes.
10. Turn the muffins out of the pan and serve warm, or transfer to a rack to cool completely.

Yield: 10 to 12 muffins

SPICED AUTUMN PUMPKIN MUFFINS

The flavor of fresh pumpkin truly denotes the arrival of fall, and these muffins celebrate the season. For best results, use fresh pumpkin cut into quarters and seeded. Bake in the oven at 375° for about 1¼ hours, or until the flesh is soft enough to pierce with a paring knife. Peel off the skin and chop the flesh, transfer to a saucepan, and cook down over medium heat for about 20 minutes or until completely tender; then purée in a food processor or blender. Fresh pumpkin has a lighter, more delicate flavor than canned, but canned purée will work. You can use any sweet squash, such as zucchini, yellow crookneck, hubbard, or acorn squash, for this recipe. Squash lovers may want to track down my squash poster (to order, see page 215), which shows these and about 25 other types of squash.

Dry Ingredients

2½ cups all-purpose flour

¾ cup granulated sugar

2 teaspoons baking powder

1 teaspoon baking soda

1 teaspoon salt

½ teaspoon ground allspice

¼ teaspoon ground nutmeg

½ teaspoon ground ginger

½ cup chopped pecans, toasted (optional, page 209)

¾ cup chocolate chips (optional)

½ cup vegetable oil

¾ cup milk

2 cups pumpkin purée

2 eggs, beaten

1 tablespoon minced orange zest (optional)

1. Preheat the oven to 375°.
2. Combine the dry ingredients and sift into a mixing bowl.
3. Stir in the pecans and chocolate chips. Set aside.
4. In a separate mixing bowl, whisk the oil, milk, pumpkin, eggs, and orange zest.
5. With a wooden spoon, stir the dry ingredients into the pumpkin mixture just until combined. Do not overmix; some of the flour should still be visible.
6. Lightly coat a muffin pan with softened butter or oil, and lightly dust with all-purpose flour.
7. Spoon the batter into the muffin pan, filling each cup just to the top.
8. Bake for 25 to 30 minutes, or until golden brown and a toothpick or paring knife comes out clean when inserted in one of the muffins in the middle of the pan.
9. Let cool in the pan for 5 minutes.
10. Turn the muffins out of the pan and serve warm, or transfer to a rack to cool completely.

Yield: 10 to 12 muffins

BLUE CORN-MAPLE MUFFINS

In the New England states and in Canada, watery, slightly sweet maple sap is harvested each spring (not in fall or winter, as many people think), then boiled down and refined into syrup. It takes about 35 to 40 gallons of sap to produce 1 gallon of maple syrup—something to think about the next time you slather pancakes or French toast with it! If possible, buy the thicker, darker, and more syrupy grade B (or even grade C) maple syrup rather than the more refined grade A; the roastiness and caramelized flavors of grade B syrup give these muffins greater depth and more character. (Grade B is also less expensive than Grade A.) Maple syrup and blue corn are a delicious combination, and the yellow corn kernels create an attractive color contrast. This is a variation of an old recipe devised by Marie O'Shea, one of our opening sous chefs at Coyote Cafe. It's a great bread for a southwestern brunch or with a bowl of posole or chowder.

Dry Ingredients

¾ cup blue cornmeal

2 cups all-purpose flour

½ cup maple sugar or firmly packed brown sugar

1 tablespoon baking powder

1 teaspoon salt

½ cup piñon nuts, toasted (optional, page 209)

½ cup corn kernels, roasted (page 209)

¾ cup maple syrup

¾ cup butter, melted

1 cup milk

3 eggs, beaten

1. Preheat the oven to 375°.
2. Combine the dry ingredients and sift into a mixing bowl.
3. Stir in the piñon nuts and corn kernels. Set aside.
4. In a separate mixing bowl, whisk the maple syrup, butter, milk, and eggs.
5. With a wooden spoon, stir the dry ingredients into the maple syrup mixture just until combined. Do not overmix; some of the flour should still be visible.
6. Lightly coat a muffin pan with softened butter or oil, and lightly dust with all-purpose flour.
7. Spoon the batter into the muffin pan, filling each cup just to the top.
8. Bake for 25 to 30 minutes, or until golden brown and a toothpick or paring knife comes out clean when inserted in one of the muffins in the middle of the pan.
9. Let cool in the pan for 5 minutes.
10. Turn the muffins out of the pan and serve warm, or transfer to a rack to cool completely.

Yield: 10 to 12 muffins

BLUEBERRY MUFFINS

This innovative recipe departs from the norm by introducing tones of lemon and ginger, which complement the blueberries and lift their flavor. It's an intriguing combination that also works well for blueberry desserts, such as cobblers, tarts, and compotes. Blueberries are widely cultivated in the United States, but many prefer the more tart wild northern blueberries from Maine and Michigan, especially for making desserts. I remember picking blueberries in the Maine woods as a kid—I never returned hungry! Blueberries freeze well when sealed properly, so buy them in bulk during the summer and enjoy them year-round.

Dry Ingredients

3¼ cups all-purpose flour

½ cup whole-wheat flour

2 teaspoons baking powder

½ cup granulated sugar

1 teaspoon salt

½ teaspoon ground nutmeg

2 teaspoons ground ginger

2 cups fresh or frozen blueberries (thawed if frozen)

1 cup butter, melted

¾ cup milk

¾ cup firmly packed brown sugar

¼ cup honey

1 teaspoon pure vanilla extract

1 teaspoon grated lemon zest

3 eggs, beaten

1. Preheat the oven to 375°.
2. Combine the dry ingredients and sift into a mixing bowl.
3. Stir in the blueberries. Set aside.
4. In a separate mixing bowl, whisk the butter, milk, brown sugar, honey, vanilla, lemon zest, and eggs.
5. With a wooden spoon, stir the dry ingredients into the milk mixture just until combined. Do not overmix; some of the flour should still be visible.
6. Lightly coat a muffin pan with softened butter or oil, and lightly dust with all-purpose flour.
7. Spoon the batter into the muffin pan, filling each cup just to the top.
8. Bake for 25 to 30 minutes, or until golden brown and a toothpick or paring knife comes out clean when inserted in one of the muffins in the middle of the pan.
9. Let cool in the pan for 5 minutes.
10. Turn the muffins out of the pan and serve warm, or transfer to a rack to cool completely.

Yield: 10 to 12 muffins

BUTTERMILK BISCUITS

Biscuits are probably the descendants of scones, which were brought to the South by eighteenth-century Scottish immigrants. A little later, pioneers introduced biscuits to Texas and the Southwest. In frontier days, biscuits were often cooked in Dutch ovens over campfires and eaten with posole and stews. They have remained a popular bread of the region ever since. These foolproof, classic home-style biscuits are tangy, light, and puffy, and best eaten warm from the oven. They are just the thing to go with chile stews and, of course, any dish with gravy. It's important not to overwork this dough. The charm of really good buttermilk biscuits is their flaky, delicate texture, so gently fold in—rather than stirring in—the buttermilk, mixing it with the dry ingredients just until they are barely combined. Minimal mixing also gives these biscuits a charming rustic look. Most folks are surprised to learn that, despite its name, buttermilk contains less fat than whole milk.

Dry Ingredients

2½ cups all-purpose flour
2½ teaspoons baking powder
1 teaspoon sugar
1 teaspoon salt

1 cup chilled butter, diced
1 cup buttermilk

1. Preheat the oven to 375°.
2. Combine the dry ingredients and sift into a mixing bowl.
3. Add the butter to the dry ingredients and rub them together between your thumbs and fingers until thoroughly combined and the mixture resembles coarse cornmeal.
4. Add the buttermilk and gently fold in with a wooden spoon just until the mixture is combined.
5. Turn the dough out onto a well-floured work surface and dust with additional flour.
6. With a rolling pin, roll out the dough to a thickness of 1½ inches.
7. Cut into 2½ - to 3-inch rounds or the shape of your choice.
8. Place at least 2 inches apart on a nonstick or black steel baking sheet.
9. Bake for 18 to 20 minutes, or until golden brown.
10. Serve warm or transfer the biscuits to a rack to cool completely.

Yield: 6 to 8 biscuits

RANGE SAGE SCONES

Scones may have originated in Scotland, but they have successfully made the journey to the New World. One thing is for certain: the Celtic variety never contained the earthy, aromatic combination of sage and pecans. These fragrant morsels are warming and satisfying, and summon images of crisp, chilly campfire mornings on the open range—though I have never heard about any leathery old cowpokes rustling up scones like these! A wonderful accompaniment for stews or soups, these scones are light if not overmixed.

Dry Ingredients

3 cups all-purpose flour

2½ teaspoons baking powder

½ teaspoon baking soda

½ teaspoon salt

½ teaspoon freshly ground black pepper

2 tablespoons dried sage

8 fresh sage leaves, minced

¾ cup chilled butter, diced

¼ cup firmly packed brown sugar

½ cup chopped pecans, toasted (page 209)

1 tablespoon honey

1 cup buttermilk

½ cup whipping cream

1. Preheat the oven to 375°.
2. Combine the dry ingredients and sift into a mixing bowl. Stir in the dried and fresh sage.
3. Add the butter to the dry ingredients, and rub them together between your thumbs and fingers until thoroughly combined and the mixture resembles coarse cornmeal.
4. Add the brown sugar, pecans, honey, buttermilk, and cream and stir with a wooden spoon just until the mixture is combined.
5. Turn the dough out onto a well-floured work surface and dust with additional all-purpose flour.
6. With a rolling pin, roll out the dough to a thickness of 1½ inches.
7. Cut into 2½ - to 3-inch rounds, triangles, or the shape of your choice. Alternatively, divide the dough into two pieces, roll into 1-inch-thick circles about 8 inches in diameter, and cut into pie-shaped wedges.
8. Place at least 2 inches apart on a nonstick or black steel baking sheet.
9. Bake for 18 to 20 minutes, or until golden brown on top.
10. Serve warm or transfer the scones to a rack to cool completely.

Yield: 12 to 15 scones

CURRANT & BRANDY SCONES

Dried currants are probably the most widely used flavoring ingredient for scones, but chopped raisins, golden raisins (sultanas), golden currants, dried cherries, dried cranberries, or dried blueberries work just as well. Brandy goes well with these dried fruits and others, such as prunes, because the flavors are complementary. In these scones, the hint of brandy highlights the flavor of the currants and awakens the taste buds. It's a quick, easy recipe that's perfect for breakfast or tea time.

Dry Ingredients

2 cups all-purpose flour

6 tablespoons whole-wheat flour

¼ cup sugar

2 teaspoons baking powder

½ teaspoon salt

½ teaspoon ground cinnamon

½ cup chilled butter, diced

2 tablespoons brandy

½ cup milk

½ cup whipping cream

2 cups dried currants

1. Preheat the oven to 375°.
2. Combine the dry ingredients and sift into a mixing bowl.
3. Add the butter to the dry ingredients, and rub them together between your thumbs and fingers until thoroughly combined and the mixture resembles coarse cornmeal.
4. Add the brandy, milk, cream, and currants and stir with a wooden spoon just until the mixture is combined.
5. Turn the dough out onto a well-floured work surface and dust with additional all-purpose flour.
6. With a rolling pin, roll out the dough to a thickness of 1½ inches.
7. Cut into 2½ - to 3-inch rounds, triangles, or the shape of your choice. Alternatively, divide the dough into two pieces, roll into 1-inch-thick circles about 8 inches in diameter, and cut into pie-shaped wedges.
8. Place at least 2 inches apart on a nonstick or black steel baking sheet.
9. Bake for 18 to 20 minutes, or until golden brown on top.
10. Serve warm or transfer the scones to a rack to cool completely.

Yield: 12 to 15 scones

HONEY HIGHLAND SCONES

Given that scones are of Scottish descent, we've included this recipe which is flavored with Drambuie, a liqueur based on Scotch whisky that's made with herbs and honey. The Drambuie and honey make these scones a bit sweet—ideal for serving with afternoon tea.

Dry Ingredients

1¾ cups all-purpose flour

½ cup whole-wheat flour

1 teaspoon baking powder

½ teaspoon salt

¼ cup chilled butter, diced

¼ cup Drambuie

2 tablespoons dark honey

¼ cup whipping cream

½ teaspoon pure vanilla extract

1 egg, beaten

1. Preheat the oven to 375°.
2. Combine the dry ingredients and sift into a mixing bowl.
3. Add the butter to the dry ingredients and rub them together between your thumbs and fingers until thoroughly combined and the mixture resembles coarse cornmeal.
4. Add the Drambuie, honey, cream, vanilla, and egg and stir with a wooden spoon just until the mixture is combined.
5. Turn the dough out onto a well-floured work surface and dust with additional all-purpose flour.
6. With a rolling pin, roll out the dough to a thickness of 1½ inches.
7. Cut into 2½- to 3-inch rounds, triangles, or the shape of your choice. Alternatively, divide the dough into two pieces, roll into 1-inch circles about 8 inches in diameter, and cut into pie-shaped wedges.
8. Place at least 2 inches apart on a nonstick or a black steel baking sheet.
9. Bake for 18 to 20 minutes, or until golden brown on top.
10. Serve warm or transfer the scones to a rack to cool completely.

Yield: 12 to 15 scones

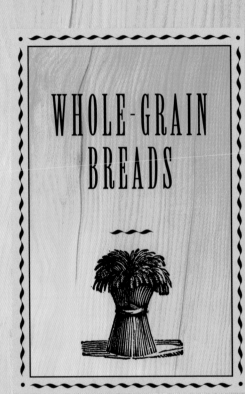

WHOLE-GRAIN
BREADS

Sweet smelling crusty wheat bread and toasted bran, chewy oatmeal, heady dark rye, tangy cider and walnuts, and rich raisins—these are just some of the captivating qualities of the big, full-flavored whole-grain breads in this chapter. Whole-grain breads are robust, healthy, and the perfect medium for intense flavors.

Grains have been the basis of our diet since at least the beginning of recorded history, long before the age of breakfast cereals. The cultivated grains we eat today are descended from the seeds of domesticated grasses that were cultivated thousands of years ago in such different regions as the fertile Nile Valley and Mesopotamia, the Russian Steppes, the wetlands of southern China, the river valleys of Mexico, and the African Savannah. All grains are high in protein and contain significant amounts of carbohydrates, vitamins, and trace elements, and facilitated small hunter-gatherer groups' cultural transformation into large, sedentary, agrarian-based communities that formed the basis of civilizations. In the New World, corn has been the most important cereal grain (for more about this, see pages 208–209), although in the Andes regions of South America, quinoa and amaranth have also been significant crops. In Europe, wheat, rye, oats and barley have been the most commonly used grains, while rice has dominated the Asian diet for centuries. In Africa, millet and sorghum are the main staples.

The breads in this chapter feature many of these grains, but especially wheat and rye, which, because of the suitable climate and growing conditions in Europe, were the preferred grains for traditional European breads. Their use can be traced back at least to medieval times; paintings by Breughel and Vermeer, for example, document the large, dense wheat and rye loaves. Introduced to the colonies by European immigrants, wheat and rye became the grains of choice for modern American bread baking.

Wheat was introduced to Europe from the Middle East, where it has been cultivated for at least 8,000 years. It is unique in containing relatively high amounts of gluten compared with other grains; this provides the necessary elasticity for making leavened breads. It was approximately 5,000 years ago that the Egyptians discovered that the combination of yeast and gluten resulted in airy, textured loaves. Wheat became the basis of the Egyptian economy and, later, the Romans spread the use of wheat far and wide across the temperate zones of Europe.

In ancient times, bread was an especially labor-intensive food because flour had to be ground by hand. The process of milling wheat into flour was revolutionized around 800 BC in Mesopotamia, when animal, water, and wind power were harnessed for the first time to turn the large stones used for grinding. This made the process of removing the tough outer layer of grain and separating the bran much easier and more efficient. Although these parts of the grain contain much of the healthful protein, fiber, and nutrients, they also contain the oils that contribute to rancidity and perishability. In any event, the resulting white flour, while less nutritious, stored better and became the standard ingredient for baking. It also became a symbol of culture and civilization during the Middle Ages; no doubt the whiteness and "purity" of refined wheat flour were reasons bread became a central part of Christian ritual, such as the Eucharist, the sacrament of Holy Communion in which bread (and wine) are consecrated and consumed as symbols of the flesh (and blood) of Christ.

Refined white bread became a symbol of elegance and nobility, while the separated and less digestible germ and bran (together with its nutritional value) were relegated to animal fodder. George III of England, who enjoyed eating brown bread and probably recognized its healthful qualities, was mockingly referred to as "Brown George," even by his poorer subjects, for whom white bread was regarded as the only type fit for consumption. The introduction of the first commercial metal rollers for milling wheat in the mid-1800s once again revolutionized flour production and bread making, ushering in the modern era of mass production. The germ and bran invariably continued to be separated to preserve the illusory all-important pristine integrity and status of white bread.

The practice of making bread with "refined" flour, and the belief in the superiority of white bread, has only recently begun to change. My generation grew up eating soft, white, bleached, bland bread, which was the norm at the time. Fortunately, we are now in the midst of a revival in whole-grain breads, in which the germ and bran are added back to the flour and special emphasis is placed on wholesome, healthful ingredients. There is also renewed interest in organic grains, stone grinding, and home milling. Organic grains offer superior flavor, enhanced nutritional qualities, and environmental benefits—the fewer chemicals we put into our bodies or the ground, the better. Stone grinding keeps the temperature of the grain low enough that the nutrients and vitamins (and consequently, the flavor) contained in the germ and bran are preserved. In addition, the texture is generally superior. I recommend using only organic, stone-ground flour in these breads. Especially with modern refrigeration and transportation techniques and improved storage and packaging, the susceptibility of fresh whole grains to spoilage is much less of an issue.

Grains provide plenty of flavor and texture, and the breads in this chapter capitalize on these innate characteristics, as well as on the deliberate addition of other pronounced flavorings. All of these breads are made with yeast, so plan for the longer rising time they require. Finally, many of the breads in this chapter and those that follow have been tested specifically in bread machines. Instructions for preparing the dough or making the bread in bread machines are given at the end of the recipes.

WHOLE-WHEAT CHILE BREAD

This is a signature Coyote Cafe bread; if you've ever eaten at one of our restaurants, chances are you've tried it. We get requests for the recipe all the time, so here it is. It's a handsome bread, with a red tinge to the crumb and red and green chile speckles throughout. Vary the type of chile powder for a different effect; for example, substitute cayenne for the milder chile molido if you like fiery flavors, or use complex, smoky chipotle chile powder, which is available at Mexican markets or from the Coyote Cafe General Store (see page 210). Chile caribe is the Spanish term for a fresher form of the dried red pepper flakes you commonly find on the table in Italian restaurants. This is an all-purpose bread that goes well with most kinds of southwestern foods, especially grilled meats.

1¼ cups lukewarm water

2 tablespoons olive oil

2 teaspoons honey

2½ teaspoons active dry yeast

Dry Ingredients

1 cup stone-ground whole-wheat flour

1 cup bread flour

1 cup all-purpose flour

2 teaspoons salt

4 teaspoons chile molido (freshly ground pure chile powder)

4 teaspoons chile caribe (red pepper flakes)

½ cup roasted, peeled, stemmed, seeded, and diced New Mexico green chile (page 209)

1. Combine the water, olive oil, and honey in the bowl of a heavy-duty electric mixer or in a large mixing bowl.

2. Sprinkle the yeast over the mixture, stir in, and let sit for 2 minutes.

3. Add the dry ingredients.

4. Mix with the dough hook (or knead by hand) for 8 to 10 minutes, or until the dough appears silky and resilient.

5. Mix or knead the green chile into the dough until thoroughly incorporated.

6. Transfer the dough to a lightly oiled bowl and cover with plastic wrap.

7. Let rise in a warm place for 1½ hours, or until approximately doubled in volume.

8. Punch the dough down, re-cover with plastic wrap, and let rise again in a warm place for 30 minutes.

9. Place a baking stone on the middle rack in the oven and preheat to 400°.

10. Place the dough on a lightly floured work surface and cut into 2 equal pieces.

11. Grease two loaf pans or generously dust a baking sheet with whole-wheat flour.

12. Shape the dough into oblong loaves. Alternatively, shape it into 2 round loaves or 14 to 16 rolls. (See photos and additional instructions on pages 206–207.)

13. Place the loaves in the prepared pans or on the baking sheet (or place the rolls on the baking sheet), cover with lightly oiled plastic wrap, and let rise again in a warm place for 20 minutes.

14. Uncover the loaves (or rolls) and, using a spray bottle, spritz them with water and lightly dust with whole-wheat flour.

15. Make 2 or 3 diagonal slashes in the tops of the loaves with a serrated knife to allow the dough to expand in the hot oven.

16. Using the spray bottle, spritz the oven walls with water. Work quickly so the oven does not lose heat.

17. Set the loaf pans or baking sheet on the hot stone.

18. Bake for 35 to 40 minutes (20 to 25 minutes for rolls). The bread is done when the crust is dark and firm and the loaves sound hollow when tapped on the bottom.

19. Let the bread cool in the pans or on the baking sheet for 10 minutes.

20. Transfer the loaves (or rolls) to a rack and cool before cutting.

Yield: 2 loaves or 14 to 16 rolls

Bread Machine Instructions

1. Combine all the ingredients, except the green chile, in the bread pan in the order specified by the manufacturer's instructions.

2. Process on the sweet or raisin bread setting (#8).

3. Add the roasted chile at the beeps.

PILGRIM BROWN BREAD

This is a dark, moist New England–style bread with colonial roots and, before that, English origins. The essential ingredient is molasses, the nutritious syrupy byproduct of sugar cane refining. I grew up in New England, and my first brown bread came out of the B & M brand can—I vividly recall the blue label—which is how it's still sold today. In my youth, I never dreamed you could actually make *brown bread! Most Saturday nights, we'd have the canned brown bread, spread thickly with sweet butter, and Boston baked beans, which my mother cooked with molasses, mustard, and a clove-studded onion. She served the beans in a large brown crock, just like the one on the bread can label! It was considerably later that I learned you could eat brown bread without baked beans. For an authentic touch, you could use the empty, tall cylindrical B & M can as a bread mold; just grease it with softened butter. This dense, sweet bread also makes excellent rolls. Either way, it's great on its own, or with meats (especially game), pot roasts, rich sauces, and, of course, baked beans.*

1½ cups lukewarm water
½ cup dark molasses
¼ cup canola oil
1 tablespoon active dry yeast

Dry Ingredients

3 cups whole-wheat flour
2¼ cups bread flour
1 tablespoon salt

1 cup raisins (optional)
1 cup hot water (optional)

1. Combine the water, molasses, and oil in the bowl of a heavy-duty electric mixer or in a large mixing bowl.
2. Sprinkle the yeast over the mixture, stir in, and let sit for 2 minutes.
3. Add the dry ingredients.
4. Mix with the dough hook (or knead by hand) for 8 to 10 minutes, or until the dough appears silky and resilient.
5. Meanwhile, place the raisins in a bowl, add the hot water, and let them plump for 10 minutes.
6. Drain the raisins and mix or knead into the dough until thoroughly incorporated.
7. Transfer the dough to a lightly oiled bowl and cover with plastic wrap.
8. Let rise in a warm place for 1½ hours, or until approximately doubled in volume.
9. Punch the dough down, re-cover with plastic wrap, and let rise again in a warm place 30 minutes.
10. Place a baking stone on the middle rack in the oven and preheat to 400°.

11. Place the dough on a lightly floured work surface and cut into 2 equal pieces.

12. Grease two loaf pans or generously dust a baking sheet with whole-wheat flour.

13. Shape the dough into oblong loaves. Alternatively, shape it into 2 round loaves or 14 to 16 rolls. (See photos and additional instructions on pages 206–207.)

14. Place the loaves in the prepared loaf pans or on the baking sheet (or place the rolls on the baking sheet), cover with lightly oiled plastic wrap, and let rise again in a warm place for 20 minutes.

15. Uncover the loaves (or rolls) and, using a spray bottle, spritz them with water and lightly dust with whole-wheat flour.

16. Make 2 or 3 diagonal slashes in the tops of the loaves with a serrated knife to allow the dough to expand in the hot oven.

17. Using the spray bottle, spritz the inside of the oven with water. Work quickly so the oven does not lose heat.

18. Set the loaf pans or baking sheet on the hot stone.

19. Bake for 35 to 40 minutes (20 to 25 minutes for rolls). The bread is done when the crust is dark and firm, and the loaves sound hollow when tapped on the bottom.

20. Transfer the loaves (or rolls) to a rack and let cool for 10 minutes before cutting.

Yield: 2 loaves

Bread Machine Instructions

1. Combine all the ingredients in the bread pan in the order specified by the manufacturer's instructions.

2. Process on the whole-wheat medium setting (#5).

COYOTE'S COUNTRY LOAF

The European tradition of bread making has prospered in the Southwest since the early seventeenth century—as long as anywhere else in the United States. The Spanish brought wheat and the technology to use it to the region, and just to the south of Santa Fe is a wonderfully preserved old mill, Las Golandrinas, which was founded in the 1600s. It provided a way station on the Camino Real, the main route northward from Mexico, and attracted Hispanic settlers. Mills were an important symbol of wheat's civilizing influence on the Americas, especially in the agrarian corn-based culture that existed in the Southwest at the time.

This is our simple, straightforward rendition of a basic wheat loaf like the kind that has been made in and around Santa Fe for centuries. It has a rustic, free-form shape—although you can make it into a long, thin, French baguette if you prefer—a tender texture, and a light, soft crust. It's very versatile—it goes well with most meals, it's great toasted, and it's ideal for making bread crumbs or croutons. Try topping it with garlic oil or cheese, and toasting it to make crostini. The wheat flavor is enhanced by the addition of whole-wheat flour.

1 cup plus 6 tablespoons lukewarm water
¼ cup butter, melted
2 teaspoons active dry yeast

Dry Ingredients

2½ cups all-purpose flour
1½ cups bread flour
¼ cup whole-wheat flour
2½ teaspoons salt

1. Pour the water and butter into the bowl of a heavy-duty electric mixer or into a large mixing bowl.

2. Sprinkle the yeast over the water, stir in, and let sit for 2 minutes.

3. Add the dry ingredients.

4. Mix with the dough hook (or knead by hand) for 8 to 10 minutes, or until the dough appears silky and resilient.

5. Transfer the dough to a lightly oiled bowl and cover with plastic wrap.

6. Let rise in a warm place for 1½ hours, or until approximately doubled in volume.

7. Punch the dough down, re-cover with plastic wrap, and let rise again in a warm place for 30 minutes.

8. Place a baking stone on the middle rack in the oven and preheat to 400°.

9. Place the dough on a lightly floured work surface and cut into 2 equal pieces.

10. Generously dust a baking sheet with cornmeal.

11. Shape the dough into round loaves. Alternatively, shape it into long, thin baguettes. (See photos and additional instructions on pages 206–2070.)

12. Place the loaves seam side down on the prepared baking sheet, cover with lightly oiled plastic wrap, and let rise again in a warm place for 20 minutes.

13. Uncover the loaves and, using a spray bottle, spritz them with water, then lightly dust with all-purpose flour.

14. Make 2 or 3 diagonal slashes in the top of the loaves with a serrated knife to allow the dough to expand in the hot oven.

15. Using the spray bottle, spritz the oven walls with water. Work quickly so the oven does not lose heat.

16. Set the baking sheet on the hot stone.

17. Bake for 35 to 40 minutes. The bread is done when the crust is a deep, golden brown and the loaves sound hollow when tapped on the bottom.

18. Transfer the loaves to a rack and let cool for 10 minutes before cutting.

Yield: 2 loaves

Bread Machine Instructions

1. Combine all the ingredients in the bread pan in the order specified by the manufacturer's instructions.
2. Process on the basic medium setting (#2).

STONE-GROUND WHEAT BREAD

This is about as simple as bread recipes get! This is the king of the grain breads. It's ideal with meals featuring strong flavors and spicy foods, and it's perfect for toast or sandwiches. Healthful home-baked breads using stone-ground whole-wheat flour are the antithesis of the Age of Tasteless White Bread, during which many of us grew up. Thankfully, Americans are increasingly embracing hearty, flavorful breads like this one.

Stone-ground flour is preferable to regular flour, which is ground with large metal rollers, because more of the nutrients and flavors of the flour are retained; metal rollers tend to overheat the flour, diminishing these qualities. Use stone-ground flour as quickly as possible, as it loses its freshness more quickly than standard flour. Ideally, you can grind your own whole-wheat berries at home, using the grain mill attachment that comes with a heavy-duty mixer. The Whole Earth Catalog and Sunset magazine are good sources for these machines.

1½ cups lukewarm water
¼ cup canola oil
2 teaspoons active dry yeast

Dry Ingredients

2 cups whole-wheat flour (preferably stone ground)
1¼ cups bread flour
¼ cup whole-wheat flakes
1 tablespoon salt

1. Pour the water and oil into the bowl of a heavy-duty electric mixer or into a large mixing bowl.
2. Sprinkle the yeast over the water, stir, and let sit for 2 minutes.
3. Add the dry ingredients.
4. Mix with the dough hook (or knead by hand) for 8 to 10 minutes, or until the dough appears silky and resilient.
5. Transfer the dough to a lightly oiled bowl and cover with plastic wrap.
6. Let rise in a warm place for 1½ hours, or until approximately doubled in volume.
7. Punch the dough down, re-cover with plastic wrap, and let rise again in a warm place for 30 minutes.
8. Place a baking stone on the middle rack of the oven and preheat to 400°.
9. Place the dough on a lightly floured work surface and cut into 2 equal pieces.
10. Grease two loaf pans or generously dust a baking sheet with whole-wheat flour.

11. Shape the dough into oblong loaves. Alternatively, shape it into 2 round loaves or 14 to 16 rolls. (See photos and additional instructions on pages 206–207.)

12. Place the loaves in the prepared greased loaf pans or on the baking sheet (or place the rolls on the baking sheet), cover with lightly oiled plastic wrap, and let rise again in a warm place for 20 minutes.

13. Uncover the loaves (or rolls) and, using a spray bottle, spritz them with water then lightly dust with whole-wheat flour.

14. Make 2 or 3 diagonal slashes in the tops of the loaves with a serrated knife to allow the dough to expand in the hot oven.

15. Using the spray bottle, spritz the oven walls with water. Work quickly so the oven does not lose heat.

16. Set the loaf pans or baking sheet on the hot stone.

17. Bake for 35 to 40 minutes (20 to 25 minutes for rolls). The bread is done when the crust is crisp and dark and the loaves sound hollow when tapped on the bottom.

18. Transfer the loaves (or rolls) to a rack and let cool for 10 minutes before cutting.

Yield: 2 loaves or 14 to 16 rolls

Bread Machine Instructions

1. Combine all the ingredients in the bread pan in the order specified by the manufacturer's instructions.

2. Process on the whole-wheat medium setting (#5).

PASTRAMI RYE

Pastrami is dry-cured, smoked beef, usually made with brisket or round, but venison, duck, and other lean meats can be processed the same way to make pastrami. The word pastrami is Romanian in origin. The meat was initially popularized in the United States by patrons of New York's kosher delicatessens. Coyote never met a pastrami sandwich he didn't like, and this hearty rye bread is almost a sandwich in itself—it certainly has all the elements of the classic pastrami with mustard on rye.

Mustard is the chosen partner for many cold meats, and here we use a combination of the smooth and sharp-flavored Dijon-style mustard and the rustic whole-grain variety. You can use a flavored mustard if you prefer; one of our favorites is made with fiery habanero chiles, which gives this recipe some extra zip. This delicious bread has a soft crust and a firm but delicate texture that makes it ideal for sandwiches—especially grilled ones with a pastrami or cheese filling. Because the bread should be kept refrigerated, the crust will soften. You can recrisp it by misting it with water and warming in a 400° oven for 3 to 4 minutes. Vegetarians (and especially vegetarian mustard lovers) can take heart; this recipe is equally delicious if you hold the pastrami.

¼ cup lukewarm water

½ cup lukewarm milk

1 cup lukewarm heavy cream

2 tablespoons butter, melted

¼ cup Dijon-style mustard

¼ cup whole-grain mustard

1 tablespoon active dry yeast

Dry Ingredients

1½ cups rye flour

2½ cups bread flour

1 tablespoon firmly packed brown sugar

1 teaspoon cracked black peppercorns, toasted (page 210)

2 teaspoons salt

2 tablespoons minced yellow onion

4 ounces sliced pastrami, cut into ¼-inch strips

1. Combine the water, milk, cream, butter, and mustards in the bowl of a heavy-duty electric mixer or in a large mixing bowl.

2. Sprinkle the yeast over the mixture, stir in, and let sit for 2 minutes.

3. Add the dry ingredients.

4. Mix with the dough hook (or knead by hand) for 8 to 10 minutes, or until the dough appears silky and resilient.

5. Mix or knead in the onion and pastrami until thoroughly incorporated.

6. Transfer the dough to a lightly oiled bowl and cover with plastic wrap.

7. Let rise in a warm place for 1½ hours, or until approximately doubled in volume.

8. Punch the dough down, re-cover with plastic wrap, and let rise again in a warm place for 30 minutes.

9. Place a baking stone on the middle rack in the oven and preheat to 400°.

10. Place the dough on a lightly floured work surface and cut into 2 equal pieces.

11. Generously dust a baking sheet with rye flour.

12. Shape the dough into round loaves. (See photos and additional instructions on pages 206–207.)

13. Place the loaves seam side down on the prepared baking sheet, cover with lightly oiled plastic wrap, and let rise again in a warm place for 30 minutes.

14. Uncover the loaves and, using a spray bottle, spritz them with water and lightly dust with rye flour.

15. Make 2 or 3 diagonal slashes in the tops of the loaves with a serrated knife to allow the dough to expand in the hot oven.

16. Using the spray bottle, spritz the oven walls with water. Work quickly so the oven does not lose heat.

17. Set the baking sheet on the hot stone.

18. Bake for 40 to 45 minutes. The bread is done when the crust is brown on top and crisp and the loaves sound hollow when tapped on the bottom.

19. Let the loaves cool on the baking sheet for 10 minutes.

20. Transfer the loaves to a rack and cool completely before cutting.

21. When cool, transfer to an airtight plastic bag and store in the refrigerator.

Yield: 2 loaves

Bread Machine Instructions

1. Combine all the ingredients, except the pastrami, in the bread pan in the order specified by the manufacturer's instructions.

2. Process on the sweet or raisin bread setting (#8).

3. Add the pastrami at the beeps.

RED SAGE QUINOA BREAD

This bread is named after Red Sage, the Washington, D.C., sister restaurant of Coyote Cafe. We are often asked if there is such a herb. Yes, red sage really does exist, although it is relatively rare and not easily available to the home cook. Its bright red flowers look like a miniature version of Indian paintbrush.

Quinoa is a remarkable supergrain that contains double the amount of protein of most other grains. Like amaranth, it is a complete protein in that it contains all the essential amino acids, is low in carbohydrates, and is a source of important nutrients; for example, quinoa has more calcium than milk. Quinoa is native to the South American Andes, where it has been cultivated for thousands of years. It was such an important staple of the Inca civilization that it was referred to as the "mother grain." It was often eaten in the form of a porridgelike mush, or shaped into flat cakes. On a recent trip to Bolivia, I enjoyed quinoa in a salad, mixed with tomatoes, garlic, and fresh herbs. Quinoa is becoming increasingly popular in the United States, and is even being grown in Colorado and the Northwest; it's available at most natural food stores. When cooked, quinoa has a pleasantly crunchy texture, rather like caviar. The combination of sage and quinoa results in an aromatic, earthy bread that's good with chicken dishes, including chicken soup. The soft texture of this bread also makes great rolls.

1 cup quinoa
2½ cups water

1 cup lukewarm water
2 tablespoons lukewarm milk
2 tablespoons canola or corn oil
2 teaspoons active dry yeast

Dry Ingredients

½ cup whole-wheat flour
3 cups bread flour
3 tablespoons dried rubbed sage
12 fresh sage leaves, coarsely chopped
1 tablespoon chile molido (freshly ground pure
   chile powder)
2½ teaspoons salt

1. Place the quinoa and 2½ cups water in a saucepan and bring to a boil.
2. Lower the heat to a simmer and cook for 20 to 25 minutes, or until the quinoa expands and becomes fluffy.
3. Drain the quinoa and place in a mixing bowl; there should be about 2 cups of cooked quinoa. Set aside.
4. Combine the 1 cup water, the milk, and oil in the bowl of a heavy-duty electric mixer or in a large mixing bowl.
5. Sprinkle the yeast over the mixture, stir in, and let sit for 2 minutes.
6. Add the cooked quinoa and dry ingredients.
7. Mix with the dough hook (or knead by hand) for 8 to 10 minutes, or until the dough appears silky and resilient.

8. Transfer the dough to a lightly oiled bowl and cover with plastic wrap.

9. Let rise in a warm place for 1½ hours, or until approximately doubled in volume.

10. Punch the dough down, re-cover with plastic wrap, and let rise again in a warm place for 30 minutes.

11. Place a baking stone on the middle rack in the oven and preheat to 400°.

12. Place the dough on a lightly floured work surface and cut into 2 equal pieces.

13. Grease two loaf pans or generously dust a baking sheet with whole-wheat flour.

14. Shape the dough into oblong loaves. Alternatively, divide it into 14 to 16 rolls. (See photos and additional instructions on pages 206–207.)

15. Place the loaves in the prepared loaf pans or on the baking sheet (or place the rolls on the baking sheet), cover with lightly oiled plastic wrap, and let rise again in a warm place for 30 minutes.

16. Uncover the loaves (or rolls) and, using a spray bottle, spritz them with water and lightly dust with rye flour.

17. Make 2 or 3 diagonal slashes in the tops of the loaves with a serrated knife to allow the dough to expand in the hot oven.

18. Using the spray bottle, spritz the oven walls with water. Work quickly so the oven does not lose heat.

19. Set the loaf pans or baking sheet on the hot stone.

20. Bake for 35 to 40 minutes (20 to 25 minutes for rolls). The bread is done when the crust is crisp and dark brown and the loaves sound hollow when tapped on the bottom.

21. Let the bread cool in the pans or on the baking sheet for 10 minutes.

22. Transfer the loaves (or rolls) to a rack and cool before cutting.

Yield: 2 loaves or 14 to 16 rolls

Bread Machine Instructions

1. Combine the ingredients, except the fresh sage, in the bread pan in the order specified by the manufacturer's instructions.

2. Process on the sweet or raisin bread setting (#8).

3. Add the fresh sage at the beeps.

CINNAMON-BUCKWHEAT BREAD

This has been a signature bread at Coyote Cafe since we opened in 1987. Its subtle sweetness and great aroma provide a satisfying contrast to savory, spicy foods (especially those containing chiles), which is the main reason the bread is so popular at the restaurant. It makes great toast, whether for breakfast, snacks, or grilled sandwiches, and is also a terrific match for red meats and hearty stews.

Botanically, buckwheat (also known as kasha) is a herb rather than a grain, although in most respects it resembles and cooks like a grain. It is native to Central Asia, and primarily grown for animal feed and as a cover crop. Buckwheat flour is a dark gray-brown color and is available in gourmet markets and natural foods stores. Buckwheat is most commonly used for human consumption in Russia, where it is made into blini and pancakes. On a trip to Bhutan, a tiny country nestled in the Himalayas, I was served buckwheat as a cereal and as the starch with a main course. It is robust in texture and flavor, and because it contains very little gluten, it must be combined with wheat flour to produce satisfactory bread.

1¼ cups lukewarm water
¼ cup butter, melted
2½ teaspoons dry active yeast

Dry Ingredients
¾ cup buckwheat flour
¼ cup buckwheat (kasha) kernels
1½ cups bread flour
¾ cup all-purpose flour
4 teaspoons ground cinnamon
1 tablespoon sugar
2 teaspoons salt

1. Combine the water and butter in the bowl of a heavy-duty electric mixer or in a large mixing bowl.
2. Sprinkle the yeast over the mixture, stir in, and let sit for 2 minutes.
3. Add the dry ingredients.
4. Mix with the dough hook (or knead by hand) for 8 to 10 minutes, or until the dough appears silky and resilient.
5. Transfer the dough to a lightly oiled bowl and cover with plastic wrap.
6. Let rise in a warm place for 1½ hours, or until approximately doubled in volume.
7. Punch the dough down, re-cover with plastic wrap, and let rise again in a warm place for 30 minutes.
8. Place a baking stone on the middle rack in the oven and preheat to 400°.
9. Place the dough on a lightly floured work surface and cut into 2 equal pieces.
10. Grease two loaf pans or generously dust a baking sheet with rye flour.

11. Shape the dough into oblong loaves. (See photos and additional instructions on pages 206–207.)

12. Place the loaves in the prepared loaf pans or on the baking sheet, cover with lightly oiled plastic wrap, and let rise again in a warm place for 30 minutes.

13. Uncover the loaves and, using a spray bottle, spritz them with water and lightly dust with rye flour.

14. Make 2 or 3 diagonal slashes in the tops of the loaves with a serrated knife to allow the dough to expand in the hot oven.

15. Using the spray bottle, spritz the oven walls with water. Work quickly so the oven does not lose heat.

16. Set the loaf pans or baking sheet on the hot stone.

17. Bake for 35 to 40 minutes. The bread is done when the crust is crisp and deep brown, and the loaves sound hollow when tapped on the bottom.

18. Let the bread cool in the pans or on the baking sheet for 10 minutes.

19. Transfer the loaves to a rack and cool completely before cutting.

Yield: 2 loaves

Bread Machine Instructions

1. Combine the ingredients in the bread pan in the order specified by the manufacturer's instructions.

2. Process on the whole-wheat medium setting (#5).

ZUNI PEPITA

Without Native Americans, there would be no pumpkin pie at Thanksgiving—they were the ones who introduced the pilgrims to pumpkins and other squash. There are hundreds of types of squash that are indigenous to North, Central, and South America. Naturally, these plants and their seeds figure prominently in the diets of native groups throughout the continent, including the agrarian Zuni of Arizona. Native Americans commonly ground the pumpkin seeds (pepitas) into flour, which is what we do in this recipe. Combined with whole-wheat flour and blue cornmeal, the ground seeds make rich, hearty, and satisfying loaves. The bread is a wonderful partner for fall or winter soups and stews, especially those containing pumpkin or squash. Buy pumpkin seed oil and fresh pumpkin seeds at gourmet markets or natural foods stores. Before buying the seeds taste one or two to make sure they are not rancid—they should be bright green and taste sweet and fresh. Buy only as many as you need, as their natural oils can become stale quickly; roast any you have left over, which is the preserving technique used by generations of Native Americans.

1¾ cups lukewarm water

1 egg, beaten

¼ cup pumpkin seed oil or corn oil

1½ teaspoons active dry yeast

1½ cups shelled pumpkin seeds, toasted (page 210)

Dry Ingredients

2½ cups bread flour

1 cup whole-wheat flour

1 cup blue cornmeal

1 tablespoon chopped fresh sage

2 teaspoons salt

2 egg whites, beaten

½ cup shelled untoasted pumpkin seeds

1. Combine the water, egg, and oil in the bowl of a heavy-duty electric mixer or in a large mixing bowl.

2. Sprinkle the yeast over the mixture, stir in, and let sit for 2 minutes.

3. Grind the toasted pumpkin seeds in a coffee grinder or spice mill until finely ground.

4. Add the ground pumpkin seeds and dry ingredients to the yeast mixture.

5. Mix with the dough hook (or knead by hand) for 8 to 10 minutes, or until the dough appears silky and resilient.

6. Transfer the dough to a lightly oiled bowl and cover with plastic wrap.

7. Let rise in a warm place for 1½ hours, or until approximately doubled in volume.

8. Punch the dough down, re-cover with plastic wrap, and let rise again in a warm place for 30 minutes.

9. Place a baking stone on the middle rack of the oven and preheat to 400°.

10. Place the dough on a lightly floured work surface and cut into 2 equal pieces.

11. Generously dust a baking sheet with cornmeal.

12. Shape the dough into round loaves. (See photos and additional instructions on pages 206–207.)

13. Place the loaves seam side down on the prepared baking sheet, cover with lightly oiled plastic wrap, and let rise again in a warm place for 20 minutes.

14. Uncover the loaves and, using a pastry brush, brush with the egg whites.

15. Sprinkle the ½ cup raw pumpkin seeds on top of the loaves and gently press with your hands to adhere the seeds to the loaves.

16. Make 2 or 3 diagonal slashes in the tops of the loaves with a serrated knife to allow the dough to expand in the hot oven.

17. Using the spray bottle, spritz the oven walls with water. Work quickly so the oven does not lose heat.

18. Set the baking sheet on the hot stone.

19. Bake for 35 to 40 minutes. The bread is done when the crust is crisp and caramel brown, and the loaves sound hollow when tapped on the bottom.

20. Let the bread cool on the baking sheet for 10 minutes.

21. Transfer the loaves to a rack and cool completely before cutting.

Yield: 2 loaves

Bread Machine Instructions

1. Combine all the ingredients, except the egg whites and raw pumpkin seeds, in the bread pan in the order specified by the manufacturer's instructions. You will not use the egg whites or raw pumpkin seeds.

2. Process on the whole-wheat medium setting (#5).

KILLARNEY IRISH OATMEAL BREAD

Many of us have early memories of oatmeal for breakfast, but centuries ago in Europe it was often the main meal of the day—and back then, it was served sans maple syrup or plump raisins! Oats are a highly nutritious grain that are probably native to central or eastern Europe and, like rye, they thrive in cool, moist climates such as that of Ireland. In the mid-1700s, Samuel Johnson wrote that oats were mostly fed to horses in England, "but which in Scotland supports the people." The English may have caught up with the Scots in the consumption of porridge, but it is still true that animals consume 70 percent of the world's oat supply. This is partly because animals have a different digestive process than humans, and are able to process the tough outer husk and capitalize on its full nutritive value. It is relatively difficult to remove the husk, so for human consumption, oats must be toasted or steamed and cleaned, as well as hulled. Another reason oats are less favored is they have a higher fat content than most grains, which gives them a shorter storage life and leads to a higher spoilage rate. They also lack gluten, making them unsuitable for using by themselves in leavened bread.

This classic loaf has a crisp, crunchy crust and a soft, delicate texture that is interspersed with the contrasting chewy oats. It's just the thing for a New England boiled dinner—corned beef and cabbage or stews—or to celebrate St. Patrick's Day. It toasts well and is an ideal snacking bread with jam or jelly.(Killarney Irish Oatmeal rolls are pictured on page 68.)

1¼ cups water

2½ cups rolled oats

2 tablespoons dark molasses

½ cup milk, at room temperature

2 teaspoons active dry yeast

Dry Ingredients

2 cups bread flour

½ cup whole-wheat flour

2¼ teaspoons salt

1. Combine the water, 2 cups of the oats, and molasses in a saucepan, bring to a simmer, and cook over medium heat for 8 to 10 minutes, stirring occasionally.

2. Transfer the mixture to the bowl of a heavy-duty electric mixer or a large mixing bowl, and let cool to room temperature. Add the milk.

3. Sprinkle the yeast over the mixture, stir in, and let sit for 2 minutes.

4. Add the dry ingredients.

5. Mix with the dough hook (or knead by hand) for 8 to 10 minutes, or until the dough appears silky and resilient.

6. Transfer the dough to a lightly oiled bowl and cover with plastic wrap.

7. Let rise in a warm place for 1½ hours, or until approximately doubled in volume.

8. Punch the dough down, re-cover with plastic wrap, and let rise again in a warm place for 30 minutes.

9. Place the baking stone on the middle rack in the oven and preheat to 400°.

10. Place the dough on a lightly floured work surface and cut into 2 equal pieces.

11. Grease two loaf pans or generously dust a baking sheet with whole-wheat flour.

12. Shape the dough into oblong loaves. Alternately, divide it into 14 to 16 rolls. (See photos and additional instructions on pages 206–207.)

13. Place the loaves in the prepared pans or on the baking sheet, cover with lightly oiled plastic wrap, and let rise again in a warm place for 30 minutes.

14. Uncover the loaves and, using a spray bottle, spritz them with water and lightly dust with rye flour.

15. Sprinkle the remaining ½ cup of oats on top of the loaves and gently press with your hands to adhere the oats to the loaves.

16. Make 2 or 3 diagonal slashes in the tops of the loaves with a serrated knife to allow the dough to expand in the hot oven.

17. Using the spray bottle, spritz the oven walls with water. Work quickly so the oven does not lose heat.

18. Set the loaf pans or baking sheet on the stone.

19. Bake for 35 to 40 minutes (20 to 25 minutes for rolls). The bread is done when the crust is crisp and deep brown, the oats are toasty, and the loaves sound hollow when tapped on the bottom.

20. Let the bread cool in the pans or on the baking sheet for 10 minutes.

21. Transfer the loaves to a rack and cool completely before cutting.

Yield: 2 loaves

Bread Machine Instructions

1. Combine the ingredients in the bread pan in the order specified by the manufacturer's instructions.
2. Process on the whole-wheat medium setting (#5).

OLDE ENGLISH CIDER-WALNUT BREAD

The aroma of freshly pressed cider and the musty, woody smell of cider presses are sure signs of autumn, with all its mellow fruitfulness. When I was growing up in New England, I always looked forward to our fall trips to the apple orchards, where we'd buy bushels of apples for desserts, sauces, and apple butter, as well as for fresh cider. The tradition of cider originates in Somerset, the county in southwestern England famous for its apple orchards and where the practice of combining cider with walnuts in bread, especially for feast days and special occasions, dates back to medieval times. Cider is the primary liquid in this bread, so the flavor really comes through. Try to find the heartiest, rust-colored unfiltered cider for this recipe. The unfiltered type is far preferable to the clear, filtered variety because it contains all the nutrients and more flavor; it's available in the refrigerated case at stores in the fall and in the freezer case at other times. Best of all, buy it from local farms or at farmers markets in the early fall, when the apple orchards are being harvested. The sweetness imbued by the apple cider makes this bread ideal for breakfast toast on a chilly fall day. It also complements cheese and will stand up to the flavors of wild game as a dinner bread. (Olde English Cider–Walnut Bread is pictured with Killarney Irish Oatmeal rolls [page 66].)

1 cup lukewarm unfiltered fresh apple cider

¼ cup cider vinegar

1 tablespoon dark molasses

1½ teaspoons active dry yeast

Dry Ingredients

2 cups bread flour

1 cup whole-wheat flour

1 tablespoon dry or powdered milk

1½ teaspoons salt

1 cup chopped walnuts or pecans, toasted
   (page 209)

1. Combine the cider, vinegar, and molasses in the bowl of a heavy-duty electric mixer or in a large mixing bowl.

2. Sprinkle the yeast over the mixture, stir in, and let sit for 2 minutes.

3. Add the dry ingredients.

4. Mix with the dough hook (or knead by hand) for 8 to 10 minutes, or until the dough appears silky and resilient.

5. Mix or knead the walnut pieces into the dough until evenly distributed.

6. Transfer the dough to a lightly oiled bowl and cover with plastic wrap.

7. Let rise in a warm place for 1½ hours, or until approximately doubled in volume.

8. Punch the dough down, re-cover with plastic wrap, and let rise again in a warm place for 30 minutes.

9. Place a baking stone on the middle rack in the oven and preheat to 400°.

(continued)

10. Place the dough on a lightly floured work surface.

11. Grease a loaf pan or generously dust a baking sheet with whole-wheat flour.

12. Shape the dough into an oblong loaf. (See photos and additional instructions on pages 206–207.)

13. Place the loaf in the prepared loaf pan or on the baking sheet, cover the loaf with lightly oiled plastic wrap, and let rise again in a warm place for 20 minutes.

14. Uncover the loaf and, using a spray bottle, spritz with water and lightly dust with whole-wheat flour.

15. Make 2 or 3 diagonal slashes in the top of the loaf with a serrated knife to allow the dough to expand in the hot oven.

16. Using the spray bottle, spritz the oven walls with water. Work quickly so the oven does not lose heat.

17. Set the loaf pan or baking sheet on the hot stone.

18. Bake for 35 to 40 minutes. The bread is done when the crust is caramel brown and firm and the loaf sounds hollow when tapped on the bottom.

19. Let the loaf cool in the pan or on the baking sheet for 10 minutes.

20. Transfer the loaf to a rack and cool completely before cutting.

Yield: 1 large loaf

Bread Machine Instructions

1. Combine all the ingredients, except the walnuts, in the bread pan in the order specified by the manufacturer's instructions.

2. Process on the sweet or raisin bread setting (#8).

3. Add the walnuts at the beeps.

LIBERTY ALE RYE

Liberty Ale is a hearty beer made by San Francisco's Anchor Brewing Company, which also produces Anchor Steam beer. For a darker, more intense bread, use a stout.

1½ cups Liberty Ale beer, at room temperature
2 tablespoons dark molasses
1 tablespoon olive oil
2½ teaspoons dry active yeast

Dry Ingredients
1¼ cups rye flour
2 cups bread flour
2½ teaspoons salt

1. Combine the beer, molasses, and oil in the bowl of a heavy-duty electric mixer or in a large mixing bowl. Sprinkle the yeast over the mixture, stir in, and let sit for 2 minutes.
2. Add the dry ingredients.
3. Mix with the dough hook (or knead by hand) for 8 to 10 minutes, or until the dough appears silky and resilient.
4. Transfer the dough to a lightly oiled bowl and cover with plastic wrap.
5. Let rise in a warm place for 1½ hours, or until approximately doubled in volume.
6. Punch the dough down, re-cover with plastic wrap, and let rise again in a warm place for 30 minutes.
7. Place a baking stone on the middle rack in the oven and preheat to 400°.
8. Place the dough on a lightly floured work surface and cut into 2 equal pieces.
9. Grease two loaf pans or generously dust a baking sheet with rye flour.

10. Shape the dough into oblong loaves. (See photos and additional instructions on pages 206–207.)
11. Place the loaves in the prepared loaf pans or on the baking sheet, cover with lightly oiled plastic wrap, and let rise again in a warm place for 30 minutes.
12. Uncover the loaves and, using a spray bottle, spritz them with water, then dust with rye flour.
13. Make 2 or 3 diagonal slashes in the tops of the loaves with a serrated knife to allow the dough to expand in the hot oven.
14. Using the spray bottle, spritz the oven walls with water. Work quickly so the oven does not lose heat.
15. Set the loaf pans or baking sheet on the hot stone.
16. Bake for 35 to 40 minutes, or until the crust is crisp and deep brown and the loaves sound hollow when tapped on the bottom.
17. Transfer the loaves to a rack and cool completely before cutting.

Yield: 2 loaves

Bread Machine Instructions
1. Combine the ingredients in the bread pan in the order specified by the manufacturer's instructions.
2. Process on the whole-wheat medium setting (#5).

HEARTY FIVE-GRAIN BREAD

If white flour and white bread have been considered pure and symbolic of affluence and "civilization" throughout history, then this coarsely textured dark bread is aligned with the natural world and rustic living. We vote for nature every time! The combination of bread, whole-wheat, buckwheat, and rye flour, along with cornmeal and brown rice, produces a tightly grained, moist, dense bread that goes with all meals and is good for sandwiches (which means it also keeps well). This multigrain bread is a little out of the traditional mold because of the unusual addition of rice and cornmeal. It's a little too dense to make into rolls, but it slices and toasts well. If you prefer, you can bake this bread in loaf pans, rather than free form. You'll find the rye and whole-wheat flakes, which are similar to rolled oats in that the grain berries are flattened when they're passed through heavy steel rollers, at gourmet markets and natural foods stores.

2 cups lukewarm water

2 tablespoons firmly packed brown sugar

1½ teaspoons active dry yeast

Dry Ingredients

3 cups bread flour

¾ cup whole-wheat flour

¾ cup rye flour

¼ cup buckwheat flour

½ cup coarse cornmeal

1 cup cooked brown rice

1 tablespoon salt

2 tablespoons rye flakes

2 tablespoons whole-wheat flakes

1. Combine the water and brown sugar in the bowl of a heavy-duty electric mixer or in a large mixing bowl.

2. Sprinkle the yeast over the mixture, stir in, and let sit for 2 minutes.

3. Add the dry ingredients.

4. Mix with the dough hook (or knead by hand) for 8 to 10 minutes, until the dough appears silky and resilient.

5. Transfer the dough to a lightly oiled bowl and cover with plastic wrap.

6. Let rise in a warm place for 1½ hours, or until approximately doubled in volume.

7. Punch the dough down, re-cover with plastic wrap, and let rise again in a warm place for 30 minutes.

8. Place a baking stone on the middle rack in the oven and preheat to 400°.

9. Place the dough on a lightly floured work surface and cut into 2 equal pieces.

10. Generously dust a baking sheet with whole-wheat flour.

11. Shape the dough into round loaves. (See photos and additional instructions on pages 206–207.)

12. Place the loaves seam side down on the prepared baking sheet, cover with lightly oiled plastic wrap, and let rise again in a warm place for 30 minutes.

13. Uncover the loaves and, using a spray bottle, spritz them with water.

14. Sprinkle the rye flakes and whole-wheat flakes on top of the loaves and gently press with your hands to adhere the flakes to the loaves.

15. Make 2 or 3 diagonal slashes in the tops of the loaves with a serrated knife to allow the dough to expand in the hot oven.

16. Using the spray bottle, spritz the oven walls with water. Work quickly so the oven does not lose heat.

17. Set the baking sheet on the hot stone.

18. Bake for 40 to 45 minutes. The bread is done when the crust is medium brown and firm and the loaves sound hollow when tapped on the bottom.

19. Let the bread cool on the baking sheet for 10 minutes.

20. Transfer the loaves to a rack and cool completely before cutting.

Yield: 2 loaves

Bread Machine Instructions

1. Combine all the ingredients, except the rye flakes and wheat flakes, in the bread pan in the order specified by the manufacturer's instructions. You will not use the rye flakes or wheat flakes.

2. Process on the whole-wheat medium setting (#5).

INCA AMARANTH BREAD

Amaranth, native to Central and South America and cultivated by both the Aztecs and Incas, is one of the smallest of all grains. Aztec healers used the seeds and leaves, and amaranth tamales played a role in their religious rituals. It is a strikingly beautiful plant, with dense clusters of crimson, purple, or green flowers that produce the seeds, or "grain," and it is usually grown as a row crop in fields of corn and squash. Amaranth is highly prolific and drought resistant, and after suffering a sharp decline in use after the Spanish conquest of the New World, it has made a comeback relatively recently in the Andes and Mexico. Now it is also generating great mainstream interest in the United States. It has a pronounced, slightly sweet and pleasantly nutty flavor, and is high in protein and nutritional value—so much so that it's often described as a supergrain. Amaranth seeds can be ground and made into a flour, but here the cooked seeds make a coarsely textured, grainy rustic loaf that's great fresh or toasted with salads or for sandwiches.

1¼ cups dried amaranth
2½ cups water

1 cup lukewarm water
1 tablespoon firmly packed brown sugar
2 tablespoons olive oil
1½ teaspoons active dry yeast

Dry Ingredients
2½ cups bread flour
1 cup whole-wheat flour
½ cup cornmeal
1½ teaspoons salt

1. Place the amaranth in a sauté pan and toast over medium heat for 3 to 4 minutes, stirring occasionally.
2. Transfer the amaranth to a saucepan, add the 2½ cups water, and bring to a boil.
3. Lower the heat and simmer for 40 to 45 minutes, or until tender.
4. Drain off any excess water and set aside.
5. Combine the 1 cup water, the brown sugar, and olive oil in the bowl of a heavy-duty electric mixer or in a large mixing bowl.
6. Sprinkle the yeast over the mixture, stir in, and let sit for 2 minutes.
7. Add the cooked amaranth and dry ingredients.
8. Mix with the dough hook (or knead by hand) for 8 to 10 minutes, or until the dough appears silky and resilient.
9. Transfer the dough to a lightly oiled bowl and cover with plastic wrap.
10. Let rise in a warm place for 1½ hours, or until approximately doubled in volume.

11. Punch the dough down, re-cover with plastic wrap, and let rise again in a warm place for 30 minutes.

12. Place a baking stone on the middle rack of the oven and preheat to 400°.

13. Place the dough on a lightly floured work surface and cut into 2 equal pieces.

14. Grease two loaf pans or generously dust a baking sheet with whole-wheat flour.

15. Shape the dough into oblong loaves. (See photos and additional instructions on pages 206–207.)

16. Place the loaves in the prepared pans or on the baking sheet, cover the loaves with lightly oiled plastic wrap, and let rise again in a warm place for 20 minutes.

17. Uncover the loaves and, using a spray bottle, spritz them with water and lightly dust with whole-wheat flour.

18. Make 2 or 3 diagonal slashes in the tops of the loaves with a serrated knife to allow the dough to expand in the hot oven.

19. Using the spray bottle, spritz the oven walls with water. Work quickly so the oven does not lose heat.

20. Set the loaf pans or baking sheet on the hot stone.

21. Bake for 35 to 40 minutes. The bread is done when the crust is golden brown and crisp and the loaves sound hollow when tapped on the bottom.

22. Let the bread cool in the pans or on the baking sheet for 10 minutes.

23. Transfer the loaves to a rack and cool completely before cutting.

Yield: 2 loaves

Bread Machine Instructions

1. Combine the ingredients in the bread pan in the order specified by the manufacturer's instructions.
2. Process on the basic dark setting (#3).

MILLET-RAISIN WHEAT BREAD

Millet, the small pale yellow round seed often used in birdseed mixtures, is a high-protein grain that is cultivated as a staple in Africa and Asia, where it has been farmed for at least 6,000 years. There are several distinct types of millet, which grows in arid climates and poor soil. In Europe and the United States, it is grown mostly for animal feed. Millet is available in health food stores and natural food groceries. Because it has a bland but slightly nutty taste and an interesting texture, it is an ideal vehicle for stronger flavorings.

1½ cups lukewarm water
¾ cup millet
1 tablespoon honey
2½ teaspoons active dry yeast

Dry Ingredients

1 cup all-purpose flour
1¾ cups bread flour
1 cup whole-wheat flour
2½ teaspoons salt

1 cup raisins
1 cup hot water

1. Combine the 1½ cups water and millet in the bowl of a heavy-duty electric mixer or in a large mixing bowl.
2. Let sit for at least 2 hours (or as long as overnight) to allow the millet to soften.
3. Stir in the honey.
4. Sprinkle the yeast over the mixture, stir in, and let sit for 2 minutes.
5. Add the dry ingredients.
6. Mix with the dough hook (or knead by hand) for 8 to 10 minutes, or until the dough appears silky and resilient.
7. Meanwhile, place the raisins in a bowl, add the hot water, and let them plump for 10 minutes.
8. Drain the raisins and mix or knead them into the dough until thoroughly incorporated.
9. Transfer the dough to a lightly oiled bowl and cover with plastic wrap.
10. Let rise in a warm place for 1½ hours, or until approximately doubled in volume.
11. Punch the dough down, re-cover with plastic wrap, and let rise again in a warm place for 30 minutes.
12. Place a baking stone on the middle rack in the oven and preheat to 400°.
13. Place the dough on a lightly floured work surface and cut into 2 equal pieces.

14. Grease two loaf pans or generously dust a baking sheet with whole-wheat flour.

15. Shape the dough into oblong loaves. Alternatively, shape it into 2 round loaves or 14 to 16 rolls. (See photos and additional instructions on pages 206–207.)

16. Place the loaves in greased loaf pans or on the baking sheet (or place the rolls on the baking sheet), cover with lightly oiled plastic wrap, and let rise again in a warm place for 20 minutes.

17. Uncover the loaves (or rolls) and, using a spray bottle, spritz them with water and lightly dust with whole-wheat flour.

18. Make 2 or 3 diagonal slashes in the tops of the loaves with a serrated knife to allow the dough to expand in the hot oven.

19. Using the spray bottle, spritz the oven walls with water. Work quickly so the oven does not lose heat.

20. Set the loaf pans or baking sheet on the hot stone.

21. Bake for 35 to 40 minutes (or 20 to 25 minutes for rolls). The bread is done when the crust is dark and firm and the loaves sound hollow when tapped on the bottom.

22. Let the bread cool in the pan or on the baking sheet for 10 minutes.

23. Transfer the loaves (or rolls) to a rack and cool completely before cutting.

Yield: 2 loaves or 14 to 16 rolls

Bread Machine Instructions

1. Combine the ingredients in the bread pan in the order specified by the manufacturer's instructions.
2. Process on the whole-wheat medium setting (#5).

FLATBREADS, CRACKERBREADS, & BREADSTICKS

Flatbreads are the oldest form of bread, dating back more than 5,000 years before ancient Egyptian times. Most cuisines of the world have flatbreads in some form, from the tortillas of Mexico, the naans of India and Pakistan, the Mandarin flatbreads of China, the pita and lavash of the Middle East, and the Scottish bannock to the fougasse and focacce of the Mediterranean. Flatbreads preceded leavened bread, which was first made by the Egyptians, and they existed before wheat was commonly used for breads, using instead all types of grain as well as beans and tubers. Flatbreads may or may not include a leavener, and they do not necessarily rely on gluten for airiness or structure, hence their name. Instead, flatbreads often depend on heat, which converts the moisture in the batter or dough into steam, which causes the bread to rise and take shape.

Eventually, unleavened flatbread came to play an important ritual role in the Jewish religion. The tradition of Passover incorporates the week-long Feast of Unleavened Bread, which symbolizes the exodus from Egypt, when the Hebrews, led by Moses, fled from slavery before the leavened bread they had prepared had time to rise.

As recorded in the Bible, Moses told the Hebrews:

> Seven days shalt thou eat unleavened bread, and in the
> Seventh day shall be a feast to the Lord…and there shall be no
> unleavened bread be seen with thee, neither shall there be
> leaven seen with thee in all thy quarters…Thou shalt therefore
> keep this ordnance in his season from year to year.

During Passover, rising agents and leavened products (especially grain breads) must be removed from the home, and nothing containing leavening must be eaten. Likewise, all grains from which bread might be made are forbidden, except for kosher matzo flour, which is mixed with water and made into a flatbread for the seder meal.

Historically, the earliest flatbreads existed before ovens—they were cooked on hot stones or other natural surfaces. In the African Sahara, for example, I have eaten flatbreads that were baked in less than an hour in the hot desert sand. Because flatbreads cook quickly and thus are fuel efficient, they are particularly suited to regions where fuel is scarce. Since ovens began to be used in ancient Mediterranean cultures (the Spanish then introduced them to the New World), flatbreads have most commonly been baked, but they can be fried (like the relatively new Native American fry bread), grilled, or steamed.

Above all, flatbreads are practical and can be a great medium for other ingredients and flavorings. In India and parts of the Middle East, flatbreads are used instead of silverware, which makes eating and sopping up delicious sauces much more fun and entertaining. Other flatbreads, such as focaccia, can be used as a base for toppings, rather like pizza. Because flatbreads often don't need to proof, they are quick and easy to make fresh, and perfect for novice bakers.

With the rustic recipes that follow, you'll find that the longer the dough sits and ferments, the better the flavor and texture due to the action of the various chemical processes. For the most part, these flatbread recipes are our modern interpretations of traditional styles, combining new and exciting flavors while using old ideas and techniques. We have included recipes for crackerbreads and breadsticks, which make an interesting and welcome addition to dinner table bread baskets. Crackerbreads are flat, crisp, cracker-style flatbreads, rather in the style of lavash—a thin, dry Middle Eastern bread that has been made for thousands of years and stores well (which is what made it ideal for nomadic life). Breadsticks provide a different, crunchier texture, having a far higher crust-to-interior ratio. Perhaps the most famous advocate of breadsticks was Napoleon, who loved grissini (Italian breadsticks). Because there was no equivalent in France, he had them sent daily to his palace in Paris.

Once you have mastered the basic flatbread-baking techniques, experiment with your favorite flavorings and feel free to borrow combinations from recipes in other chapters. And here's one final tip: most of the flatbread and rustic bread doughs are sticky, so it helps to flour your hands and the work surface generously when handling them.

SUNDRIED TOMATO FLATBREAD

Most people think tomatoes originated in Italy, but they are another of the great botanical and culinary gifts that the New World gave the Old World. The same misconception applies to the provenance of sundried tomatoes; the practice of sundrying tomatoes began in the Spanish missions of the Southwest and California, and was probably based on the Native American tradition of sundrying foods. Native Americans made jerky from sundried (and sometimes fire-dried) game meats such as buffalo and venison, and they also sundried corn, chiles, and squash, among other foods. They strung both chiles and slices of squash in ristras to dry for the winter months; red chile ristras are still a hallmark of the Southwest.

The best, sweetest sundried tomatoes I ever tasted were from an organic farm near Los Cabos, in Baja California. Their intense flavor was probably due to the region's rich soil and constant sunshine. The tomatoes give this bread distinct Mediterranean flavors, which is one reason it goes so well with pastas, pestos, eggplant dishes, and most Italian or Provençal foods. Try this bread at cocktail hour with a hearty Rioja wine, or for sandwiches with goat cheese or coppacola ham. If you use sundried tomatoes packed in oil rather than rehydrating the (unsalted) dried tomatoes, use only 2 to 3 tablespoons of olive oil in this recipe.

¾ cup milk

1 cup lukewarm water

2 teaspoons active dry yeast

2 cups bread flour

22 to 24 whole dry-packed sundried tomatoes, rehydrated

¼ cup extra virgin olive oil

½ cup semolina flour

2 teaspoons salt

½ teaspoon freshly ground black pepper

4 teaspoons chopped fresh oregano, or 2 teaspoons dried oregano

2 tablespoons chopped fresh parsley, or 1 tablespoon dried parsley

1. Combine the milk and ½ cup of the water in the bowl of a heavy-duty electric mixer or in a large mixing bowl.

2. Sprinkle the yeast over the mixture, stir in, and let sit for 2 minutes.

3. Mix in 1 cup of the bread flour with the dough hook (or knead in by hand).

4. Cover the bowl with plastic wrap and let sit for 2½ hours.

5. In a food processor, purée half of the sundried tomatoes and the olive oil. Add to the bowl.

6. Add the remaining ½ cup water, the remaining 1 cup bread flour, and the semolina, salt, and pepper.

7. Mix with the dough hook (or knead by hand) for 8 to 10 minutes, or until the dough appears silky and resilient.

8. Coarsely chop the remaining sundried tomatoes.

9. Mix or knead the chopped sundried tomatoes, oregano, and parsley into the dough until evenly distributed.

10. Transfer the dough to a lightly oiled bowl and cover with plastic wrap.

11. Let rise in a warm place for 2 hours.

12. Turn over a baking sheet and sprinkle with cornmeal or semolina flour. Set aside.

13. Place the dough on a work surface generously sprinkled with semolina flour and cut into 2 equal pieces.

14. Gently pull and stretch each piece of dough into an 8-inch round or a 7-inch square.

15. Press each flatbread into the semolina flour, then flip to coat the other side.

16. Transfer to the prepared baking sheet.

17. Cover with plastic wrap and let rise in a warm place for 45 minutes to 1 hour.

18. Place a baking stone on the middle rack in the oven and preheat to 450°.

19. Using a spray bottle, spritz the oven walls with water. Work quickly so the oven does not lose heat.

20. Slide the flatbreads onto the hot stone.

21. Bake for 14 to 16 minutes, or until the bread browns.

22. Transfer the flatbreads to a rack to cool completely before cutting.

Yield: 2 flatbreads

Bread Machine Instructions
To prepare the dough in a bread machine:
1. Combine all the ingredients, except the sundried tomatoes and herbs, in the bread pan in the order specified by the manufacturer's instructions.
2. Process on the dough setting (#9).
3. When the cycle is complete, turn the dough out on a well-floured work surface.
4. Continue with step 9 of the recipe.

ARUGULA-WATERCRESS FLATBREAD

People tend to do a double-take when they first set eyes on this bright green bread. When they taste it, the spicy aromatic greens have the same effect on the palate! Arugula, also called rocket, has a peppery, pleasantly savory flavor. Use it as soon as possible as it loses its spark after a day or two. It has always been popular in Italian cuisine, and Italian markets are among the best places to find it. Arugula is easy to grow from seed, and can be successfully cultivated in window boxes if you don't have a garden. If it's unavailable, you can substitute a mixture of mustard greens and spinach, or use equal quantities of watercress, cilantro, and mint.

This picante, refreshing flatbread makes great toast and crostini, and goes well with bean and other vegetable soups, antipasti, and most dishes with tomatoes, cheese, and lentils. It makes a good pizza-type base for toppings such as sliced fresh tomatoes, and stands up well to white wines such as Sauvignon Blanc, Gewürztraminer, and Riesling.

¾ cup milk

1 cup lukewarm water

2 teaspoons active dry yeast

2½ cups bread flour

2 teaspoons salt

30 arugula leaves, coarsely chopped

20 sprigs watercress, coarsely chopped

1. Combine the milk and ½ cup of the water in the bowl of a heavy-duty electric mixer or in a large mixing bowl.

2. Sprinkle the yeast over the mixture, stir in, and let sit for 2 minutes.

3. Mix in 1 cup of the bread flour with the dough hook (or knead in by hand).

4. Cover the bowl with plastic wrap and let sit for 2½ hours.

5. Add the remaining ½ cup water, the remaining 1½ cups bread flour, and salt.

6. Mix with the dough hook (or knead by hand) for 8 to 10 minutes, or until the dough appears silky and resilient.

7. Fold or knead the arugula and watercress into the dough until evenly distributed.

8. Transfer the dough to a lightly oiled bowl and cover with plastic wrap.

9. Let rise in a warm place for 2 hours.

10. Turn over a baking sheet and sprinkle with cornmeal or semolina flour.

11. Place the dough on a work surface generously sprinkled with semolina flour and cut into 2 equal pieces.

12. Gently pull and stretch each piece of dough into an 8-inch round or a 7-inch square.

13. Press each flatbread into the semolina flour, then flip to coat the other side.

14. Transfer to the prepared baking sheet.

15. Cover with plastic wrap and let rise in a warm place for 45 minutes to 1 hour.

16. Place a baking stone on the middle rack in the oven and preheat to 450°.

17. Using a spray bottle, spritz the oven walls with water. Work quickly so the oven does not lose heat.

18. Slide the flatbreads onto the hot stone.

19. Bake for 14 to 16 minutes, or until the bread browns.

20. Transfer the flatbreads to a rack to cool.

Yield: 2 flatbreads

Bread Machine Instructions
To prepare the dough in a bread machine:

1. Combine all the ingredients, except the arugula and watercress, in the bread pan in the order specified by the manufacturer's instructions.

2. Process on the dough setting (#9).

3. When the cycle is complete, turn the dough out onto a well-floured work surface.

4. Knead the arugula and watercress into the dough until evenly distributed.

5. Continue with step 8 of the recipe.

VELARDE GREEN CHILE FLATBREAD

Velarde is an agricultural community in the Rio Grande Valley, which is north of Santa Fe and known for its green chiles and apples. When you fly from Albuquerque to Denver, the Velarde area is a striking sight from the air: its thin, verdant strip of fertile fields parallels to the river, surrounded by nothing but arid-looking land as far as the eye can see. Some chile purists will tell you that the best green chiles grow in Hatch, which is in the southern part of the state, but New Mexicans have such strong opinions about this it's probably best to agree to differ. In each region, the soil, climate, and seed yield different characteristics so that the heat and flavor nuances of chiles grown there differ from year to year.

Each fall, the fiery aroma of roasting green chiles perfumes the air in and around Santa Fe as the harvest is preserved, enabling chileheads to indulge their addiction throughout the year. Because roasted chiles freeze well (to order frozen chiles, see page 210), this fine bread can be made year-round. This is a good bread to serve for brunch, with braised pork, green chile stew, posole, and grilled chicken dishes.

¾ cup lukewarm milk

1 cup lukewarm water

2 teaspoons active dry yeast

2½ cups bread flour

½ cup cornmeal

2 teaspoons salt

½ bunch fresh cilantro, stems removed

4 New Mexico green chiles, roasted, peeled, stemmed, seeded, and diced (page 209)

1. Combine the milk and ½ cup of the water in the bowl of a heavy-duty electric mixer or in a large mixing bowl.

2. Sprinkle the yeast over the mixture, stir in, and let sit for 2 minutes.

3. Mix in 1 cup of the bread flour with the dough hook (or knead in by hand).

4. Cover the bowl with plastic wrap and let sit for 2½ hours.

5. Add the remaining ½ cup water, the remaining 1½ cups bread flour, the cornmeal, and the salt.

6. Mix with the dough hook (or knead by hand) for 8 to 10 minutes, or until the dough appears silky and resilient.

7. Chop the cilantro leaves.

8. With the mixer running on low speed, add the chopped cilantro and green chiles to the dough and mix until evenly distributed. Alternatively, knead the cilantro and chile into the dough by hand. (The chiles add moisture

to the dough; you may need to add up to ¼ cup more bread flour if the dough appears too wet.)

9. Transfer the dough to a lightly oiled bowl and cover with plastic wrap.

10. Let rise in a warm place for 2 hours.

11. Turn over a baking sheet and sprinkle with cornmeal or semolina flour.

12. Place the dough on a work surface generously sprinkled with semolina flour and cut into 2 equal pieces.

13. Gently pull and stretch each piece of dough into an 8-inch round or a 7-inch square.

14. Press each flatbread into the semolina flour, then flip to coat the other side.

15. Transfer to the prepared baking sheet.

16. Cover with plastic wrap and let rise in a warm place for 45 minutes to 1 hour.

17. Place a baking stone on the middle rack in the the oven and preheat to 450°.

18. Using a spray bottle, spritz the oven walls with water to create some humidity. Work quickly so the oven does not lose heat.

19. Slide the flatbreads onto the hot stone.

20. Bake for 14 to 16 minutes, or until the bread browns.

21. Transfer the flatbreads to a rack to cool.

Yield: 2 flatbreads

> **Bread Machine Instructions**
> **To prepare the dough in a bread machine:**
> *1. Combine all the ingredients, except the chiles and cilantro, in the bread pan in the order specified by the manufacturer's instructions.*
> *2. Process on the dough setting (#9).*
> *3. When the cycle is complete, turn the dough out onto a well-floured work surface. Chop the cilantro.*
> *4. Knead in the chiles and cilantro until evenly distributed.*
> *5. Continue with step 9 of the recipe.*

WILD MUSHROOM FLATBREAD

Here's a delicious flatbread from the forest. Wild mushrooms have always enjoyed a reputation as an exotic, magical food, probably because they have such different growing habits and characteristics than other plants. They mysteriously appear overnight and grow quickly, often in eerie and forbidding locations, such as deep, dark forests rather than open fields. And of course they are close cousins to hallucinogenic and poisonous fungi, which makes them suspect to many people. When I worked at Chez Panisse in Berkeley during the late 1970s, a high proportion of our clientele would avoid wild mushrooms or stop eating them if they realized what they were. These days this has changed, and wild mushrooms are recognized as the delicacy they truly are. Wild mushrooms have always been revered in Europe, and they are one of my favorite foods. This recipe works just as well with any type of wild mushroom or with white- or brown-cap mushrooms.

This bread is the perfect partner for game or red meats; serve the same wine with the meal that you use in the dough. The bread can also be served with vegetarian dishes—for example, it's great with a robust salad. It's also satisfying dipped in garlic oil, as garlic and mushrooms have a real affinity for each other. We recommend chef Michael Chiarello's Consorzio brand of flavored oils.

¾ cup lukewarm milk

½ cup lukewarm water

2 teaspoons active dry yeast

2 cups bread flour

¼ cup olive oil

½ cup thinly sliced shallots

2 cups thickly sliced mushrooms, such as chanterelles, porcini, portobellos, black trumpets, morels, or shiitakes

½ cup red wine, such as Cabernet Sauvignon or Merlot

½ cup whole-wheat flour

2 teaspoons salt

1 teaspoon freshly ground black pepper

1. Combine the milk and water in the bowl of a heavy-duty electric mixer or in a large mixing bowl.

2. Sprinkle the yeast over the mixture, stir in, and let sit for 2 minutes.

3. Mix in 1 cup of the bread flour with the dough hook (or knead in by hand).

4. Cover the bowl with plastic wrap and let sit for 2½ hours.

5. Meanwhile, heat the olive oil in a sauté pan and sauté the shallots and mushrooms over medium-high heat for 2 to 2½ minutes, or until the shallots are translucent and the mushrooms are tender. Set aside to cool.

6. Add the red wine, the remaining 1 cup bread flour, the whole-wheat flour, salt, and pepper to the dough.

7. Mix with the dough hook (or knead by hand) for 8 to 10 minutes, or until the dough appears silky and resilient.

8. Add the cooled shallot and mushroom mixture to the dough and fold or knead in until evenly distributed.

9. Transfer the dough to a lightly oiled bowl and cover with plastic wrap.

10. Let rise in a warm place for 2 hours.

11. Turn over a baking sheet and sprinkle with cornmeal or semolina flour.

12. Place the dough on a work surface generously sprinkled with semolina flour and cut into 2 equal pieces.

13. Gently pull and stretch each piece of dough into an 8-inch round or a 7-inch square.

14. Press each flatbread into the semolina flour, then flip to coat the other side.

15. Transfer to the prepared baking sheet.

16. Cover with plastic wrap and let rise in a warm place for 45 minutes to 1 hour.

17. Place a baking stone on the middle rack in the oven and preheat to 450°.

18. Using a spray bottle, spritz the oven walls with water. Work quickly so the oven does not lose heat.

19. Slide the flatbreads onto the hot stone.

20. Bake for 14 to 16 minutes, or until the bread browns.

21. Transfer the flatbreads to a rack to cool.

Yield: 2 flatbreads

Bread Machine Instructions
To prepare the dough in a bread machine:
1. Combine all the ingredients, except the oil, shallots, and mushrooms, in the bread pan in the order specified by the manufacturer's instructions.
2. Process on the dough setting (#9).
3. While the dough is rising, sauté the shallots and mushrooms as directed in step 5 of the recipe.
4. When the cycle is complete, turn the dough out onto a well-floured work surface.
5. Knead the sautéed shallots and mushrooms into the dough until evenly distributed.
6. Continue with step 9 of the recipe.

RED BELL PEPPER-SMOKED TOMATO FLATBREAD

Nothing quite matches the unique flavor of home-smoked tomatoes. They are easy to make and a wonderful addition to soups, chile sauces, huevos rancheros, and pizza sauces. You can use a covered barbecue grill for smoking—just soak some hickory, mesquite, or fruit wood chips in water for about an hour and then add them to a low fire in the base of the grill. It's important to smoke foods gently, or they may get bitter and too smoky. We highly recommend investing in a small, inexpensive home smoker. They are available at camping, hardware, and even some sporting stores for less than $50. If you don't want to go to the trouble of smoking, oven-dried tomatoes will also give this recipe an intense flavor. Or even better, brush the halved tomatoes very lightly with liquid smoke before you put them in the oven to dry. Serve this bread with red wine and smoked meats, smoked or sharp cheeses such as Cheddar or aged goat cheese, and smoked fish such as salmon, gravlax, or trout. This full-flavored bread is also marvelous for picnics.

¾ cup milk

1 cup lukewarm water

2 teaspoons active dry yeast

2 cups bread flour

5 plum tomatoes, cut in half lengthwise and seeded

½ cup semolina flour

2 teaspoons salt

½ teaspoon freshly ground black pepper

8 to 10 fresh basil leaves, or 2 teaspoons dried basil

1 large red bell pepper, cut in half, seeded, and diced

1. Preheat the oven to 250°.

2. Combine the milk and ½ cup of the water in the bowl of a heavy-duty electric mixer or in a large mixing bowl.

3 Sprinkle the yeast over the mixture, stir in, and let sit for 2 minutes.

4. Mix in 1 cup of the bread flour with the dough hook (or knead in by hand).

5. Cover the bowl with plastic wrap and let sit for 2½ hours.

6. Meanwhile, lightly sprinkle the tomato halves with salt and place cut side down on a rack resting on a baking sheet.

7. Transfer rack and baking sheet to the preheated oven and dry the tomatoes for 2 hours.

8. Soak 3 cups (½ pound) mesquite or apple or cherry wood in water for 1 hour.

9. Prepare the smoker or a grill. Add the soaked wood chips to the smoker or grill.

10. Smoke the tomatoes over very low heat for about 1 hour.

11. While the tomatoes are smoking, add the remaining ½ cup water, the remaining 1 cup bread flour, the semolina flour, salt, and pepper to the yeast mixture.

12. Mix with the dough hook (or knead by hand) for 8 to 10 minutes, or until the dough appears silky and resilient.

13. Transfer the dough to a lightly oiled bowl and cover with plastic wrap.

14. Let rise in a warm place for 2 hours.

15. Coarsely chop the smoked tomatoes, then combine with the basil and bell pepper.

16. Fold or knead the tomato mixture into the dough until evenly distributed.

17. Turn over a baking sheet and sprinkle with cornmeal or semolina flour.

18. Place the dough on a work surface generously sprinkled with semolina flour and cut into 2 equal pieces.

19. Gently pull and stretch each piece of dough into an 8-inch round or a 7-inch square.

20. Press each flatbread into the semolina flour, then flip to coat the other side.

21. Transfer to the prepared baking sheet.

22. Cover with plastic wrap and let rise in a warm place for 45 minutes to 1 hour.

23. Place a baking stone on the middle rack in the oven and preheat to 450°.

24. Using a spray bottle, spritz the oven walls with water. Work quickly so the oven does not lose heat.

25. Slide the flatbreads onto the hot stone.

26. Bake in the preheated oven for 14 to 16 minutes, or until the bread browns.

27. Transfer the flatbreads to a rack to cool.

Yield: 2 flatbreads

Bread Machine Instructions
To prepare the dough in a bread machine:
1. Combine all the ingredients, except the smoked tomatoes, basil, and bell pepper, in the bread pan in the order specified by the manufacturer's instructions.
2. Process on the dough setting (#9).
3. While the dough is rising, smoke the tomatoes, as directed in steps 6 through 10 of the recipe.
4. When the cycle is complete, turn the dough out onto a well-floured work surface.
5. Knead the smoked tomatoes, basil, and bell pepper into the dough until evenly distributed.
6. Continue with step 17 of the recipe.

ORANGE-CUMIN RUSTIC RYE BREAD

Orange and cumin are a classic Middle Eastern combination; the rye flour contributes a rustic, robust flavor. Oranges are native to southeast Asia, and their name is derived from the Sanskrit word meaning "fragrant." If you don't already own one, invest in a good-quality citrus zester, which makes zesting a lot easier and leaves the bitter white pith behind. We have regularly served Orange-Cumin Bread at Coyote Cafe since we opened, which goes to show that it complements southwestern foods very well. Nothing goes better with this bread than a classic black bean soup or a hearty bowl of chili. Try it with other spicy foods, salads, and shellfish, too. If you prefer, you can substitute a mixture of cumin, ground fennel seed, and anise or equal amounts of fennel and anise for the cumin.

This bread requires advance planning and preparation. However, the recipe is straightforward and you will gain an enhanced wheaty flavor from letting the sponge sit overnight due to the longer fermentation process.

Sponge

1 cup lukewarm water
½ teaspoon active dry yeast
1 cup bread flour
1 tablespoon ground cumin

Dough

1 cup lukewarm freshly squeezed orange juice
1 teaspoon active dry yeast
2 cups bread flour
½ cup rye flour
2¼ teaspoons salt
Zest of 2 oranges, minced

1. To prepare the sponge, place the water in a mixing bowl.
2. Sprinkle the yeast over the water, stir in, and let sit for 2 minutes.
3. Mix in the bread flour and cumin.
4. Cover the bowl with plastic wrap and let sit overnight or for 14 to 16 hours.
5. To prepare the dough, place the orange juice in the bowl of a heavy-duty electric mixer or in a mixing bowl.
6. Sprinkle the yeast over the top, stir in, and let sit for 2 minutes.
7. Add the sponge, bread flour, rye flour, salt, and orange zest.
8. Mix with the dough hook for 2 minutes, or until the ingredients are combined. Or beat vigorously by hand with a wooden spoon for 8 to 10 minutes.
9. Let the dough rest for 15 minutes.
10. Resume mixing and continue for 12 to 14 minutes, or until the dough is silky and elastic and pulls away from the sides of the bowl.

The dough should be very wet and sticky, but still elastic.

11. Transfer the dough to a lightly oiled bowl and cover with plastic wrap.

12. Let rise in a warm place for 1½ hours, or until approximately doubled in volume.

13. Turn over a baking sheet and sprinkle with cornmeal or semolina flour.

14. Place the dough on a well-floured work surface, handling it gently to preserve as much volume as possible, and cut into 2 equal pieces.

15. Gently pull and stretch each piece of dough into a flat round, about 1¼ inches thick.

16. Transfer to the prepared baking sheet.

17. Cover with plastic wrap and let rise in a warm place for 45 minutes to 1 hour.

18. Place a baking stone on the middle rack in the oven and preheat to 450°.

19. Using a spray bottle, spritz the oven walls with water. Work quickly so the oven does not lose heat.

20. Slide the loaves onto the hot stone.

21. Bake for 16 to 18 minutes, or until the bread browns.

22. Transfer the flatbreads to a rack to cool.

Yield: 2 flatbreads

Bread Machine Instructions
To prepare the dough in a bread machine
(this is also a 2-day process):
1. On the first day, place the sponge ingredients in the bread pan.
2. Process on the dough setting (#9).
3. Let sit in the machine for 14 to 16 hours.
4. On the second day, add the dough ingredients and process again on the dough setting.
5. When the cycle is complete, turn the dough out onto a well-floured work surface.
6. Continue with step 11 of the recipe.

CURRY-CARDAMOM BREAD

Here's a bread to serve with Indian food or with nothing more than a chilled glass of white wine. It's best served with spicy foods that do not contain delicate flavors—a lentil or vegetable curry, for example. Cardamom is related to ginger. It is a pungent, aromatic spice with green tones that is usually sold in small pods. It's a digestive and breath freshener, which is why it's often offered at the end of Indian meals instead of mints. Cardamom is available in Indian and Middle Eastern stores, where it is usually cheaper and fresher. Sometimes, it comes preground, which increases the risk that it will be less fresh. The fresher it is, the less you are likely to need, so use it sparingly and err on the side of caution! The same goes for the curry powder, but if you have a high heat tolerance, you might consider substituting a hot or even a vindaloo curry powder. Stick to a mild blend if you like spicy flavors, but don't particularly enjoy hot foods.

This bread requires advance planning and preparation. Letting the sponge sit overnight enhances the bread's wheaty flavor (due to the longer fermentation process).

Sponge

1 cup lukewarm water

½ teaspoon active dry yeast

1 cup bread flour

Dough

1 cup lukewarm water

1 teaspoon active dry yeast

2¾ cups bread flour

2¼ teaspoons salt

1 tablespoon curry powder

2 teaspoons freshly ground cardamom

3 scallions, green parts only, chopped (about
 ½ cup)

1. To prepare the sponge, place the water in a mixing bowl.
2. Sprinkle the yeast over the water, stir in, and let sit for 2 minutes.
3. Mix in the bread flour.
4. Cover the bowl with plastic wrap and let sit overnight or for 14 to 16 hours.
5. To prepare the dough, place the water in the bowl of a heavy-duty electric mixer or in a mixing bowl.
6. Sprinkle the yeast over the top, stir in, and let sit for 2 minutes.
7. Add the sponge, bread flour, salt, cardamom, and curry powder.
8. Mix with the dough hook for 2 minutes, or until the ingredients are combined. Or beat vigorously with a wooden spoon for 8 to 10 minutes.
9. Let the dough rest for 15 minutes.
10. Resume mixing and continue for 12 to 14 minutes, or until the dough is silky and elastic and pulls away from the sides of the bowl.

The dough should be very wet and sticky, but still elastic.

11. Mix or knead the chopped scallions into the dough until evenly distributed.

12. Transfer the dough to a lightly oiled bowl and cover with plastic wrap.

13. Let rise in a warm place for 1½ hours, or until approximately doubled in volume.

14. Turn over a baking sheet and sprinkle with cornmeal or semolina flour.

15. Place the dough on a well-floured work surface, handling it gently to preserve as much volume as possible, and cut into 2 equal pieces.

16. Gently pull and stretch each piece of dough into a flat round, about 1¼ inches thick.

17. Transfer to the prepared baking sheet.

18. Cover with plastic wrap and let rise in a warm place for 45 minutes to 1 hour.

19. Place a baking stone on the middle rack in the oven and preheat to 450°.

20. Using a spray bottle, spritz the oven walls with water. Work quickly so the oven does not lose heat.

21. Slide the loaves onto the hot stone.

22. Bake for 16 to 18 minutes, or until the bread browns.

23. Transfer the flatbreads to a rack to cool.

Yield: 2 loaves

Bread Machine Instructions
To prepare the dough in a bread machine
(this is also a 2-day process):

1. On the first day, place the sponge ingredients in the bread pan.

2. Process on the dough setting (#9).

3. Let sit in the machine for 14 to 16 hours.

4. On the second day, add all the remaining ingredients, except the scallions, and process again on the dough setting.

5. When the cycle is complete, turn the dough out onto a well-floured work surface.

6. Knead the scallions into the dough until evenly distributed.

7. Continue with step 12 of the recipe.

FENNEL-BLACK OLIVE BREAD

The assertive flavors of this rustic bread conjure up sunny images of the Mediterranean. In fact, this recipe was inspired by the great fougasse breads of southern France, which feature distinctive Provençal flavors such as garlic, olives, onions, herbs, and anchovies. This bread is best with ratatouille, bouillabaisse, most pasta dishes (especially pasta primavera), vegetable crudités, herbed soft goat cheese, feta, and mozzarella. While the bread lifts the flavors of mild cheeses, it clashes with sharp Cheddar or other robust cheeses. This outdoorsy bread can be served for picnics, with al fresco salads, or with hors d'oeuvres on the patio.

This bread requires advance planning and preparation. Letting the sponge sit overnight enhances the bread's wheaty flavor (due to the longer fermentation process).

Sponge

1 cup lukewarm water

½ teaspoon active dry yeast

1 cup bread flour

Dough

1 cup lukewarm freshly squeezed orange juice

1 teaspoon active dry yeast

2 cups bread flour

1 cup semolina flour

2 teaspoons salt

½ teaspoon freshly ground black pepper

1 fennel bulb, julienned

1½ cups coarsely chopped, pitted kalamata olives

1 orange, peeled, sectioned, and coarsely chopped

1. To prepare the sponge, place the water in a mixing bowl.

2. Sprinkle the yeast over the water, stir in, and let sit for 2 minutes.

3. Mix in the bread flour.

4. Cover the bowl with plastic wrap and let sit overnight or for 14 to 16 hours.

5. To prepare the dough, place the orange juice in the bowl of a heavy-duty electric mixer or in a mixing bowl.

6. Sprinkle the yeast over the top, stir in, and let sit for 2 minutes.

7. Add the sponge, bread flour, semolina flour, salt, and pepper.

8. Mix with the dough hook for 2 minutes, or until the ingredients are combined. Or beat vigorously with a wooden spoon for 8 to 10 minutes.

9. Let the dough rest for 15 minutes.

10. Add the fennel, olives, and orange and resume mixing, continuing for 12 to 14 minutes, or until the dough is silky and elastic and pulls away from the sides of the bowl. The dough should be very wet and sticky, but still elastic.

11. Transfer the dough to a lightly oiled bowl and cover with plastic wrap.

12. Let rise in a warm place for 1½ hours, or until approximately doubled in volume.

13. Turn over a baking sheet and sprinkle with cornmeal or semolina flour.

14. Place the dough on a well-floured work surface, handling it gently to preserve as much volume as possible, and cut into 2 equal pieces.

15. Gently pull and stretch each piece of dough into a flat round about 1¼ inches thick.

16. Transfer to the prepared baking sheet.

17. Cover with plastic wrap and let rise in a warm place for 45 minutes to 1 hour.

18. Place the baking stone on the middle rack in the oven and preheat to 450°.

19. Using a spray bottle, spritz the oven walls with water to create some humidity. Work quickly so the oven does not lose heat.

20. Slide the loaves onto the hot stone.

21. Bake in the preheated oven for 16 to 18 minutes, or until the bread browns.

22. Transfer the flatbreads to a rack to cool.

Yield: 2 loaves

Bread Machine Instructions
To prepare the dough in a bread machine (this is also a 2-day process):

1. On the first day, place the sponge ingredients in the bread pan.

2. Process on the dough setting (#9).

3. Let sit in the machine for 14 to 16 hours.

4. On the second day, add all the remaining ingredients, except the fennel, olives, and orange, and process again on the dough setting.

5. When the cycle is complete, turn the dough out onto a well-floured work surface.

6. Knead the fennel, olives, and orange into the dough until evenly distributed.

7. Continue with step 11 of the recipe.

CARAMELIZED ONION BREAD

We invariably get numerous requests for this recipe every time we serve it at Coyote Cafe—it's that popular. The best type of onions for caramelizing are the naturally sweet varieties: Vidalia, from Georgia; Maui, from Hawaii; Walla Walla, from Washington State; and Texas Noonday. (The varieties are all very closely related.) If these sweet varieties are unavailable, use yellow onions, which are sweeter than the white. The technique of caramelizing onions brings out their sweet, yet savory tanginess—qualities that make this bread a good choice with minestrone, chicken soup, or any brothy soup or stew.

This bread requires advance planning and preparation. Letting the sponge sit overnight enhances the bread's wheaty flavor (due to the longer fermentation process).

Sponge

1 cup lukewarm water
½ teaspoon active dry yeast
1 cup bread flour

Caramelized Onions

2 tablespoons extra virgin olive oil
2 tablespoons firmly packed brown sugar
2 onions, sliced into ¼-inch rings

Dough

1 cup lukewarm water
1 teaspoon active dry yeast
2¼ cups bread flour
½ cup whole-wheat flour
2¼ teaspoons salt
½ teaspoon freshly ground black pepper

1. To prepare the sponge, place the water in a mixing bowl.
2. Sprinkle the yeast over the water, stir in, and let sit for 2 minutes.
3. Mix in the 1 cup bread flour.
4. Cover the bowl with plastic wrap and let sit overnight or for 14 to 16 hours.
5. To prepare the onions, heat the olive oil and sugar in a heavy-bottomed saucepan over medium heat for 1 minute.
6. Add the onions, stir well, and sauté, stirring occasionally, for 10 to 12 minutes, or until browned and caramelized.
7. Remove the pan from the heat and set aside to cool.
8. To prepare the dough, place the water in the bowl of an electric mixer or in a mixing bowl.
9. Sprinkle the yeast over the top, stir in, and let sit for 2 minutes.
10. Add the sponge, bread flour, whole-wheat flour, salt, and pepper.
11. Mix with the dough hook for 2 minutes, or until the ingredients are combined. Or beat vigorously with a wooden spoon for 8 to 10 minutes.

12. Let the dough rest for 15 minutes.

13. Add the caramelized onions and resume mixing, continuing for 12 to 14 minutes, or until the dough is silky and elastic and pulls away from the sides of the bowl. The dough should be very wet and sticky, but still elastic.

14. Transfer the dough to a lightly oiled bowl and cover with plastic wrap.

15. Let rise in a warm place for 1½ hours, or until doubled in volume.

16. Turn over a baking sheet and sprinkle with cornmeal or semolina flour.

17. Place the dough on a well-floured work surface, handling it gently to preserve as much volume as possible, and cut into 2 equal pieces.

18. Gently pull and stretch each piece of dough into a flat round, about 1¼ inches thick.

19. Transfer to the prepared baking sheet.

20. Cover with plastic wrap, and let rise in a warm place for 45 minutes to 1 hour.

21. Place a baking stone on the middle rack in the oven and preheat to 450°.

22. Using a spray bottle, spritz the oven walls with water. Work quickly so the oven does not lose heat.

23. Slide the loaves onto the hot stone.

24. Bake for 16 to 18 minutes, or until the bread browns.

25. Transfer the flatbreads to a rack to cool.

Bread Machine Instructions
To make the dough in a bread machine (this is also a 2-day process):

1. On the first day, place the sponge ingredients in the bread pan.

2. Process on the dough setting (#9).

3. Let sit in the machine for 14 to 16 hours.

4. On the second day, add all the remaining ingredients, except the caramelized onions, and process again on the dough setting.

5. While the dough is rising, prepare the caramelized onions as directed in steps 5 through 7 of the recipe.

6. When the cycle is complete, turn the dough out onto a well-floured work surface.

7. Knead the caramelized onions into the dough until evenly distributed.

8. Continue with step 14 of the recipe.

ZUCCHINI-PARMESAN BREAD

This is a great way to use the annual surfeit of summer squash. Yellow zucchini or crook-neck squash works just as well as the green varieties. Likewise, you can use other semihard cheeses such as (nonsalty) Romano or Asiago instead of the Parmesan. Adding vegetables to bread is sometimes a clever way to slip children nutrients and vitamins, but we've found that they like this bread's flavor and interesting coloration anyway. Serve this bread with salads, lasagna, minestrone soup, herb-roasted chicken, tomato-based stews or sauces, pastas, pesto dishes—just about anything that's Italian. It's also a good picnic bread.

This bread requires advance planning and preparation. Letting the sponge sit overnight enhances the bread's wheaty flavor (due to the longer fermentation process).

Sponge

1 cup lukewarm water
½ teaspoon active dry yeast
1 cup bread flour

Dough

1 cup lukewarm water
1 teaspoon active dry yeast
1¾ cups bread flour
½ cup semolina flour
¼ cup whole-wheat flour
2¼ teaspoons salt
½ teaspoon freshly ground black pepper
4 teaspoons chopped fresh oregano, or
   2 teaspoons dried oregano
2 small zucchini, unpeeled, cut lengthwise into
   2 inch-long strips, then into 1/4-inch julienne
¾ cup grated Parmesan cheese

1. To prepare the sponge, place the water in a mixing bowl.
2. Sprinkle the yeast over the water, stir in, and let sit for 2 minutes.
3. Mix in the 1 cup bread flour.
4. Cover the bowl with plastic wrap and let sit overnight or for 14 to 16 hours.
5. To prepare the dough, place the water in the bowl of a heavy-duty electric mixer or in a mixing bowl.
6. Sprinkle the yeast over the top, stir in, and let sit for 2 minutes.
7. Add the sponge, 1¾ cups bread flour, the semolina flour, whole-wheat flour, salt, pepper, and oregano.
8. Mix with the dough hook for 2 minutes, or until the ingredients are combined. Or beat vigorously by hand with a wooden spoon for 8 to 10 minutes.
9. Let the dough rest for 15 minutes.
10. Resume mixing the dough and continue for 12 to 14 minutes, or until it is silky and elastic and pulls away from the sides of the bowl. The dough should be very wet and sticky, but also elastic.

11. Add the zucchini and cheese to the dough.

12. Continue mixing or kneading for 2 to 3 minutes, or until the zucchini and cheese are evenly distributed.

13. Transfer the dough to a lightly oiled bowl and cover with plastic wrap.

14. Let rise in a warm place for 1½ hours, or until approximately doubled in volume.

15. Turn over a baking sheet and sprinkle with cornmeal or semolina flour.

16. Place the dough on a well-floured work surface, handling it gently to preserve as much volume as possible, and cut into 2 equal pieces.

17. Gently pull and stretch each piece of dough into a flat round about 1¼ inches thick.

18. Transfer to the prepared baking sheet.

19. Cover with plastic wrap and let rise in a warm place for 45 minutes to 1 hour.

20. Place a baking stone on the middle rack in the oven and preheat to 450°.

21. Using a spray bottle, spritz the oven walls with water. Work quickly so the oven does not lose heat.

22. Slide the loaves onto the hot stone.

23. Bake for 16 to 18 minutes, or until the bread browns.

24. Transfer the flatbreads to a rack to cool.

Yield: 2 loaves

Bread Machine Instructions
To prepare the dough in a bread machine (this is also a two-day process):

1. On the first day, place the sponge ingredients in the bread pan.

2. Process on the dough setting (#9).

3. Let sit in the machine for 14 to 16 hours.

4. On the second day, add all the remaining ingredients, except the oregano, zucchini, and cheese, and process again on the dough setting.

5. When the cycle is complete, turn the dough out onto a well-floured work surface.

6. Knead the oregano, zucchini, and cheese into the dough until evenly distributed.

7. Continue with step 13 of the recipe.

HERBED FOCACCIA

Focaccia is a traditional northern Italian round flatbread, from the Genoa region. Its name is derived from the Latin word focus *which means "hearth," which is where the bread was originally baked. Until recently, focaccia could only be found in the United States in the old-fashioned Italian bakeries in San Francisco and New York, but in the last few years, it has broken into the mainstream and become popular all over. Focaccia is not only a wonderful bread in its own right, it is the ultimate pizza dough; you can make delicious pizzas by topping focaccia dough with sliced fresh mozzarella, fresh tomatoes, a drizzle of extra virgin olive oil, and a sprinkle of black pepper. This aromatic bread also pairs beautifully with meats, game, and fowl, as well as with soups and salads, and can certainly be enjoyed plain, or dipped into a good extra virgin olive oil.*

1¾ cups lukewarm water

¼ cup extra virgin olive oil

2 teaspoons active dry yeast

3 cups bread flour

¾ cup all-purpose flour

2 teaspoons salt

1 teaspoon freshly ground black pepper

2 tablespoons chopped fresh oregano, or
   1 tablespoon dried oregano

6 fresh basil leaves, chopped, or 2 teaspoons
   dried basil

8 fresh sage leaves, chopped, or 2 teaspoons
   dried sage

2 teaspoons chopped fresh rosemary needles,
   or 1 teaspoon dried rosemary

1. Combine the water and 3 tablespoons of the olive oil in the bowl of a heavy-duty electric mixer or in a mixing bowl.

2. Sprinkle the yeast over the mixture, stir in, and let sit for 2 minutes.

3. Add the bread flour and all-purpose flour.

4. Mix with the dough hook (or knead by hand) for 6 to 8 minutes, or until the dough is silky and elastic.

5. Add the salt and continue mixing or kneading for 1 minute.

6. Add the pepper and herbs and mix or knead into the dough for 1½ to 2 minutes, or until evenly distributed.

7. Transfer the dough to a lightly oiled bowl and cover with plastic wrap.

8. Let rise in a warm place for 1 hour, until approximately doubled in volume.

9. Punch the dough down and let rise for 30 minutes longer.

10. Turn over a baking sheet and sprinkle generously with cornmeal.

11. Place a baking stone on the middle rack in the oven and preheat to 450°.

12. Place the dough on a well-floured work surface.

13. Gently pull and stretch the dough into a 14 x 10-inch rectangle or a 12-inch circle.

14. Brush the top of the dough with the remaining 1 tablespoon olive oil, and sprinkle lightly with salt.

15. Transfer to the prepared baking sheet.
16. Cover with plastic wrap and let rise again for 15 minutes.
17. Using a spray bottle, spritz the oven walls with water. Work quickly so the oven does not lose heat.
18. Using a fingertip, create dimples in the top of the dough.
19. Slide the focaccia onto the hot stone.
20. Bake for 14 to 16 minutes, or until the focaccia is golden brown.
21. Transfer the focaccia to a rack to cool.

Yield: 1 focaccia

Bread Machine Instructions

1. Combine all the ingredients, except the pepper and herbs, in the bread pan in the order specified by the manufacturer's instructions.

2. Process on the dough setting (#9).

3. When the cycle is complete, turn the dough out onto a well-floured work surface.

4. Knead`the pepper and herbs into the dough until evenly distributed.

5. Continue with step 7 of the recipe.

ASIAGO FOCACCIA

This focaccia is like a pizza minus the tomatoes. If you'd like to make a focaccia pizza, just add a sprinkling of chopped black olives, shredded prosciutto or ham, fresh or sundried tomatoes, and a drizzle of extra virgin olive oil before baking the dough. Served plain, this bread is perfect for almost any Italian meal. It also makes great bruschetta, and is wonderful with grilled meats or antipasto plates featuring black olives, cured meats such as prosciutto or coppacola ham, or marinated hot peppers. Asiago is a rich, semihard Italian cheese; good alternatives are Parmesan or Romano. An optional finishing touch is to sprinkle the warm (but not hot) focaccia with a few sea salt flakes or crystals, or minced fresh thyme or rosemary needles.

1¾ cups lukewarm water

¼ cup extra virgin olive oil

2 teaspoons active dry yeast

3¾ cups bread flour

2 teaspoons salt

2 cups grated Asiago cheese

10 cloves garlic, coarsely chopped

1. Combine the water and 3 tablespoons of the olive oil in the bowl of a heavy-duty electric mixer or in a mixing bowl.

2. Sprinkle the yeast over the mixture, stir in, and let sit for 2 minutes.

3. Add the bread flour.

4. Mix with the dough hook (or knead by hand) for 6 to 8 minutes, or until the dough is silky and elastic.

5. Add the salt and continue mixing or kneading for 1 minute.

6. Add 1½ cups of the Asiago cheese and mix for 1½ to 2 minutes longer, or until evenly distributed.

7. Transfer the dough to a lightly oiled bowl and cover with plastic wrap.

8. Let rise in a warm place for 1 hour, or until approximately doubled in volume.

9. Punch the dough down and let rise for 30 minutes longer.

10. Turn over a baking sheet and sprinkle with cornmeal.

11. Place a baking stone on the middle rack in the oven and preheat to 450°.

12. Place the dough on a well-floured work surface.

13. Gently pull and stretch the dough evenly into a 14 x 10-inch rectangle or a 12-inch circle.

14. Brush the top of the dough with the remaining 1 tablespoon olive oil and top with the remaining ½ cup cheese and the chopped garlic.

15. Transfer to the prepared baking sheet.

16. Cover with plastic wrap and let rise for another 15 minutes.

17. Using a spray bottle, spritz the oven walls with water. Work quickly so the oven does not lose heat.

18. Using a finger tip, create dimples in the top of the dough.

19. Slide the dough onto the hot stone.

20. Bake for 14 to 16 minutes, or until the focaccia turns golden brown.

21. Transfer the focaccia to a rack to cool.

Yield: 1 focaccia

Bread Machine Instructions
1. Combine all the ingredients, except the cheese and garlic, in the bread pan in the order specified by the manufacturer's instructions.
2. Process on the dough setting (#9).
3. When the cycle is complete, turn the dough out onto a well-floured work surface.
4. Knead 1 1/2 cups of the cheese into the dough until evenly distributed.
5. Continue with step 7 of the recipe.

POTATO FOCACCIA

Walk down a main street in a northern Italian town, and chances are you'll pass a small bakery with huge black pans sticking out of the storefront, holding focacce with different toppings. As you can imagine, the aroma from these bakeries is heavenly. Focacce are the forebears of pizza and, like pizza, they do not keep well so it's best to eat the bread the same day you make it. This variation is great with venison and red meats—an innovative approach to meat and potatoes. Like the previous recipe, you can turn this focaccia into a delicious pizza by slicing low-starch potatoes (such as new or red potatoes, or yellow Finns), placing them on the dough, drizzling extra virgin olive oil over the top, sprinkling with black pepper, and grating a hard cheese over the top. And don't forget the chiles!

2 new or red potatoes (unpeeled), diced

4 cups water

¼ cup extra virgin olive oil

2 teaspoons active dry yeast

3 cups bread flour

½ cup all-purpose flour

¼ cup whole-wheat flour

2 teaspoons coarse salt

½ teaspoon freshly ground black pepper

2 teaspoons chopped fresh thyme, or
   1½ teaspoons dried thyme

1. Place the potatoes in a large saucepan and cover with the water.

2. Bring to a boil, reduce the heat to medium, and cook for 15 to 17 minutes, or until tender.

3. Drain the potatoes, reserving the cooking liquid, and set them aside to cool.

4. Place the cooking liquid in the refrigerator or freezer to cool until just lukewarm.

5. Transfer 1½ cups of the lukewarm potato cooking liquid to the bowl of a heavy-duty electric mixer or another mixing bowl.

6. Add 3 tablespoons of the olive oil.

7. Sprinkle the yeast over the mixture, stir in, and let sit for 2 minutes.

8. Add the bread flour, all-purpose flour, and whole-wheat flour.

9. Mix with the dough hook (or knead by hand) for 6 to 8 minutes, or until the dough is silky and elastic.

10. Add the salt and continue mixing or kneading for 1 minute.

11. Add the pepper and thyme, and mix or knead for 1½ to 2 minutes longer, or until the thyme is evenly distributed.

(continued)

12. Transfer the dough to a lightly oiled bowl and cover with plastic wrap.

13. Let rise in a warm place for 1 hour, until approximately doubled in volume.

14. By hand, mix or knead two-thirds of the cooked potatoes into the dough until evenly distributed.

15. Cover with plastic wrap and let the dough rise for 30 minutes longer.

16. Turn over a baking sheet and sprinkle with cornmeal.

17. Place a baking stone on the middle rack in the oven and preheat to 450°.

18. Place the dough on a well-floured work surface.

19. Gently pull and stretch the dough evenly into a 14 x 10-inch rectangle or a 12-inch circle.

20. Brush the top of the dough with the remaining 1 tablespoon olive oil, cover with the remaining potatoes, and sprinkle lightly with salt.

21. Transfer to the prepared baking sheet.

22. Cover with plastic wrap and let rise for another 15 minutes.

23. Using a spray bottle, spritz the oven walls with water. Work quickly so the oven does not lose heat.

24. Using a fingertip, create dimples in the top of the dough.

25. Slide the dough onto the hot stone.

26. Bake for 14 to 16 minutes, or until the focaccia turns golden brown.

27. Transfer the focaccia to a rack to cool.

Yield: 1 focaccia

Bread Machine Instructions

1. Cook the potatoes as described in steps 1 through 4 of the recipe.

2. Combine 1½ cups of the lukewarm cooking liquid and all the ingredients, except the cooked potatoes and thyme, in the bread pan in the order specified by the manufacturer's instructions.

3. Process on the dough setting (#9).

4. When the cycle is complete, turn the dough out onto a well-floured work surface.

5. Continue with step 14 of the recipe.

HOPI PIKI

Piki is a traditional paper-thin, feathery light flatbread made by the Hopi people who have lived in what is now northern Arizona for centuries. In fact, piki is one of the oldest of all North American breads. Piki is made without wheat or a leavening agent and predates the introduction of baking ovens. It is made with finely ground blue cornmeal and cooked on specially selected flat stones that heat evenly when placed over a fire. Traditionally, the piki batter is also made with juniper, chamisa, or corn cob ashes, but we assume you do not have easy access to these ingredients—or a suitable piki stone. Fortunately, a heavy cast iron skillet will suffice. When I first started traveling to Santa Fe twenty-five years ago, Native American street vendors commonly sold piki. Unfortunately, those days are gone because the bread is no longer cost effective for vendors to make on a regular basis. Piki is, however, still sold at some some special events, such as at Santa Fe's Indian Market (in August) and at various powwows. Use this bread like you would use a tortilla. It is especially good with southwestern vegetable or bean dishes.

4 to 5 cups water
2 cups blue cornmeal
½ teaspoon salt
18 fresh sage leaves, or 3 tablespoons dried sage
Corn or canola oil

1. In a saucepan, bring 2 cups of the water to a boil.

2. Whisk in the cornmeal and cook, stirring, for 2 minutes.

3. Stir in the salt and remove the pan from the heat.

4. Let the mixture cool, then transfer to a large mixing bowl.

5. Preheat the oven to 425°.

6. Place the sage on a baking sheet and toast in the oven for 12 to 14 minutes, or until the leaves have burned up and only ashes remain.

7. Whisk the remaining 2 to 3 cups of water and the sage ashes into the cornmeal to make a thin batter.

8. Heat an 8- to 10-inch nonstick skillet (a crepe pan would be perfect) or a well-seasoned, heavy cast iron skillet over medium-low heat.

9. Brush the skillet with oil, coating the bottom well.

10. Ladle 2 tablespoons of the batter into the skillet and spread evenly into a very thin 6- or 7-inch circle by tilting the pan quickly from side to side.

11. Cook for 1 minute; the edges of the piki should dry out and curl up.

12. Remove the piki from the pan and immediately roll it up, making a 1- or 1½ -inch roll. Keep warm.

13. Repeat with the remaining batter. (Any unused batter will keep in the refrigerator for several days.)

14. Serve warm in a basket covered with a towel.

Yield: 10 to 12 piki

NEW MEXICO RED CHILE CRACKERBREAD

You can really let your creativity loose with this bread. Bake it in one piece, then break it up when it's cooked, or cut it into attractive shapes—tall triangles, equilateral triangles, squares, rectangles, or circles—before baking. One striking presentation is to cut the cracker-bread into pointy triangles and arrange them in a circle around some salsa or guacamole with the points sticking out toward the edge of the plate. Alternatively, top the triangles with hors d'oeuvres, such as small herb-marinated shrimp, or serve them in a basket with blue and yellow tortilla chips. The chile powder gives these crunchy crackers a lively kick. They don't keep well as they absorb moisture easily and will soften, so eat them as soon as you can or store them in an airtight container. To restore crispness, reheat them in a 300° oven for 8 to 10 minutes.

1½ cups milk, at room temperature
½ teaspoon active dry yeast

Dry Ingredients
2¼ cups all-purpose flour
½ cup whole-wheat flour
1½ teaspoons salt
2 tablespoons chile molido (freshly ground pure
    chile powder)
2 tablespoons chile caribe (red pepper flakes)
2 teaspoons ground cayenne

1 egg white, beaten

1. Place the milk in the bowl of a heavy-duty electric mixer or in a mixing bowl.
2. Sprinkle the yeast over the mixture, stir in, and let sit for 2 minutes.
3. Add the dry ingredients.
4. Mix with the dough hook (or knead by hand) for about 6 minutes, or until the dough is elastic.
5. Transfer the dough to a lightly oiled bowl and cover with plastic wrap.
6. Let rise in a warm place for 1 hour.
7. Preheat the oven to 375°.
8. Place the dough on a well-floured work surface.
9. Dust the dough with flour and roll out into a rectangle about 14 x 12 inches and ¹⁄₁₆ inch thick.
10. Cover the dough with plastic wrap and let rest for 20 minutes.
11. Cut the dough into shapes (such as triangles, squares, or circles) with a pizza cutter, pastry cutter, or paring knife. Alternatively, the dough can be baked in one piece and broken up later.
12. Sprinkle a baking sheet with cornmeal.

13. Using a spatula, transfer the crackers to the prepared baking sheet.
14. Brush the dough with the egg white.
15. Bake in the preheated oven for 25 to 30 minutes, or until browned and crisp.
16. Transfer the crackerbread(s) to a rack to cool.

Yield: 30 to 35 small crackerbreads or 1 large crackerbread

Bread Machine Instructions
1. Combine all the ingredients, except the egg white, in the bread pan in the order specified by the manufacturer's instructions.
2. Process on the dough setting (#9).
3. When the cycle is complete, turn the dough out onto a well-floured work surface.
4. Continue with step 5 of the recipe.

BLACK PEPPER-GARLIC CRISP CRACKERBREAD

The wooden cracker barrel was a fixture in western country stores during pioneering days. I even remember seeing them as a youngster in rural old-fashioned groceries in northern New England when my family went on fall leaf-peeping outings. These spicy, savory crackers make a respectable addition to any bread basket. Their crunchy texture contrasts nicely with pastas and other foods with soft textures. The flavors complement herbed or lemony chicken and fish, most soups, and shellfish—especially oysters.

1½ cups milk, at room temperature
½ teaspoon active dry yeast

Dry Ingredients
2 cups all-purpose flour
½ cup semolina flour
2 teaspoons salt
1 tablespoon freshly ground black pepper

12 cloves garlic, minced
1 egg white, beaten
1 tablespoon sesame seeds

1. Place the milk in the bowl of a heavy-duty electric mixer or in a mixing bowl.
2. Sprinkle the yeast over the mixture, stir in, and let sit for 2 minutes.
3. Add the dry ingredients and garlic.
4. Mix with the dough hook (or knead by hand) for about 6 minutes, or until the dough is elastic.
5. Transfer the dough to a lightly oiled bowl and cover with plastic wrap.
6. Let rise in a warm place for 1 hour.
7. Preheat the oven to 375°.
8. Place the dough on a well-floured work surface.
9. Dust the dough with flour and roll out into a rectangle about 14 x 12 inches and ¹⁄₁₆ inch thick.

10. Cover the dough with plastic wrap and let rest for 20 minutes.
11. Cut the dough into shapes (such as triangles, squares, or circles) with a pizza cutter, pastry cutter, or paring knife. Alternatively, the dough can be baked in one piece and broken up later.
12. Sprinkle a baking sheet with cornmeal.
13. Using a spatula, transfer the dough shapes to the prepared baking sheet.
14. Brush the shapes with the egg white and sprinkle them with the sesame seeds.
15. Bake for 25 to 30 minutes, or until browned and crisp.
16. Transfer the crackerbreads to a rack to cool.

Yield: 30 to 35 crackerbreads

Bread Machine Instructions
1. Combine all the ingredients, except the garlic, eggwhite, and sesame seeds in the bread pan in the order specified by the manufacturer's instructions.
2. Process on the dough setting (#9).
3. When the cycle is complete, turn the dough out onto a well-floured work surface.
4. Knead the garlic into the dough until evenly distributed.
5. Continue with step 5 of the recipe.

SESAME-PEANUT BREADSTICKS

The nutty-tasting, oily sesame seed is indigenous to East Africa, and many people mistakenly think that continent is also the ancestral home of the peanut, when in fact is it native to South America. The flavors go very well with most Thai dishes, Asian fare (especially stir-fries and noodles), and, of course, African food.

¾ cup lukewarm water
1 teaspoon active dry yeast
1 tablespoon olive oil
¼ cup peanut butter

Dry Ingredients

1½ cups bread flour
2 tablespoons dry or powdered milk
1 teaspoon sugar
1½ teaspoons salt

1 egg white, beaten
2 teaspoons sesame seeds

1. Place the water in the bowl of a heavy-duty electric mixer or in a mixing bowl.
2. Sprinkle the yeast over the water, stir in, and let sit for 2 minutes.
3. Add the oils, peanut butter, and dry ingredients.
4. Mix with the dough hook (or knead by hand) for about 6 minutes, or until the dough is elastic.
5. Transfer the dough to a lightly oiled bowl and cover with plastic wrap.
6. Let rise in a warm place for 1 hour.
7. Place a baking stone on the middle rack in the oven and preheat to 400°.
8. Place the dough on a well-floured work surface.
9. Cut the dough into 12 to 15 equal pieces.
10. Roll the pieces with the palm of your hand until they are about as thick as a pencil, making each about 12 inches long.
11. Sprinkle a baking sheet with cornmeal.
12. Transfer the breadsticks to the baking sheet, spacing them about 2 inches apart.
13. Cover with plastic wrap and let rise for another 20 minutes.
14. Brush the breadsticks with the egg white and sprinkle with the sesame seeds.
15. Bake for 18 to 20 minutes, or until golden brown and crisp.
16. Transfer the breadsticks to a rack to cool.

Yield: 12 to 15 breadsticks

Bread Machine Instructions

1. Combine all the ingredients, except the egg white and sesame seeds, in the bread pan in the order specified by the manufacturer's instructions.
2. Process on the dough setting (#9).
3. When the cycle is complete, turn the dough out onto a well-floured work surface.
4. Continue with step 5 of the recipe.

CUMIN-CHIPOTLE BREADSTICKS

Breadsticks are a wonderful addition to dinner bread baskets because they have a much greater ratio of crispy crust to bready interior than other breads. These smoky, savory breadsticks are delicious on their own, as well as with most southwestern food, or for hors d'oeuvres with goat cheese or crudités. We occasionally serve them at Red Sage, Coyote Cafe's sister restaurant in Washington, D.C.

8 to 10 dried chipotle chiles, stemmed
2 cups hot water

¾ cup lukewarm water
1 teaspoon active dry yeast
1 tablespoon olive oil

Dry Ingredients
1½ cups bread flour
2 tablespoons dry or powdered milk
1 teaspoon sugar
1½ teaspoons salt
2 teaspoons cumin seed, toasted and
   ground (page 210)

1 egg white, beaten

1. Finely chop the chipotle chiles in a food processor or by hand.
2. Pour the 2 cups hot water into a bowl, add the chipotles, and rehydrate for 10 minutes.
3. Place the ¾ cup lukewarm water in the bowl of a heavy-duty electric mixer or in a mixing bowl.
4. Sprinkle the yeast over the water, stir in, and let sit for 2 minutes.
5. Add the drained rehydrated chipotles, oil, and dry ingredients.
6. Mix with the dough hook (or knead by hand) for about 6 minutes, or until the dough is elastic.
7. Transfer the dough to a lightly oiled bowl and cover with plastic wrap.
8. Let rise in a warm place for 1 hour.
9. Place a baking stone on the middle rack in the oven and preheat to 400°.
10. Place the dough on a well-floured work surface.
11. Cut the dough into 12 to 15 equal pieces.
12. Roll out the pieces with the palm of your hand until about as thick as a pencil and about 12 inches long.
13. Sprinkle a baking sheet with cornmeal.
14. Transfer the breadsticks to the baking sheet, spacing them about 2 inches apart.
15. Cover with plastic wrap and let rise again in a warm place for 20 minutes.
16. Brush the breadsticks with the egg white.
17. Bake for 18 to 20 minutes, or until golden brown and crisp.
18. Transfer the breadsticks to a rack to cool.

Yield: 12 to 15 breadsticks

Bread Machine Instructions
1. Combine all the ingredients, except the beaten egg white, in the bread pan in the order specified by the manufacturer's instructions.
2. Process on the dough setting (#9).
3. When the cycle is complete, turn the dough out onto a well-floured work surface.
4. Continue with step 7 of the recipe.

JALAPEÑO-ASIAGO BREADSTICKS

Cheese and chiles—especially jalapeños—are a classic southwestern combination, as evidenced by any self-respecting plate of nachos. In this recipe, grated semihard cheeses and minced fresh jalapeños work best. Add these breadsticks to a basket of corn chips, and serve with salsa or guacamole and tall, refreshing margaritas.

¾ cup lukewarm water

1 teaspoon active dry yeast

1 tablespoon olive oil

4 jalapeño chiles, stemmed, seeded, and minced

½ cup grated Asiago or Parmesan cheese

Dry Ingredients

1½ cups bread flour

2 tablespoons dry or powdered milk

1 teaspoon sugar

1½ teaspoons salt

1 egg white, beaten

1. Place the water in the bowl of a heavy-duty electric mixer or in a mixing bowl.
2. Sprinkle the yeast over the water, stir in, and let sit for 2 minutes.
3. Add the oil, chiles, 7 tablespoons of the cheese, and the dry ingredients.
4. Mix with the dough hook (or knead by hand) for about 6 minutes, or until the dough is elastic.
5. Transfer the dough to a lightly oiled bowl and cover with plastic wrap.
6. Let rise in a warm place for 1 hour.
7. Place the baking stone on the middle rack in the oven and preheat to 400°.
8. Place the dough on a well-floured work surface.
9. Cut the dough into 12 to 15 equal pieces.
10. Roll out the pieces with the palm of your hand until about as thick as a pencil and 12 inches long.
11. Sprinkle a baking sheet with cornmeal.
12. Transfer the breadsticks to the baking sheet, spacing them about 2 inches apart.
13. Cover with plastic wrap and let rise again in a warm place for 20 minutes.
14. Brush the breadsticks with the egg white and sprinkle with the remaining 1 tablespoon Asiago cheese.
15. Bake for 16 to 20 minutes, or until golden brown and crisp.
16. Transfer the breadsticks to a rack to cool.

Yield: 12 to 15 breadsticks

Bread Machine Instructions

1. Combine all the ingredients, except the jalapeños, cheese, and egg white, in the bread pan in the order specified by the manufacturer's instructions.

2. Process on the dough setting (#9).

3. When the cycle is complete, turn the dough out onto a well-floured work surface.

4. Knead the jalapeños and 7 tablespoons of the cheese into the dough until evenly distributed.

5. Continue with step 5 of the recipe.

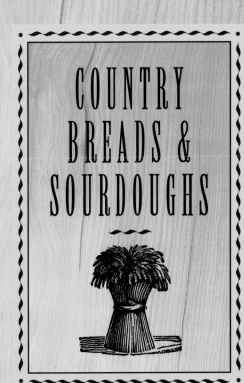

COUNTRY
BREADS &
SOURDOUGHS

In the centuries before the Industrial Revolution, most of the European population lived in the countryside rather than in towns and cities. Because the rural economy was mostly self-sustaining and there were no bakeries outside the main towns, bread making was primarily a domestic task. Typically, loaves were substantial, dense, and fine-crumbed, in the tradition of the English cottage loaf and the French *paysan* bread. The loaves were large enough to feed the family and field hands for several days—whether with hefty wedges of cheese for ploughman's lunches or for sopping up soups, stews, and sauces. The same was true for the bread made in the early days of the American colonies. The rustic yeast breads in this chapter follow in this tradition and, like the people they have nourished in times gone by, they have plenty of personality and individualism. We have added some contemporary flavorings that reflect cuisines from around the United States and the rest of the world, giving old classics a new twist.

Sourdough is a style of rustic bread that is based on a living starter that essentially consists of yeast, flour, and water or milk. Once established, the starter can be continuously replenished with just flour and water. Authentic sourdough is one of the oldest types of bread, dating back approximately 5,000 years, and is said to have been carried to the New World by Columbus. In any event, sourdough was popularized in the United States by the '49ers, the nineteenth-century prospectors and miners who flocked to California, the Yukon, and Alaska to seek their fortunes during the Gold Rush. Many of these fortune-seekers were immigrants from central and eastern Europe, who were used to fresh-baked bread. Of course, there were no bakeries in the places the '49ers staked their claims, so sourdough was the ideal bread for these pioneers. The highly prized, self-perpetuating starters were traditionally kept in wooden pails and made bread-making possible even in remote locations. The significance of the bread in the prospectors' diet and the esteem in which it was held is evidenced by the frontiersmen's nickname, "sourdoughs." In European professional baking families, priceless heirloom sourdough starters are still handed down from generation to generation and treated with great reverence. Many restaurants in the United States likewise pride themselves on the age of their sourdough starter.

The process of establishing and perpetuating a sourdough starter reminds us of the demanding plant in the musical *Little Shop of Horrors*. The plant constantly cajoles its human caregivers with "feed me, feed me." Sourdough cultures must be fed regularly, or they will die. This is what makes sourdough one of the most interesting types of bread—it is derived from a living, breathing entity with a potentially limitless lifetime. (This rather spooky quality led sourdough starters to be called "witches' yeast" during the nineteenth century.) Sourdough is less predictable than other breads because the degree of sourness and other flavor characteristics of the starter rarely remain consistent from one baking session to the next. Experienced bakers establish their starters with wild yeast spores, which occur naturally in the air and are trapped by grape skins, potato skins, and flour. However, starters made from wild yeast sometimes require up to 10 days to ferment and can be unreliable.

Here are some pointers for making these country breads and for removing some of the unpredictability from sourdough baking:

• Some of the country breads (like some of the flatbreads in the previous chapter) use a sponge, or a batterlike mixture, to develop the yeast. This method tends to create a moist texture and assists with the rising process by softening the flour.

• In general, the longer the starter sits and ferments, the more sour and flavorful it is likely to be.

• Use bottled spring water or some type of purified water in sourdough starter because chlorine, fluoride, and other natural or added chemicals and minerals in tap water tend to inhibit the action of yeast.

• The purity of the grain from which the flour is milled is an important factor in establishing and replenishing the starter. Organic, stone-ground, unbleached flour provides the best medium for sustaining yeast.

• If the starter refuses to bubble, becomes moldy, or dries up, start over.

• Once established, keep your starter refrigerated in a nonreactive (preferably glass or ceramic) container; never use metal.

• If a layer of dark liquid, the "hooch," rises to the top, and the starter has been replenished recently, simply stir the liquid into the mixture and return to the refrigerator.

• Feed your sourdough starter at least every 4 weeks by whisking in ½ cup water and ½ cup all-purpose flour until smooth. The starter should be the consistency of pancake batter.

TEXAS HILL COUNTRY RASHER BREAD

There is something magical about the Texas Hill Country, which is in the heart of the Lone Star State, bordered to the east by Austin, the hospitable state capital. In spring, waves of bluebonnets (the state flower) carpet the hillsides; during the summer, the rolling landscape shimmers under seemingly relentless waves of heat; in the fall, the vines of the wineries turn crimson and harvesting begins for the production of award-winning wines; in winter, the countless streams and rivers surge through the canyons, powered by the season's fierce rains. An important stop in Hill Country is Fredericksburg, one of several communities in the state settled by immigrants from Germany and central Europe in the mid-1800s. These communities are renowned for their smoked meats, a tradition the town's founders brought with them from Europe. One theory holds that the famed Texas barbecue originated in the smokehouses established by these early settlers.

Fortunately, Texas is also wild boar (or javelina) country, and in hunting season, they're popular quarry. Wild boar is also raised commercially in the state, where it is made into deliciously rich, flavorful, and slightly gamey smoked bacon. If you can't get wild boar bacon, regular, high-quality lean bacon or another smoked meat can be used in its place. This is a real comfort-food bread, and at the risk of sounding politically, or rather, culinarily incorrect, you can cut it into thick Texas toast–style slices, dip it in melted bacon fat or spread it with butter, and toast for breakfast with eggs—we recommend eggs over easy.

¾ cup lukewarm water

½ cup lukewarm milk

1 teaspoon honey

2 teaspoons active dry yeast

6 ounces lean wild boar bacon (6 to 8 strips, ⅛ inch thick)

Dry Ingredients

2 cups bread flour

1 cup whole-wheat flour

½ tablespoon salt

½ teaspoon freshly ground black pepper

1. Combine the water, milk, and honey in the bowl of a heavy-duty electric mixer or in a large mixing bowl.
2. Sprinkle the yeast over the mixture, stir in, and let sit for 2 minutes.
3. Place the bacon in a sauté pan and fry over medium heat, turning once, until crisp, about 6 to 8 minutes.
4. Remove the bacon, reserving 1 tablespoon of the bacon fat. Drain the bacon on paper towels. Let cool.
5. Add the dry ingredients and reserved cooled bacon fat to the yeast mixture.
6. Mix with the dough hook (or knead by hand) for 4 to 6 minutes, or until the dough is silky and elastic.

7. Slice the cooled bacon into ¼-inch strips and add to the dough.

8. Continue mixing or kneading for 2 minutes, or until the bacon is evenly distributed.

9. Transfer the dough to a lightly oiled bowl and cover with plastic wrap.

10. Let rise in a warm place for 1½ hours, or until approximately doubled in volume.

11. Punch the dough down, re-cover with plastic wrap, and let rise again in a warm place for 1 hour.

12. Place the dough on a lightly floured work surface.

13. Generously sprinkle a baking sheet with whole-wheat flour.

14. Shape into a round, oval, or oblong loaf. (See photos and additional instructions on pages 206–207.)

15. Place the loaf on the prepared baking sheet, cover with plastic wrap, and let rise in a warm place for 30 minutes.

16. Place the baking stone on the middle rack in the oven and preheat to 400°.

17. Uncover the loaf and, using a spray bottle, spritz with water, then lightly dust with whole-wheat flour.

18. Make 2 or 3 diagonal slashes in the top of the loaf with a serrated knife to allow the dough to expand in the hot oven.

19. Using the spray bottle, spritz the oven walls with water. Work quickly so the oven does not lose heat.

20. Slide the loaf onto the hot stone.

21. Bake for 35 to 40 minutes, or until the crust is golden brown.

22. Transfer the loaf to a rack to cool.

Yield: 1 large loaf

Bread Machine Instructions
To make the bread in a bread machine:

1. Prepare the bacon as directed in steps 3 and 4 of the recipe.

2. Combine all the ingredients, including the cooled bacon fat but excluding the bacon, in the bread pan in the order specified by the manufacturer's instructions.

3. Process on the sweet or raisin bread setting (#8).

4. Add the cooked bacon at the beeps.

To prepare the dough in a bread machine:

1. Prepare the bacon as directed in steps 3 and 4 of the recipe.

2. Combine all the ingredients, including the 1 tablespoon cooled bacon fat but excluding the bacon, in the bread pan in the order specified by the manufacturer's instructions.

3. Process on the dough setting (#9).

4. When the cycle is complete, turn the dough out onto a well-floured work surface.

5. Knead the bacon into the dough until evenly distributed.

6. Continue with step 9 of the recipe.

GREEN CHILE-BEEF JERKY BREAD

For centuries, the Plains Indians made buffalo, elk, and venison jerky to sustain them through the harsh winters. They cured the meat with herbs and berries and dried it slowly over fires or in the sun. When the pioneers and frontier trappers came along, jerky became a popular form of preserved meat among them as well. Then, in the late nineteenth century, when cattle became a fixture of the western range, beef jerky became popular. As this recipe proves, beef and green chiles are a delicious combination. The jerky rehydrates and softens in the bread, which can be served with most southwestern dishes, especially stews and spicy beef chilis. To preserve the freshness of the jerky, store this bread in the refrigerator as soon as it's cooled.

1 cup lukewarm water

¼ cup lukewarm milk

2 teaspoons active dry yeast

Dry Ingredients

2¾ cups bread flour

½ cup cornmeal

½ tablespoon salt

1 teaspoon honey

1 tablespoon olive oil

4 New Mexico green chiles, roasted, peeled, stemmed, seeded, and diced (page 209)

8 ounces beef jerky, cut into ¼-inch-wide strips

1. Combine the water and milk in the bowl of a heavy-duty electric mixer or in a large mixing bowl.

2. Sprinkle the yeast over the mixture, stir in, and let sit for 2 minutes.

3. Add the dry ingredients, honey, and olive oil to the yeast mixture.

4. Mix with the dough hook (or knead by hand) for 4 to 6 minutes, or until the dough is silky and elastic.

5. Add the chiles and jerky and continue mixing or kneading for 2 minutes, or until they are evenly distributed.

6. Transfer the dough to a lightly oiled bowl and cover with plastic wrap.

7. Let rise in a warm place for 1½ hours, or until approximately doubled in volume.

8. Punch the dough down, re-cover with plastic wrap, and let rise again in a warm place for 1 hour.

9. Place the dough on a lightly floured work surface and cut into 2 equal pieces.

10. Generously sprinkle a baking sheet with cornmeal.

11. Shape the dough into rounds, ovals, or oblong loaves. (See photos and additional instructions on page 206-207.)

12. Place the loaves on the prepared baking sheet, cover with plastic wrap, and let rise in a warm place for 30 minutes.

13. Place a baking stone on the middle rack in the oven and preheat to 400°.

14. Uncover the loaves and, using a spray bottle, spritz them with water, then sprinkle with cornmeal.

15. Make 2 or 3 diagonal slashes in the tops of the loaves with a serrated knife to allow the dough to expand in the hot oven.

16. Using the spray bottle, spritz the oven walls with water. Work quickly so the oven does not lose heat.

17. Slide the loaves onto the hot stone.

18. Bake for 35 to 40 minutes, or until the crust is golden brown.

19. Transfer the loaves to a rack to cool.

Yield: 2 loaves

Bread Machine Instructions
To make the bread in a bread machine:
1. Combine all the ingredients, except the chiles and jerky, in the bread pan in the order specified by the manufacturer's instructions.
2. Process on the sweet or raisin bread setting (#8).
3. Add the chiles and jerky at the beeps.

To prepare the dough in a bread machine:
1. Combine all the ingredients, except the chiles and jerky, in the bread pan in the order specified by the manufacturer's instructions.
2. Process on the dough setting (#9).
3. When the cycle is complete, turn the dough out onto a well-floured work surface.
4. Knead the chiles and jerky into the dough until evenly distributed.
5. Continue with step 6 of the recipe.

MUSTARD GREENS & GRITS BREAD

Stephan Pyles, a good friend and the owner of the nationally acclaimed southwestern restaurant Star Canyon in Dallas was once asked the difference between down-home Southern grits and the upscale, popular polenta. "About $7.50 a plate," he replied. They are indeed, for all intents and purposes, the same thing. In Stephan's book, The New Texas Cuisine, *he reports that a Texan once wrote that the best batch of grits is one that's made and then thrown out. Abused as grits are outside their native region, they are a staple in the South and about as ever present on southern plates as chard and collard, turnip, and mustard greens. The slightly bitter, warming heat of the mustard greens gives this bread a truly unique taste, and its green color is striking. The coarse-grained texture and the fresh-tasting greens make the bread a perfect partner for ribs, fried chicken, chicken fried steak, and barbecued meats. It's also a good choice for picnics or Fourth of July cookouts.*

¾ cup lukewarm water

½ cup lukewarm milk

2 teaspoons active dry yeast

Dry Ingredients

2 cups bread flour

¾ cup grits

½ cup whole-wheat flour

2 teaspoons salt

1 teaspoon honey

1 tablespoon olive oil

5 to 6 cups chopped mustard greens, spinach, chard, or kale

1. Combine the water and milk in the bowl of a heavy-duty electric mixer or in a large mixing bowl.
2. Sprinkle the yeast over the mixture, stir in, and let sit for 2 minutes.
3. Add the dry ingredients, honey, and olive oil.
4. Mix with the dough hook (or knead by hand) for 4 to 6 minutes, or until the dough is silky and elastic.
5. Add the mustard greens and continue mixing or kneading for 2 minutes, or until the greens are evenly distributed.
6. Transfer the dough to a lightly oiled bowl and cover with plastic wrap.
7. Let rise in a warm place for 1½ hours, or until approximately doubled in volume.
8. Punch the dough down, re-cover with plastic wrap, and let rise again in a warm place for 1 hour.
9. Place the dough on a lightly floured work surface and cut into 2 equal pieces.
10. Generously sprinkle a baking sheet with cornmeal.

11. Shape the dough into rounds, ovals, or oblong loaves. (See photos and additional instructions on pages 206–207.)

12. Place the loaves on the prepared baking sheet, cover with plastic wrap, and let rise in a warm place for 30 minutes.

13. Preheat the oven to 400° and place a baking stone on the middle rack.

14. Uncover the loaves and, using a spray bottle, spritz them with water, then sprinkle with cornmeal.

15. Make 2 or 3 diagonal slashes in the tops of the loaves with a serrated knife to allow the dough to expand in the hot oven.

16. Using the spray bottle, spritz the oven walls with water. Work quickly so the oven does not lose heat.

17. Slide the loaves onto the hot stone.

18. Bake for 35 to 40 minutes, or until the crust is golden brown.

19. Transfer the loaves to a rack to cool.

Yield: 2 loaves

Bread Machine Instructions
To make the bread in a bread machine:

1. Combine all the ingredients, except the mustard greens, in the bread pan in the order specified by the manufacturer's instructions.

2. Process on the sweet or raisin bread setting (#8).

3. Add the mustard greens at the beeps.

To prepare the dough in a bread machine:

1. Combine all the ingredients, except the mustard greens, in the bread pan in the order specified by the manufacturer's instructions.

2. Process on the dough setting (#9).

3. When the cycle is complete, turn the dough out onto a well-floured work surface.

4. Knead the mustard greens into the dough until evenly distributed.

5. Continue with step 6 of the recipe.

CAJUN SPICE BREAD

Be sure to take this bread with you when you travel down to New Orleans for Mardi Gras or gator wrassling on the bayou. If you prefer, instead of making up the spice blend, you can use 1 tablespoon of a premixed Cajun spice blend; we recommend our good friend Paul Prud-homme's original Cajun Magic brand, which is available in most supermarkets nationwide. This recipe will also make 8 to 10 long rolls ideal for Po-Boy sandwiches. So deep-fry those clams or oysters, blacken some redfish, sauté a mess of soft-shell crabs or Andouille sausage, pile 'em all in between this bread, put on some of that down-home zydeco music—Queen Ida will do nicely—and feast "Nawlins" style.

1 cup lukewarm water

1½ tablespoons honey

2 teaspoons Worcestershire sauce

1½ teaspoons active dry yeast

Spice Blend

¼ teaspoon ground cayenne

½ teaspoon dried thyme

½ teaspoon dried oregano

½ teaspoon garlic powder

½ teaspoon onion powder

½ teaspoon freshly ground black pepper

Dry Ingredients

2 cups bread flour

½ cup cornmeal

½ cup whole-wheat flour

2 teaspoons salt

1 cup peeled, seeded, and diced plum tomatoes (page 210)

1. Combine the water, honey, and Worcestershire sauce in the bowl of a heavy-duty electric mixer or in a large mixing bowl.

2. Sprinkle the yeast over the mixture, stir in, and let sit for 2 minutes.

3. Combine the spice blend ingredients in a small bowl.

4. Add the dry ingredients and the spice blend to the yeast mixture.

5. Mix with the dough hook (or knead by hand) for 4 to 6 minutes, or until the dough is silky and elastic.

6. Add the tomatoes and continue mixing or kneading for 2 minutes, or until the tomatoes are evenly distributed.

7. Transfer the dough to a lightly oiled bowl and cover with plastic wrap.

8. Let rise in a warm place for 1½ hours, or until approximately doubled in volume.

9. Punch the dough down. (For longer fermentation and to develop a wheaty, fuller, and more complex flavor, cover the dough and refrigerate it overnight at this point. The next day, bring the dough to room temperature, punch down again, and continue as recipe directs.)

10. Place the dough on a well-floured work surface and cut into 2 equal pieces.

11. Sprinkle a baking sheet with cornmeal.

12. Shape the dough into round loaves. (See photos and additional instructions on pages 206–207.)

13. Place the loaves on the prepared baking sheet, cover with plastic wrap, and let rise in a warm place for 1 hour.

14. Place a baking stone on the middle rack in the oven and preheat to 400°.

15. Uncover the loaves and, using a spray bottle, spritz them with water, then lightly dust with whole-wheat or all-purpose flour.

16. Make 2 or 3 diagonal slashes in the top of the loaves with a serrated knife to allow the dough to expand in the hot oven.

17. Using the spray bottle, spritz the oven walls with water. Work quickly so the oven does not lose heat.

18. Slide the loaves onto the hot stone.

19. Bake for 35 to 40 minutes, or until the crust is golden brown.

20. Transfer the loaves to a rack to cool.

Yield: 2 loaves

> ***Bread Machine Instructions***
> ***To make the bread in a bread machine:***
> *1. Combine all the ingredients, except the spice blend and tomatoes, in the bread pan in the order specified by the manufacturer's instructions.*
> *2. Process on the sweet or raisin bread setting (#8).*
> *3. Add the spice blend and tomatoes at the beeps.*
>
> ***To prepare the dough in a bread machine:***
> *1. Combine all the ingredients, except the spice blend and tomatoes, in the bread pan in the order specified by the manufacturer's instructions.*
> *2. Process on the dough setting (#9).*
> *3. When the cycle is complete, turn the dough out onto a well-floured work surface.*
> *4. Knead the spice blend and tomatoes into the dough until evenly distributed.*
> *5. Continue with step 7 of the recipe.*

BLACK BEAN–CHIPOTLE BREAD

Here's another tasty and nutritional bread we've been serving at Coyote Cafe for years. It contains the traditional southwestern flavors of black beans and chipotle chiles (which are smoked, dried jalapeños). The rich black beans provide the perfect backdrop for the smoky, fiery qualities of the chipotles, and this recipe recalls the flavors of the classic black bean soup. The type of black beans on the market these days does not usually require soaking overnight, which can save considerable time. Or, you can always used drained canned beans. Just be sure to reserve ¾ cup of the liquid. Serve this bread with southwestern food or as a snack any time. Mexican oregano is more aromatic and intense than regular oregano; if unavailable locally, it can be ordered through the mail (see page 210). If you prepare the sponge the night before baking, you might want to cook the beans then, too, to save time.

Sponge

1 cup lukewarm water
1 teaspoon active dry yeast
¾ cup bread flour
¼ cup whole-wheat flour

5 cups water
1½ cups dried black beans, picked through and
    rinsed
1 teaspoon active dry yeast

Dry Ingredients

2½ cups bread flour
½ cup whole-wheat flour
2 teaspoons salt
½ teaspoon ground cumin
½ teaspoon dried Mexican oregano, or
    1 teaspoon dried regular oregano

6 dried chipotle chiles, stemmed and chopped
    (about 3½ teaspoons), or 4 teaspoons canned
    minced chipotles
1 tablespoon barbecue sauce

1. To prepare the sponge, place the water in a mixing bowl.
2. Sprinkle 1 teaspoon yeast over the water, stir in, and let sit for 2 minutes.
3. Mix in the flours.
4. Cover the bowl with plastic wrap and let sit for 14 to 16 hours or overnight.
5. Place the water and black beans in a saucepan, and bring to a boil.
6. Reduce the heat to a simmer and cook for about 2 hours, or until the beans are tender.
7. Let the beans cool, then drain them, reserving ¾ cup of the cooking liquid.
8. To prepare the dough, heat the reserved cooking liquid in a saucepan until it is lukewarm.
9. Pulse the cooked beans in a food processor until they are chunky, but not puréed.
10. Pour the lukewarm cooking liquid into the bowl of a heavy-duty electric mixer or into a large mixing bowl.
11. Add the beans and sponge to the cooking liquid.
12. Sprinkle the remaining 1 teaspoon yeast over the bean mixture, stir in, and let sit for 2 minutes.

13. Add the dry ingredients, chiles, and barbecue sauce.

14. Mix with the dough hook (or knead by hand) for 6 to 8 minutes, or until the dough is silky and elastic. If the dough seems too wet, add up to ¼ cup more bread flour.

15. Transfer the dough to a lightly oiled bowl and cover with plastic wrap.

16. Let rise in a warm place for 1½ hours, or until approximately doubled in volume.

17. Punch the dough down, transfer to a well-floured work surface, and cut into 2 equal pieces. Alternatively, do not divide.

18. Sprinkle a baking sheet with cornmeal.

19. Shape the dough into round loaves. (See photos and additional instructions on pages 206–207.)

20. Place the loaves on the baking sheet, cover with plastic wrap, and let rise again in a warm place for 1 hour.

21. Place a baking stone on the middle rack in the oven and preheat to 425°.

22. Uncover the loaves and, using a spray bottle, spritz them with water, then lightly dust with whole-wheat flour.

23. Make 2 or 3 diagonal slashes in the tops of the loaves with a serrated knife to allow the dough to expand in the hot oven.

24. Using the spray bottle, spritz the oven walls with water. Work quickly so the oven does not lose heat.

25. Slide the loaves onto the hot stone.

26. Bake for 35 to 40 minutes, or until the crust is caramel brown.

27. Transfer the loaves to a rack to cool.

Yield: 2 small loaves or 1 large loaf

Bread Machine Instructions
To make the bread in a bread machine (this is also a 2-day process):

1. On the first day, combine the sponge ingredients in the bread pan.

2. Process on the dough setting (#9).

3. Let sit in the machine for 14 to 16 hours.

4. On the second day, prepare the beans (see steps 5 through 9).

5. Add the ¾ cup lukewarm cooking liquid from the beans to the sponge, along with the processed beans.

6. Add the remaining ingredients, except the chipotles and oregano.

7. Process on the sweet or raisin bread setting (#8).

8. Add the chipotles and oregano at the beeps.

To prepare the dough in a bread machine (this is also a 2-day process:

1. On the first day, combine the sponge ingredients in the bread pan.

2. Process on the dough setting (#9).

3. Let sit in the machine for 14 to 16 hours.

4. On the second day, prepare the beans (see steps 5 through 9).

5. Add the ¾ cup lukewarm cooking liquid, the beans, and the remaining ingredients, except the chipotles and oregano, to the sponge in the bread pan in the order specified by the manufacturer's instructions.

6. Process on the dough setting (#9).

7. When the cycle is complete, turn the dough out onto a well-floured work surface.

8. Knead the chipotles and oregano into the dough until evenly distributed.

9. Continue with step 15 of the recipe.

SPICY CHORIZO-RED CHILE BREAD

Chorizo is the traditional spicy pork sausage the Spaniards introduced to Mexico. It is usually served crumbled or loose or in patties, rather than in sausage casings, and it is often used as a filling for enchiladas, quesadillas, or tacos, as well as an accompaniment for eggs. Spanish chorizo is a hard sausage from Andalusia made with hand-chopped pork that is cured with spices and plenty of garlic, and is not the type used in this recipe. You can buy ready-made chorizo—we particularly recommend Bruce Aidells's bulk sausage from the San Francisco Bay Area—or you can make your own, using the recipe in my first book, Coyote Cafe. *Alternatively, you can substitute a crumbly spicy Italian sausage, but the flavor won't be quite the same. This bread is a natural with huevos rancheros, scrambled eggs, or Spanish omelets. Be sure to keep it refrigerated.*

Sponge

1 cup lukewarm water

1 teaspoon active dry yeast

¾ cup bread flour

¼ cup whole-wheat flour

¾ cup lukewarm water

1 teaspoon active dry yeast

Dry Ingredients

3 cups bread flour

¼ cup whole-wheat flour

2 teaspoons salt

1 tablespoon chile molido (freshly ground pure chile powder)

6 ounces chorizo sausage or spicy Italian sausage, cooked, cooled, and diced

1. To prepare the sponge, place the water in a mixing bowl.
2. Sprinkle the yeast over the water, stir in, and let sit for 2 minutes.
3. Mix in the flours.
4. Cover the bowl with plastic wrap and let sit for 14 to 16 hours, or overnight.
5. To prepare the dough, place the water and sponge in the bowl of a heavy-duty electric mixer or in a large mixing bowl.
6. Sprinkle the yeast over the mixture, stir in, and let sit for 2 minutes.
7. Add the dry ingredients.
8. Mix with the dough hook (or knead by hand) for 6 to 8 minutes, or until the dough is silky and elastic.
9. Add the chorizo and mix just until it is evenly distributed, about 1 or 2 minutes.
10. Transfer the dough to a lightly oiled bowl and cover with plastic wrap.
11. Let rise in a warm place for 1½ hours, or until approximately doubled in volume.
12. Punch the dough down, transfer to a well-floured work surface, and cut into 2 equal pieces. Alternatively, do not divide.

13. Sprinkle a baking sheet with cornmeal.

14. Shape into round loaves. (See photos and additional instructions on pages 206–207.)

15. Place the loaves on the baking sheet, cover with plastic wrap, and let rise in a warm place for 1 hour.

16. Place the baking stone on the middle rack in the oven and preheat to 425°.

17. Uncover the loaves and, using a spray bottle, spritz them with water.

18. Make 2 or 3 diagonal slashes in the tops of the loaves with a serrated knife to allow the dough to expand in the hot oven.

19. Using the spray bottle, spritz the oven walls with water. Work quickly so the oven does not lose heat.

20. Slide the loaves onto the hot stone.

21. Bake for 35 to 40 minutes, or until the crust is caramel brown.

22. Transfer the loaves to a rack to cool.

23. When completely cool, place in an airtight plastic bag and store in the refrigerator.

Yield: 2 small loaves or 1 large loaf

Bread Machine Instructions
To make the bread in a bread machine (this is also a 2-day process):
1. On the first day, combine the sponge ingredients in the bread pan.
2. Process on the dough setting (#9).
3. Let sit in the machine for 14 to 16 hours.
4. On the second day, add the remaining ingredients, except the chorizo, in the order specified by the manufacturer's instructions.
5. Process on the sweet or raisin bread setting (#8).
6. Add the chorizo at the beeps.

To prepare the dough in a bread machine (this is also a 2-day process):
1. On the first day, combine the sponge ingredients in the bread pan.
2. Process on the dough setting (#9).
3. Let sit in the machine for 14 to 16 hours.
4. On the second day, add the remaining ingredients, except the chorizo, in the order specified by the manufacturer's instructions.
5. Process on the dough setting (#9).
6. When the cycle is complete, turn the dough out onto a well-floured work surface.
7. Knead the chorizo into the dough until evenly distributed.
8. Continue with step 10 of the recipe.

ANASAZI BEAN & RAJAS BREAD

Anasazi beans are named for "the ancient ones," believed to be the agrarian predecessors of the Pueblo Indians of New Mexico's Rio Grande Valley and other Native American groups in the Southwest. The Anasazi, who occupied the region over 1,000 years ago, lived in hollowed-out caves along the steep faces of mesas and in elaborate adobe buildings tucked within the contours of the cliffs. Mesa Verde, the dramatic cliff city preserved in the Four Corners area of southwestern Colorado, was the one of the centers of the Anasazi culture. The Anasazi farmed corn on top of the mesas and beans and squash on the valley floor and, together with other agrarian native groups in North America, they genetically selected and cultivated hundreds of varieties of beans as well as corn. Anasazi beans, which have been found in archaeological digs, are some of the prettiest beans of all (but when cooked, their dappled red color turns a uniform pink). Rajas is the term for julienned (or sliced) bell peppers and other chiles. Serve this bread with southwestern dishes, minestrone and bean soups, or with barbecued ribs and fresh corn.

Sponge

1 cup lukewarm water
1 teaspoon active dry yeast
¾ cup bread flour
¼ cup rye flour

5 cups water
1½ cups dried anasazi or pinto beans
1 teaspoon active dry yeast

Dry Ingredients

2 cups bread flour
½ cup rye flour
2 teaspoons ground cumin
2 teaspoons salt
2 teaspoons dried Mexican oregano, or
    1 tablespoon regular oregano

1 large red bell pepper, roasted, stemmed,
    seeded, peeled, and julienned (page 209)

1. To prepare the sponge, place the water in a mixing bowl.
2. Sprinkle the yeast over the water, stir in, and let sit for 2 minutes.
3. Mix in the flours.
4. Cover the bowl with plastic wrap and let sit for 14 to 16 hours, or overnight.
5. Place the water and anasazi beans in a saucepan, and bring to a boil.
6. Reduce the heat to a simmer and cook for about 2 hours, or until the beans are tender.
7. Let the beans cool, then drain them, reserving ¾ cup of the cooking liquid.
8. To prepare the dough, heat the excess cooking liquid in a saucepan until lukewarm.
9. Pulse the cooked beans in a food processor until they are chunky, but not puréed.
10. Pour the lukewarm cooking liquid into the bowl of a heavy-duty electric mixer or a large mixing bowl.
11. Add the beans and the sponge to the cooking liquid.

12. Sprinkle the yeast over the bean mixture, stir in, and let sit for 2 minutes.

13. Add the dry ingredients.

14. Mix with the dough hook (or knead by hand) for 6 to 8 minutes, or until the dough is silky and elastic.

15. Add the red pepper strips and mix or knead just until evenly distributed, about 1 or 2 minutes.

16. Transfer the dough to a lightly oiled bowl and cover with plastic wrap.

17. Let rise in a warm place for 1½ hours, or until approximately doubled in volume.

18. Punch the dough down, transfer to a well-floured work surface, and cut into 2 equal pieces. Alternatively, do not divide.

19. Sprinkle a baking sheet with cornmeal.

20. Shape the dough into round loaves. (See photos and additional instructions on pages 206–207.)

21. Place the loaves on the baking sheet, cover with plastic wrap, and let rise in a warm place for 1 hour.

22. Place a baking stone on the middle rack in the oven and preheat to 425°.

23. Uncover the loaves and, using a spray bottle, spritz them with water.

24. Make 2 diagonal slashes in the tops of the loaves with a serrated knife to allow the dough to expand in the hot oven.

25. Using the spray bottle, spritz the oven walls with water. Work quickly so the oven does not lose heat.

26. Slide the loaves onto the hot stone.

27. Bake for 35 to 40 minutes, or until the crust is dark caramel brown.

28. Transfer to a rack to cool.

Yield: 2 small loaves

Bread Machine Instructions
To make in a bread machine (this is also a 2-day process):

1. On the first day, combine the sponge ingredients in the bread pan.

2. Process on the dough setting (#9).

3. Let sit in the machine for 14 to 16 hours.

4. On the second day, prepare the beans (see steps 5 through 9).

5. Add the ¾ cup lukewarm cooking liquid to the sponge, along with the processed beans.

6. Add the remaining ingredients, except the oregano and red pepper strips.

7. Process on the sweet or raisin bread setting (#8).

8. Add the oregano and red pepper strips at the beeps.

To prepare the dough in a bread machine (this is also a 2-day process):

1. On the first day, combine the sponge ingredients in the bread pan.

2. Process on the dough setting (#9).

3. Let sit in the machine for 14 to 16 hours.

4. On the second day, prepare the beans (see steps 5 through 9).

5. Add the ¾ cup lukewarm cooking liquid, the beans, and the remaining ingredients, except the oregano and red pepper strips, to the sponge in the bread pan in the order specified by the manufacturer's instructions.

6. Process on the dough setting (#9).

7. When the cycle is complete, turn the dough out onto a well-floured work surface.

8. Knead the oregano and red pepper strips into the dough until evenly distributed.

9. Continue with step 16 of the recipe.

SONOMA JACK BREAD

The Sonoma Valley is a beautiful wine-growing region between the coast and Napa Valley to the north of San Francisco. Connoisseurs will probably always argue which of the valleys produces the better wines or is more scenic. If you get the chance, it is well worth the drive to visit the valley and the town of Sonoma, with its old-fashioned town square and California's northernmost mission at the square's northeast corner. Sonoma Valley is cooler than its rival, mainly because the fog regularly drifts in from the coast, creating perfect conditions for the delicate pinot noirs and chardonnays for which Sonoma is famous.

Another product of the valley is Sonoma Jack cheese, a semisoft, quick-ripening mild cheese. The first cheeses made in North America were produced in the missions the Spanish established in California and the Southwest, and Monterey jack was first made at the mission on the Monterey peninsula. Jack is an essential cheese in southwestern cuisine, mostly because its texture, richness, and flavor make a good foil for picante chiles, salsas, and sauces. One of the most appealing qualities of this bread is the aroma while it's baking, another is the golden melted cheese that blankets the crust. It's the cheese that gives this bread an appealing density and richness. If Sonoma Jack cheese is unavailable in your area, order it through the mail (see page 210) or use Muenster, Monterey, a creamy Havarti, or another jack cheese.

1 cup lukewarm water
1½ tablespoons honey
1½ teaspoons active dry yeast

Dry Ingredients
2¼ cups bread flour
½ cup whole-wheat flour
2 teaspoons salt

2 cups grated Sonoma Jack cheese

1. Combine the water and honey in the bowl of a heavy-duty electric mixer or in a large mixing bowl.

2. Sprinkle the yeast over the mixture, stir in, and let sit for 2 minutes.

3. Add the dry ingredients.

4. Mix with the dough hook (or knead by hand) for 4 to 6 minutes, or until the dough is silky and elastic.

5. Add 1½ cups of the cheese and continue mixing or kneading for 2 minutes, or until the cheese is evenly distributed.

6. Transfer the dough to a lightly oiled bowl and cover with plastic wrap.

7. Let rise in a warm place for 1½ hours, or until approximately doubled in volume.

8. Punch the dough down. (For longer fermentation and to develop a wheaty, fuller, and

more complex flavor, cover the dough and refrigerate it overnight at this point. The next day, bring the dough to room temperature, punch down again, and continue as the recipe directs.)

9. Transfer the dough to a well-floured work surface and cut it into 2 equal pieces.

10. Sprinkle a baking sheet with cornmeal.

11. Shape into round loaves. (See photos and additional instructions on pages 206–207.)

12. Place on the prepared baking sheet, cover with plastic wrap, and let rise in a warm place for 1 hour.

13. Preheat the oven to 400° and place a baking stone on the middle rack.

14. Uncover the loaves and, using a spray bottle, spritz them with water.

15. Sprinkle the remaining ½ cup cheese on top of the loaves and gently press with your hands to adhere it to the loaves.

16. Make 2 or 3 diagonal slashes in the tops of the loaves with a serrated knife to allow the dough to expand in the hot oven.

17. Using the spray bottle, spritz the oven walls with water. Work quickly so the oven does not lose heat.

18. Slide the loaves onto the hot stone.

19. Bake for 35 to 40 minutes, or until the crust is golden brown.

20. Transfer the loaves to a rack to cool.

Yield: 2 loaves

Bread Machine Instructions
To make the bread in a bread machine:
1. Combine all the ingredients, except the cheese, in the bread pan in the order specified by the manufacturer's instructions.
2. Process on the sweet or raisin bread setting (#8).
3. Add 1½ cups of the cheese at the beeps. You will not use the remaining ½ cup cheese.

To prepare the dough in a bread machine:
1. Combine all the ingredients, except the cheese, in the bread pan in the order specified by the manufacturer's instructions.
2. Process on the dough setting (#9).
3. When the cycle is complete, turn the dough out onto a well-floured work surface.
4. Knead in 1½ cups of the cheese until evenly distributed.
5. Continue with step 6 of the recipe.

SPANISH MANCHEGO, CAPER, & ANCHOVY BREAD

Manchego is the most famous Spanish cheese. It is made from the milk of sheep grazed on the renowned plains of La Mancha—Don Quixote country. It is a firm cheese with a hard, dark rind and creamy texture. Cheddar or another semisoft cheese can be substituted. This rich, savory bread pairs beautifully with most seafood and fresh fish, and it will delight all anchovy lovers. Buy Spanish, Portuguese, or French anchovies packed in olive oil—we find anchovies packed in other types of oil inferior. You can also serve this bread with tomato dishes or salads. As you take a bite of the bread, imagine you're in an exotic tapas bar listening to flamenco music and clacking castanets, or on a sunlit villa patio by the azure waters of the Mediterranean, waiting for the spit-grilled fresh-caught fish to finish cooking…

1 cup lukewarm water
1½ tablespoons honey
1½ teaspoons active dry yeast

Dry Ingredients
2 cups bread flour
¾ cup semolina flour
1 teaspoon salt

1½ cups grated manchego cheese or Cheddar
¼ cup chopped capers
6 canned anchovy fillets, chopped

1. Combine the water and honey in the bowl of a heavy-duty electric mixer or in a large mixing bowl.
2. Sprinkle the yeast over the mixture, stir in, and let sit for 2 minutes.
3. Add the dry ingredients.
4. Mix with the dough hook (or knead by hand) for 4 to 6 minutes, or until the dough is silky and elastic.
5. Add the cheese, capers, and anchovies, and continue mixing or kneading for 2 minutes, or until evenly distributed.
6. Transfer the dough to a lightly oiled bowl and cover with plastic wrap.
7. Let rise in a warm place for 1½ hours, or until approximately doubled in volume.
8. Punch the dough down. (For longer fermentation and to develop a tangy flavor, cover the dough and refrigerate it overnight at this point. The next day, bring the dough to room temperature, punch down again, and continue as the recipe directs.)
9. Transfer the dough to a well-floured work surface and cut it into 2 equal pieces.

10. Sprinkle a baking sheet with cornmeal.

11. Shape into round loaves. (See photos and additional instructions on pages 206–207.)

12. Place on the prepared baking sheet, cover with plastic wrap, and let rise in a warm place for 1 hour.

13. Place a baking stone on the middle rack in the oven and preheat to 400°.

14. Uncover the loaves and, using a spray bottle, spritz them with water, then lightly dust with semolina flour.

15. Make 2 or 3 diagonal slashes in the tops of the loaves with a serrated knife to allow the dough to expand in the hot oven.

16. Using the spray bottle, spritz the oven walls with water. Work quickly so the oven does not lose heat.

17. Slide the loaves onto the hot stone.

18. Bake for 35 to 40 minutes, or until the crust is golden brown.

19. Transfer to a rack to cool.

Yield: 2 loaves

Bread Machine Instructions
To make the bread in a bread machine:

1. Combine all the ingredients, except the cheese, capers, and anchovies, in the bread pan in the order specified by the manufacturer's instructions.
2. Process on the sweet or raisin bread setting (#8).
3. Add the cheese, capers, and anchovies at the beeps.

To prepare the dough in a bread machine:

1. Combine all the ingredients, except the cheese, capers, and anchovies, in the bread pan in the order specified by the manufacturer's instructions.
2. Process on the dough setting (#9).
3. When the cycle is complete, turn the dough out onto a well-floured work surface.
4. Knead the cheese, capers, and anchovies into the dough until evenly distributed.
5. Continue with step 6 of the recipe.

CORIANDER-MINT COUNTRY BREAD

Coriander, the name given to the seed of the fresh cilantro herb, is an aromatic spice related to parsley that is native to Asia and used extensively in Indian and Mediterranean cooking. Toasting coriander eliminates its raw edge and pulls out its complex, roasty flavor. Coriander seed and fresh cilantro have quite different characteristics and are not interchangeable. However, for those who insist they don't like cilantro, coriander is a flavorful way to enjoy this plant.

The coriander and cooling mint in this bread are a natural match for lamb (especially braised shanks and kebabs) or red meats with strong flavors. The combination is also used in Indian cuisine in the yogurt-based raita—a cooling accompaniment to curry—as well as in crispy poppadums and naan breads. Try this bread with southwestern food, tabouli, or marinated grain or bean salads. The dough also makes good rolls or baguette-style loaves.

1 cup lukewarm water

1½ tablespoons honey

1½ teaspoons active dry yeast

Dry Ingredients

2¾ cups bread flour

2 teaspoons salt

2 teaspoons ground toasted coriander plus
   additional for sprinkling (page 210)

2 cups mint leaves, coarsely chopped

1. Combine the water and honey in the bowl of a heavy-duty electric mixer or in a large mixing bowl.

2. Sprinkle the yeast over the mixture, stir in, and let sit for 2 minutes.

3. Add the dry ingredients.

4. Mix with the dough hook (or knead by hand) for 4 to 6 minutes, or until the dough is silky and elastic.

5. Add the mint leaves and continue mixing or kneading for 2 minutes, or until the mint is evenly distributed.

6. Transfer the dough to a lightly oiled bowl and cover with plastic wrap.

7. Let rise in a warm place for 1½ hours, or until approximately doubled in volume.

8. Punch the dough down. (For longer fermentation and to develop a tangy flavor, cover the dough and refrigerate it overnight at this point. The next day, bring the dough to room temperature, punch down again, and continue as the recipe directs.)

9. Transfer the dough to a well-floured work surface and cut into 2 equal pieces.

10. Sprinkle a baking sheet with cornmeal.

11. Shape into round loaves. (See photos and additional instructions on pages 206–207.)

12. Place on the prepared baking sheet, cover with plastic wrap, and let rise in a warm place for 1 hour.

13. Place a baking stone on the middle rack in the oven and preheat to 400°.

14. Uncover the loaf and, using a spray bottle, spritz the loaf with water, then sprinkle with ground coriander.

15. Make 2 or 3 diagonal slashes in the top of the loaf with a serrated knife to allow the dough to expand in the hot oven.

16. Using the spray bottle, spritz the oven walls with water. Work quickly so the oven does not lose heat.

17. Slide the loaf onto the hot stone.

18. Bake for 35 to 40 minutes, or until the crust is golden brown.

19. Transfer the loaf to a rack to cool.

Yield: 1 large loaf

Bread Machine Instructions
To make the bread in a bread machine:

1. Combine all the ingredients, except the mint, in the bread pan in the order specified by the manufacturer's instructions.

2. Process on the sweet or raisin bread setting (#8).

3. Add the mint at the beeps.

To prepare the dough in a bread machine:

1. Combine all the ingredients, except the mint, in the bread pan in the order specified by the manufacturer's instructions.

2. Process on the dough setting (#9).

3. When the cycle is complete, turn the dough out onto a well-floured work surface.

4. Knead the mint into the dough until evenly distributed.

5. Continue with step 6 of the recipe.

SOURDOUGH STARTER

Picture, if you will, a swaying wagon train following a cattle drive fording the Red River in the mid-1800s as it passes north from Texas into Oklahoma, on its way to the trailhead and stockyards in Kansas City. As the pioneers set up camp, the "cookie" arranges the vittles and brings out the sourdough starter, which is much like this one, to prepare the bread. At around the same time in history, a gnarled and bearded '49er pioneer outfitted in his newfangled Levi jeans prepares for a day panning for gold in northern California by taking a piece of starter from his wooden pail and making up a sourdough loaf. Such is the stuff of culinary legend, but sourdough is rooted in this very real heritage.

San Francisco is often thought of as the sourdough capital of the United States, probably because sourdough bread has remained popular there ever since Gold Rush days. Making the initial starter is a three-day process, so plan ahead if you want to make sourdough for the first time. You may need to visit a natural foods store to find the organic stone-ground unbleached white flour.

1½ cups lukewarm milk
¼ teaspoon active dry yeast
1 teaspoon honey
2 cups unbleached white flour
¼ cup spring water

1. To prepare the starter, place the milk in a mixing bowl.
2. Sprinkle the yeast over the milk.
3. Whisk in the honey and 1½ cups of the flour.
4. Cover with plastic wrap and let sit at room temperature (72° to 76°) for 72 hours (3 days).
5. After 72 hours, stir in the ¼ cup water and whisk in the remaining ½ cup flour.
6. Cover again with plastic wrap and let sit at room temperature for 2 hours; the mixture should be bubbly and have a sour, tangy aroma and taste.
7. Remove the amount of starter the recipe calls for and set aside.

8. Transfer the remaining starter to a sterile glass jar and replenish it by mixing in ½ cup water and ½ cup flour. Cover tightly and store in the refrigerator for up to 1 month.

> ### Bread Machine Instructions
> ### (This is also a 3- or 4-day process.)
> *1. On the first day, combine the milk, yeast, honey, and 1½ cups of the flour in the bread pan.*
> *2. Process on the dough setting (#9).*
> *3. Let sit in the machine for 72 hours (3 days).*
> *4. After 72 hours, add ¼ cup water and the remaining ½ cup flour to the starter in the bread pan.*
> *5. Process again on the dough setting and let sit for 2 hours.*
> *6. Remove all but the amount of starter the recipe calls for from the machine, transferring it to a sterile glass jar. Cover tightly and store in the refrigerator for up to 1 month.*

RYE SOURDOUGH STARTER

This rye starter is for making rye sourdough loaves rather than wheat sourdoughs. Use organic flour if possible.

1 cup lukewarm milk
¼ teaspoon dry active yeast
1½ cups rye flour
½ cup lukewarm spring water

1. Place the milk in a mixing bowl.
2. Sprinkle the yeast over the milk.
3. Whisk in 1 cup of the rye flour.
4. Cover with plastic wrap and let sit at room temperature (72° to 76°) for 72 hours (3 days).
5. After 72 hours, stir in the ½ cup water and the remaining ½ cup of rye flour.
6. Cover again with plastic wrap and let sit at room temperature for another 2 hours; the mixture should be bubbly and have a sour, tangy aroma and taste.
7. Remove the amount of starter the recipe calls for and set aside. Transfer the remaining starter to a sterile glass jar and replenish it by mixing in ½ cup water and ½ cup rye flour. Cover tightly and store in the refrigerator for up to 1 month.

> ### *Bread Machine Instructions*
> ### *(This is also a 3- or 4-day process.)*
> *1. On the first day, combine the milk, yeast, and 1 cup of the rye flour in the bread pan.*
> *2. Process on the dough setting (#9).*
> *3. Let sit in the machine for 72 hours (3 days).*
> *4. After 72 hours, add the ½ cup water and the remaining ½ cup rye flour to the starter in the bread pan.*
> *5. Process again on the dough setting and let sit for 2 hours.*
> *6. Remove all but the amount of starter the recipe calls for from the machine, transferring it to a sterile glass jar. Cover tightly and store in the refrigerator for up to 1 month.*

PEPITA-SAGE HARVEST SOURDOUGH

For centuries Native Americans of the Southwest have relied on pumpkin seeds, or pepitas, and other squash seeds as a major food source (for more about this, see page 64). Likewise, the sage that grows wild across the region has long been used as a culinary and medicinal herb, especially in home remedies and teas. The hearty, roasted flavors of the toasted seeds complement the earthy tones of the sage in this bread, which can be served with most southwestern foods and soups—especially those made with pumpkin or squash. Pumpkin seeds are rich in natural oils and therefore turn rancid quickly; make sure you buy fresh ones.

2 cups Sourdough Starter (page 140)

1 cup lukewarm water

½ teaspoon active dry yeast

Dry Ingredients

3¼ cups bread flour

½ cup whole-wheat flour

2 teaspoons salt

½ cup toasted and finely ground pumpkin seeds (page 210)

¼ cup wheat germ

18 fresh sage leaves, coarsely chopped

2 tablespoons dried sage

¼ cup shelled untoasted pumpkin seeds

1. Place the starter and water in the bowl of a heavy-duty electric mixer or in a large mixing bowl.
2. Sprinkle the yeast over the mixture, stir in, and let sit for 2 minutes.
3. Add the dry ingredients except the sage.
4. Mix with the dough hook (or knead by hand) for 10 to 12 minutes, or until the dough is silky and elastic. Add the sage and continue mixing for 2 minutes, or until incorporated.
5. Transfer the dough to a lightly oiled bowl and cover with plastic wrap.
6. Let rise in a warm place for 4 hours, or until approximately doubled in volume.
7. Punch the dough down and turn out onto a lightly floured work surface.
8. Sprinkle a baking sheet with whole-wheat flour.
9. Gently pull and stretch the dough into a round loaf or 2 small loaves in the shape of your choice. (See photos and additional instructions on pages 206–207.)
10. Place the loaf on the prepared baking sheet.
11. Cover with plastic wrap and let rise in a warm place for 1½ to 2 hours.
12. Place a baking stone on the middle rack in the oven and preheat to 425°.

13. Uncover the loaf and, using a spray bottle, spritz it with water.

14. Sprinkle the untoasted pepitas on the top and along the sides of the loaf and gently press with your hands to adhere the seeds to the loaf.

15. Make 2 or 3 diagonal slashes in the top of the loaf with a serrated knife to allow the dough to expand in the hot oven.

16. Using the spray bottle, spritz the oven walls with water. Work quickly so the oven does not lose heat.

17. Slide the loaf onto the hot stone.

18. Bake for 40 to 45 minutes, or until the crust is dark brown.

19. Transfer the loaf to a rack to cool.

Yield: 1 large loaf or 2 small loaves

Bread Machine Instructions
To prepare the dough in a bread machine:
1. Place the starter in the bread pan.
2. Add the water, yeast, and dry ingredients to the starter.
3. Process on the dough setting (#9).
4. When the cycle is complete, turn the dough out onto a well-floured work surface.
5. Continue with step 5, but omit step 14 (you will not use the untoasted pumpkin seeds).

ALMOND-CHERRY SOURDOUGH

Only two nuts are mentioned in the Bible: almonds and pistachios, which indicates their region of origin. Almond milk was a prized ingredient in medieval Europe as it had to be transported from the Mediterranean to European destinations such as England, Germany, and northern France. Among other uses, it was a vital element in sauces. Virtually all of the almond crop in the United States (and half of the world crop) is grown in California.

The best cherries are grown in Oregon's Willamette Valley and in Michigan. Try to find organic dried cherries at natural foods stores, or order them from my friend and colleague Larry Forgione, who sells great dried cherries under his American Spoon Foods label (see page 210). Roasted almonds and cherries make a great dessert combination—in an almond and cherry tart, for example—but it's unusual to find them together in a bread. The sweet fruit and tangy sourdough provide an intriguing and delicious counterpoint to the richness of the almonds and hearty whole wheat. It makes a memorable breakfast bread—and, of course, good toast—or you can serve it for dinner with venison, duck, and other game and red meat.

1½ cups dried cherries
¾ cup water
1 tablespoon brandy (optional)

1½ cups Sourdough Starter (page 140)
1 cup lukewarm water
½ teaspoon active dry yeast

Dry Ingredients
3¼ cups bread flour
1 cup whole-wheat flour
2 teaspoons salt

1 cup sliced almonds, toasted (page 209)
½ cup untoasted sliced almonds

1. Place the cherries, water, and brandy in a saucepan and bring to a simmer over medium heat.
2. Turn off the heat and let cool for 15 minutes.
3. Place the starter and water in the bowl of a heavy-duty electric mixer or in a large mixing bowl.
4. Sprinkle the yeast over the mixture, stir in, and let sit for 2 minutes.
5. Add the dry ingredients.
6. Mix with the dough hook (or knead by hand) for 10 to 12 minutes, or until the dough is silky and elastic.
7. Drain the cherries, add to the dough along with the toasted almonds, and continue mixing or kneading until evenly distributed.
8. Transfer the dough to a lightly oiled bowl and cover with plastic wrap.
9. Let rise in a warm place for 4 hours, or until approximately doubled in volume.

10. Punch the dough down and turn it out onto a lightly floured work surface.

11. Sprinkle a baking sheet with whole-wheat flour.

12. Gently pull and stretch the dough into a round loaf or 2 small loaves in the shape of your choice. (See photos and additional instructions on pages 206–207.)

13. Place the loaf on the prepared baking sheet, cover with plastic wrap, and let rise in a warm place for 1½ to 2 hours.

14. Place a baking stone on the middle rack in the oven and preheat to 425°.

15. Uncover the loaf and, using a spray bottle, spritz it with water.

16. Sprinkle the untoasted almonds on top and along the sides of the loaf and press gently with your hands to adhere the nuts to the loaf.

17. Make 2 or 3 diagonal slashes in the top of the loaf with a serrated knife to allow the dough to expand in the hot oven.

18. Using the spray bottle, spritz the oven walls with water. Work quickly so the oven does not lose heat.

19. Slide the loaf onto the hot stone.

20. Bake for 40 to 45 minutes, or until the crust is dark brown.

21. Transfer the loaf to a rack to cool.

Yield: 1 large loaf or 2 small loaves

> ***Bread Machine Instructions***
> ***To prepare the dough in a bread machine:***
>
> *1. Place the starter in the bread pan.*
>
> *2. Prepare the cherries (see steps 1 and 2 of the recipe), and reserve.*
>
> *3. Add the lukewarm water, yeast, and dry ingredients to the starter.*
>
> *4. Process on the dough setting (#9).*
>
> *5. When the cycle is complete, turn the dough out onto a well-floured work surface.*
>
> *6. Knead the drained cherries into the dough until evenly distributed.*
>
> *7. Continue with step 8 of the recipe, omitting step 16 (you will not use the untoasted almonds).*

CHOCOLATE-CHERRY SOUROUGH

This may sound like a strange combination of flavors, but once you try it you'll be hooked! The first time Andrew tasted this unusual combination was at Nancy Silverton's La Brea Bakery in Los Angeles. He loved the innovative balance of ingredients, and especially the flavors of the bitter cocoa and sour cherries that set off the savory bread. This recipe is his version, and it really goes well with meat stews, venison, and beef. It also toasts well—try it with some Red Chile Honey (page 188) or Cinnamon Clove Honey (page 189). For this recipe, we prefer to use the dark Dutch process cocoa, such as Drost or Valhrona. Dutched cocoas are less acidic, smoother, mellower in flavor, and yield a richer, darker color than American "supermarket" cocoas.

2 cups dried sour cherries
1 cup water
1 tablespoon brandy (optional)

1½ cups Sourdough Starter (page 140)
1½ cups lukewarm water
½ teaspoon active dry yeast

Dry Ingredients

3¼ cups bread flour
¾ cup Dutch process cocoa powder
2 teaspoons salt
½ teaspoon freshly ground black pepper

1. Place the cherries, water, and brandy in a saucepan and bring to a simmer over medium heat.
2. Turn off the heat and let cool for 15 minutes.
3. Place the starter and water in the bowl of a heavy-duty electric mixer or a large mixing bowl.
4. Sprinkle the yeast over the mixture, stir in, and let sit for 2 minutes.
5. Add the dry ingredients.
6. Mix with the dough hook (or knead by hand) for 10 to 12 minutes, or until the dough is silky and elastic.
7. Drain the cherries, add to the dough, and continue mixing or kneading until evenly distributed.
8. Transfer the dough to a lightly oiled bowl and cover with plastic wrap.
9. Let rise in a warm place for 4 hours, or until approximately doubled in volume.
10. Punch the dough down and turn out onto a lightly floured work surface.
11. Sprinkle a baking sheet with whole-wheat flour.
12. Gently pull and stretch the dough into a

(continued)

round loaf or 2 small loaves in the shape of your choice. (See photos and additional instructions on page 206–207.)

13. Place the loaf on the prepared baking sheet, cover with plastic wrap, and let rise in a warm place for 1½ to 2 hours.

14. Place a baking stone on the middle rack in the oven and preheat to 425°.

15. Uncover the loaf and, using a spray bottle, spritz with water.

16. Make 2 or 3 diagonal slashes in the top of the loaf with a serrated knife to allow the dough to expand in the hot oven.

17. Using the spray bottle, spritz the oven walls with water. Work quickly so the oven does not lose heat.

18. Slide the loaf onto the hot stone.

19. Bake for 40 to 45 minutes, or until the crust is dark brown.

20. Transfer the loaf to a rack to cool.

Yield: 1 large loaf or 2 small loaves

> ***Bread Machine Instructions***
> ***To prepare the dough in a bread machine:***
> *1. Place the starter in the bread pan.*
> *2. Prepare the cherries (see steps 1 and 2 of the recipe) and reserve.*
> *3. Add the lukewarm water, yeast, and dry ingredients to the starter.*
> *4. Process on the dough setting (#9).*
> *5. When the cycle is complete, turn the dough out onto a well-floured work surface.*
> *6. Knead the drained cherries into the dough until evenly distributed.*
> *7. Continue with step 8 of the recipe.*

SOUTHWESTERN SOURDOUGH

Some believe that the City by the Bay's fog, humidity, and moderate warmth create the ideal microclimate for the unique wild yeasts that give San Francisco sourdoughs their special flavor. We think it's quite possible to make sourdough that's just as good, just about any where. This flavored bread evokes the southwestern range and makes great toast.

1½ cups Sourdough Starter (page 140)
1 cup lukewarm water
½ teaspoon active dry yeast

Dry Ingredients
3½ cups bread flour
½ cup whole-wheat flour
2 teaspoons ground cumin
2 teaspoons salt

1. Place the starter and lukewarm water in the bowl of a heavy-duty electric mixer or in a large mixing bowl.
2. Sprinkle the yeast over the mixture, stir in, and let sit for 2 minutes.
3. Add the dry ingredients.
4. Mix with the dough hook (or knead by hand) for 10 to 12 minutes, or until the dough is silky and elastic.
5. Transfer the dough to a lightly oiled bowl and cover with plastic wrap.
6. Let rise in a warm place for 4 hours, or until approximately doubled in volume.
7. Punch the dough down, and turn it out onto a lightly floured work surface.
8. Sprinkle a baking sheet with cornmeal.
9. Gently pull and stretch the dough into a round loaf or 2 small loaves in the shape of your choice. (See photos and additional instructions on pages 206–207.)

10. Place the loaf on the prepared baking sheet, cover with plastic wrap, and let rise in a warm place for 1½ to 2 hours.
11. Place a baking stone on the middle rack in the oven and preheat to 425°.
12. Uncover the loaf and, using a spray bottle, spritz with water, then lightly dust with bread flour.
13. Make 2 or 3 diagonal slashes in the top of the loaf with a serrated knife to allow the dough to expand in the hot oven.
14. Using the spray bottle, spritz the oven walls with water. Work quickly so the oven does not lose heat.
15. Slide the loaf onto the hot stone.
16. Bake for 40 to 45 minutes, or until the crust is dark brown.
17. Transfer the loaf to a rack to cool.

Yield: 1 large loaf or 2 small loaves

Bread Machine Instructions
1. Add the lukewarm water, ½ teaspoon yeast, and the dry ingredients to the starter in the bread pan.
2. Process on the dough setting (#9).
3. When the cycle is complete, turn the dough out on a well-floured work surface.
4. Continue with step 8 of the recipe.

POTATO-CHIVE SOURDOUGH

Consider, and pity, the poor misrepresented potato. It was described erroneously but colorfully at the turn of the nineteenth century by the French writer Diderot as "an Egyptian fruit whose cultivation may possibly have some value in the colonies." Later in the same century, the German philosopher and writer Nietzsche proclaimed that "a diet which consists predominantly of potatoes leads to the use of liquor." No doubt Sir Walter Raleigh, the Elizabethan English explorer who carried the potato (as well as tobacco) to Europe from Virginia, is quietly turning in his grave! Potatoes are native to the Andes of South America, where they were cultivated over 5,000 years ago, and today they are one of the world's most important crops. Potatoes and most members of the allium family, which includes onions, garlic, scallions, and chives, make fine partners in flavor, as this bread demonstrates. Enjoy it sliced simply with a dollop of sour cream, or serve it with soups, salads, and any grilled meat or fish.

1 large potato, diced

2 cups water

1½ cups Sourdough Starter (page 140)

½ teaspoon active dry yeast

Dry Ingredients

4¼ cups bread flour

1 teaspoon dried thyme

2 teaspoons salt

½ teaspoon freshly ground black pepper

1½ cups finely sliced fresh chives

1. Place the potato and water in a saucepan and bring to a simmer over medium heat.
2. Cook for 16 to 18 minutes, or until tender.
3. Turn off the heat, remove the potato and set aside. Reserve 1½ cups of the cooking water, letting it cool to lukewarm.
4. Transfer the cooking water to the bowl of a heavy-duty electric mixer or a large mixing bowl.
5. Add the starter, sprinkle the yeast over the mixture, stir in, and let sit for 2 minutes.
6. Add the dry ingredients.
7. Mix with the dough hook (or knead by hand) for 10 to 12 minutes, or until the dough is silky and elastic.
8. Chop the potato, add it to the dough along with the chives, and continue mixing until evenly distributed.
9. Transfer the dough to a lightly oiled bowl and cover with plastic wrap.
10. Let rise in a warm place for 4 hours, or until approximately doubled in volume.
11. Punch the dough down and turn out onto a lightly floured work surface.

12. Sprinkle a baking sheet with bread flour.

13. Gently pull and stretch the dough into a round loaf or 2 small loaves in the shape of your choice. (See photos and additional instructions on pages 206–207.)

14. Place the loaf on the prepared baking sheet, cover with plastic wrap, and let rise in a warm place for 1½ to 2 hours.

15. Place the baking stone on the middle rack in the oven and preheat to 425°.

16. Uncover the loaf, and using a spray bottle, spritz it with water.

17. Sprinkle the loaf with bread flour.

18. Make 2 or 3 diagonal slashes in the top of the loaf with a serrated knife to allow the dough to expand in the hot oven.

19. Using the spray bottle, spritz the oven walls with water. Work quickly so the oven does not lose heat.

20. Slide the loaf onto the hot stone.

21. Bake for 40 to 45 minutes, or until the crust is dark brown.

22. Transfer the loaf to a rack to cool.

Yield: 1 large loaf or 2 small loaves

Bread Machine Instructions
To prepare the dough in a bread machine:
1. Place the starter in the bread pan.
2. Prepare the potato (see steps 1 through 3 of the recipe), chop, and reserve.
3. Add the lukewarm potato cooking water, yeast, and dry ingredients to the starter.
4. Process on the dough setting (#9).
5. When the cycle is complete, turn the dough out onto a well-floured work surface.
6. Knead the chopped potato and chives into the dough until evenly distributed.
7. Continue with step 9 of the recipe.

RYE SOURDOUGH WITH VERMONT SHARP CHEDDAR

It's the richness of the milk that defines the quality of cheese, and the verdant pastures where Vermont's dairy cows graze ensure fine Cheddar-style cheeses. Andrew, who grew up in Vermont, recommends the local Cabot brand, which is dry, very firm in texture, and one of the sharpest tasting Cheddars around (to order, see page 210). If Vermont cheese is unavailable locally, use a sharp Wisconsin or Canadian Cheddar.

Caraway is an aromatic herb related to parsley, and it provides a crunchy burst of flavor in this bread. It's a classic ingredient in rye breads, and it's also used as a flavoring for some cheeses (such as Havarti). This is a great sandwich bread, especially with grilled cheese and vine-ripened tomatoes or for Reubens. It also makes excellent toasted croutons for soups or salads.

2 cups Rye Sourdough Starter (page 141)
1½ cups lukewarm spring water
1 teaspoon active dry yeast

Dry Ingredients
4½ cups bread flour
½ cup rye flour
1 tablespoon salt

2 tablespoons caraway seeds, toasted (page 210)
1½ cups grated sharp Vermont Cheddar cheese
1 tablespoon untoasted caraway seeds

1. Place the starter and lukewarm water in the bowl of a heavy-duty electric mixer or in a large mixing bowl.
2. Sprinkle the yeast over the mixture, stir in, and let sit for 2 minutes.
3. Add the dry ingredients.
4. Mix with the dough hook (or knead by hand) for 10 to 12 minutes, or until the dough is silky and elastic.
5. Add the toasted caraway seeds and the cheese, and continue mixing or kneading until they are evenly distributed.
6. Transfer the dough to a lightly oiled bowl and cover with plastic wrap.
7. Let rise in a warm place for 4 hours, or until approximately doubled in volume.
8. Punch the dough down and turn out onto a lightly floured work surface.
9. Sprinkle a baking sheet with rye flour.
10. Cut the dough into 2 equal pieces and shape into round, oval, or oblong loaves. (See photos and additional instructions on pages 206–207.)

11. Place the loaves on the prepared baking sheet, cover with plastic wrap, and let rise again in a warm place for 1½ to 2 hours.

12. Place a baking sheet on the middle rack in the oven and preheat to 425°.

13. Uncover the loaves and, using a spray bottle, spritz with water.

14. Sprinkle the untoasted caraway seeds on the top and along the sides of the loaves and press gently with your hands to adhere the seeds to the loaves.

15. Make 2 or 3 diagonal slashes in the tops of the loaves with a serrated knife to allow the dough to expand in the hot oven.

16. Using the spray bottle, spritz the oven walls with water. Work quickly so the oven does not lose heat.

17. Slide the loaves onto the hot stone.

18. Bake for 40 to 45 minutes, or until the crust is dark, earthy brown.

19. Transfer the loaves to a rack to cool.

Yield: 2 loaves

Bread Machine Instructions

1. Place the starter in the bread pan.

2. Add the lukewarm water, 1 teaspoon yeast, and the dry ingredients to the bread pan.

3. Process on the dough setting (#9).

4. When the cycle is complete, turn the dough out onto a well-floured work surface.

5. Knead the toasted caraway seeds and cheese into the dough until evenly distributed.

6. Continue with step 6 of the recipe, omitting step 14 (you will not use the untoasted caraway seeds).

MISSION FIG RYE SOURDOUGH

Figs were first brought to North America by the Franciscan monks who established the missions in California and the Southwest. Although there are many types of figs, the purple-black Mission fig remains one of the most popular in the United States. Make sure the dried figs you buy are moist and pliable; if they are dry and hard, they're old and will have inferior flavor and texture. Figs and rye bread are a classic combination you'll find in the loaves sold by many of the great American bakeries. In this recipe, the sweet figs are a tantalizing contrast to the tangy sourdough and the hearty, rustic rye. This bread is best plain or toasted for breakfast; it's one of the few breads in this book that's best unaccompanied by other food.

1½ cups stemmed and quartered dried Mission or Calimyrna figs

¾ cup water

¼ cup brandy (optional)

2 cups Rye Sourdough Starter (page 140)

1½ cups lukewarm water

1 teaspoon active dry yeast

Dry Ingredients

4½ cups bread flour

1 cup rye flour

1 tablespoon salt

1. Place the figs, water, and brandy in a saucepan and bring to a simmer over medium heat.
2. Turn off the heat and let cool for 15 minutes.
3. Place the starter and water in the bowl of a heavy-duty electric mixer or in a large mixing bowl.
4. Sprinkle the yeast over the mixture, stir in, and let sit for 2 minutes.
5. Add the dry ingredients.
6. Mix with the dough hook (or knead by hand) for 10 to 12 minutes, or until the dough is silky and elastic.
7. Drain the figs, add to the dough, and continue mixing or kneading until evenly distributed.
8. Transfer the dough to a lightly oiled bowl and cover with plastic wrap.
9. Let rise in a warm place for 4 hours, or until approximately doubled in volume.
10. Punch the dough down and turn out onto a lightly floured work surface.
11. Sprinkle a baking sheet with rye flour.
12. Cut the dough into 2 equal pieces and shape into round, oval, or oblong loaves. (See photos and additional instructions on pages 206–207.)

13. Place the loaves on the prepared baking sheet, cover with plastic wrap, and let rise again in a warm place for 1½ to 2 hours.

14. Place a baking stone on the middle rack of the oven and preheat to 425°.

15. Uncover the loaves and, using a spray bottle, spritz them with water, then lightly dust with rye flour.

16. Make 2 or 3 diagonal slashes in the tops of the loaves with a serrated knife to allow the dough to expand in the hot oven.

17. Using the spray bottle, spritz the oven walls with water. Work quickly so the oven does not lose heat.

18. Slide the loaves onto the hot stone.

19. Bake for 40 to 45 minutes, or until the crust is a dark, earthy brown.

20. Transfer the loaves to a rack to cool.

Yield: 2 large loaves

Bread Machine Instructions
To prepare the dough in a bread machine:
1. Prepare the figs as directed in steps 1 and 2 of the recipe.
2. Place the starter, lukewarm water, yeast, and dry ingredients in the bread pan.
3. Process on the dough setting (#9).
4. When the cycle is complete, turn the dough out onto a well-floured work surface.
5. Knead the drained figs into the dough until evenly distributed.
6. Continue with step 8 of the recipe.

BLACK OLIVE-ROSEMARY RYE SOURDOUGH

Olives and rye are another classic combination from the Mediterranean, and this bread is a natural with foods from the region's sunny climate, especially those featuring tomatoes, mozzarella cheese, pasta, and pestos. Or, if you prefer, enjoy it with nothing more than a glass of chilled Rosé from Provence, a Spanish Rioja, or an elegant Italian Chianti. Mediterranean breads always seem lighter in flavor and airier than those from northern Europe, and this bread fits into that classification. You can use large green olives if you prefer (green olives are simply immature versions of the ripe black olive). Whatever type you choose, buy olives stored in buckets of brine rather than canned or dry, salt-cured ones, which are too salty.

2 cups Rye Sourdough Starter (page 141)
1¼ cups lukewarm water
1 teaspoon active dry yeast

Dry Ingredients
4½ cups bread flour
½ cup rye flour
2 teaspoons salt

1½ cups pitted large black olives (such as kalamata)
4 teaspoons fresh rosemary needles, or 2 teaspoons dried

1. Place the starter and water in the bowl of a heavy-duty electric mixer or in a large mixing bowl.
2. Sprinkle the yeast over the mixture, stir in, and let sit for 2 minutes.
3. Add the dry ingredients.
4. Mix with the dough hook (or knead by hand) for 10 to 12 minutes, or until the dough is silky and elastic.
5. Add the olives and rosemary and continue mixing or kneading until evenly distributed.
6. Transfer the dough to a lightly oiled bowl and cover with plastic wrap.
7. Let rise in a warm place for 4 hours, or until approximately doubled in volume.
8. Punch the dough down and turn out onto a lightly floured work surface.
9. Sprinkle a baking sheet with flour.
10. Cut the dough into 2 equal pieces and shape into round, oval, or oblong loaves. (See photos and additional instructions on pages 206–207.)
11. Place the loaves on the prepared baking sheet.
12. Cover with plastic wrap and let rise again in a warm place for 1½ to 2 hours.

13. Place a baking stone on the middle rack in the oven and preheat to 425°.

14. Uncover the loaves and, using a spray bottle, spritz them with water, then lightly dust with rye flour.

15. Make 2 or 3 diagonal slashes in the tops of the loaves with a serrated knife to allow the dough to expand in the hot oven.

16. Using the spray bottle, spritz the oven walls with water. Work quickly so the oven does not lose heat.

17. Slide the loaves onto the hot stone.

18. Bake for 40 to 45 minutes, or until the crust is dark, earthy brown.

19. Transfer the loaves to a rack to cool.

Yield: 2 large loaves

Bread Machine Instructions
To prepare the dough in a bread machine:

1. Place the rye sourdough starter in the bread pan.

2. Add the water, yeast, and dry ingredients to the starter.

3. Process on the dough setting (#9).

4. When the cycle is complete, turn the dough out onto a well-floured work surface.

5. Knead the olives and rosemary into the dough until evenly distributed.

6. Continue with step 9 of the recipe.

LIGHT PAN BREADS
& BREAKFAST
BREADS

The practice of cooking breads in molds, rather than free form, originated in ancient Egypt, when batterlike dough was poured into preheated molds that were nested in an early form of oven. These molds were shaped like inverted pyramids and produced thick, tapered, cone-shaped loaves. The Greeks and Romans also used earthenware molds for a type of milk bread, but it wasn't until the late eighteenth century that baking bread in molds and pans became common as metal cookware became increasingly available and affordable due to the Industrial Revolution. While bread had occasionally been baked in earthenware and porcelain molds, metal pans and cookware revolutionized kitchen techniques, and encouraged baking in shaped forms. Metal pans and molds became even more popular when bakers recognized they could control not only the form of the bread but also the texture and color by using them. In addition, they were unbreakable.

At the same time, classical French cooking was taking root. This was an era in which food was seen in a new light: not just as sustenance, but as an art form and even as architecture. Bread became a symbol of the new bourgeois, for example, when family crests were imprinted in the molds and appeared on the baked loaves. The fluted metal brioche mold and the ornately decorated kugelhopf mold from the Alsace region of France are examples of the extent to which bread baking was transformed into edible sculpture. Even plain molds and pans provided an attractive structure, far removed from the peasant-style, free-form bread that was looked down on by sophisticated, "cultured" society. Some molds, such as the brioche, also served a practical purpose by giving breads a greater crust surface and preventing the rich, soft dough from falling.

In the modern era, large-scale commercial baking has necessitated standardized, modular loaves, both to maximize oven space and for ease in packing and shipping. The invention of the sandwich in the nineteenth century also boosted the popularity of uniformly shaped molded bread, since it is easier to slice and provides an even surface for the filling ingredients.

There are many kinds of bread molds, from the ornate to the utilitarian, and each produces different results. For example, while shiny metal molds reflect heat, dark metal pans with a dull finish absorb heat rapidly, creating thick, crisp crusts, a soft internal texture, and a browner, more attractive color. Ceramic and glass molds absorb heat more slowly, resulting in thinner but nevertheless crisp crusts. Some molds are designed to enclose the dough; for example, hinged metal cylinders prevent the dough from rising fully, creating rounded loaves of precise, standardized dimensions. Baked this way, the bread has a soft, thin crust and a dense interior. Other (open) molds are designed so that when a specific amount of dough is used, it will mushroom up and over the rim of the mold so the bread spreads attractively and assumes a distinctive shape.

It can be fun to experiment with differently shaped molds and pans made from different materials to achieve various textures and qualities. As a general rule, the dough should fill about half of the mold. The dough should be placed inside the pan or mold so it fits the contours and can only expand upward, rather than outward. King Arthur Flour is a good mail-order source for regular and specialty bread molds (for ordering information, see page 210), and most kitchen, specialty, and gourmet stores also carry an interesting selection.

The pan breads and breakfast breads in this chapter tend to be richer and moister than most of the other breads in this book. They are almost a cross between bread and pastry, and as a result are filling and satisfying. Their lively flavors are particularly suited to mornings and they are easy to make. Their sweet, rich nature is the perfect foil for the tannic and bitter tones of tea and coffee, and they are a wonderful medium for jams and preserves. Most of these breads also make great toast, and their comforting aromas and flavors are ideal for brunch or buffets. In addition, some of the loaves, such as the Sweet Potato Pecan Bread (page 164), Hazelnut Bread (page 168), Gorgonzola Blue Vein Bread (page 176), and the Herbal Goat Cheese Bread (page 178), make a splendid addition to the cheese course.

B L T B R E A D

What American sandwich is more classic than the BLT? Here, we've put the bacon, lettuce, and tomato in, rather than between, the bread. We think this is the natural evolution of the BLT! Mesclun mixes of baby lettuces, such as radicchio, frisée, Bibb, spinach, mizuna, and mustard greens, have become popular and increasingly available, even in supermarkets. Do not use iceberg lettuce in this recipe (or for any other purpose, for that matter). Plum (Roma) tomatoes or cherry tomatoes are preferable, especially in nonsummer months, because their quality tends to be more consistent year-round than regular tomatoes. However, be sure to use vine-ripened tomatoes in the summer, especially if you enjoy the luxury of picking them right off the vine yourself. Use this bread for tasty grilled cheese or chicken salad sandwiches, as well as for "double" BLTs.

1 cup lukewarm water
¼ cup lukewarm milk
2 tablespoons olive oil
2 teaspoons active dry yeast

Dry Ingredients

3½ cups bread flour
½ cup whole-wheat flour
1 teaspoon sugar
2 teaspoons salt

6 strips bacon
2 cups loosely packed mesclun lettuce or baby
    lettuces
2 plum tomatoes, cut into ¼-inch-thick slices

1. Place the water, milk, and olive oil in the bowl of a heavy-duty electric mixer or in a large mixing bowl.
2. Sprinkle the yeast over the mixture, stir in, and let sit for 2 minutes.
3. Add the dry ingredients.
4. Mix with the dough hook (or knead by hand) for 4 to 6 minutes, until the dough is silky and elastic.
5. Transfer the dough to a lightly oiled bowl and cover with plastic wrap.
6. Let rise in a warm place for 1 hour, or until approximately doubled in volume.
7. Sauté the bacon over medium heat until crisp.
8. When cool, chop coarsely.
9. Carefully fold or knead the bacon, lettuce, and tomato slices into the risen dough until evenly distributed.
10. Turn out onto a lightly floured work surface.
11. Cut the dough into 2 equal pieces and form into oblong loaves. (See photos and additional instructions on pages 206–207.)
12. Place in two oiled 8 x 4-inch loaf pans and cover with plastic wrap.

13. Let rise in a warm place for 30 minutes, or until approximately doubled in volume.

14. Preheat the oven to 400°.

15. Uncover the loaves and bake for 35 to 40 minutes, or until dark brown.

16. Let the bread cool in the pans for 10 minutes.

17. Turn the loaves out onto a rack to finish cooling.

18. When completely cool, place the loaves in airtight plastic bags and store in the refrigerator.

Yield: 2 loaves

Bread Machine Instructions
To prepare the dough in a bread machine:

1. Combine all the ingredients, except the bacon, lettuce, and tomatoes, in the bread pan in the order specified by the manufacturer's instructions.

2. Process on the dough setting (#9).

3. Cook the bacon as directed in steps 7 and 8 of the recipe.

4. When the cycle is complete, turn the dough out onto a well-floured work surface.

5. Knead the bacon, lettuce, and tomatoes into the dough until evenly distributed.

6. Continue with step 10 of the recipe.

SWEET POTATO–PECAN BREAD

This classic Coyote Cafe pan bread has been popular with our guests for years, and we've made it in various forms. Its naturally soft and delicate texture is complemented by the silky smoothness of the sweet potato. The combination of pecans and sweet potato is one we also enjoy in desserts and waffles. Both of these ingredients are indigenous to the Americas. "Pecan" is a Native American word, and although the nut is thought of as a southern crop, with the largest commercial orchards in Georgia, pecans from the Mesilla Valley in southern New Mexico rival those from any southern state. Pecan trees are rather temperamental; they need silt loam soil and long, hot summers for the shells to fill properly, so in many parts of the East Coast and California, the trees are grown mostly as ornamentals. This is an excellent holiday bread and goes well with ham dishes and most soups.

2 sweet potatoes

½ cup lukewarm water
¼ cup lukewarm milk
2 tablespoons olive oil
2 teaspoons active dry yeast

Dry Ingredients
2 cups bread flour
1 cup whole-wheat flour
2 teaspoons salt

1 teaspoon maple syrup
1 cup pecans, toasted (page 209)

1. Preheat the oven to 375°.
2. Bake the sweet potatoes on a baking sheet for 30 minutes.
3. Remove the potatoes and let cool. Turn off the oven.
4. Peel the sweet potatoes and cut into ½- to 1-inch dice.
5. Place the water, milk, and olive oil in the bowl of a heavy-duty electric mixer or in a large mixing bowl.
6. Sprinkle the yeast over the mixture, stir in, and let sit for 2 minutes.
7. Add the diced sweet potatoes to the bowl, together with the dry ingredients and the maple syrup.
8. Mix with the dough hook (or knead by hand) for 4 to 6 minutes, or until the dough is silky and elastic.
9. Add the pecans and continue mixing or kneading for 2 minutes, or until evenly distributed.
10. Transfer the dough to a lightly oiled bowl and cover with plastic wrap.

11. Let rise in a warm place for 1 hour, or until approximately doubled in volume.
12. Turn out onto a lightly floured work surface.
13. Cut the dough into 2 equal pieces and form into oblong loaves. (See photos and additional instructions on pages 206–207.)
14. Place in two oiled 8 x 4-inch loaf pans and cover with plastic wrap.
15. Let rise in a warm place for 30 minutes, or until approximately doubled in volume.
16. Preheat the oven to 400°.
17. Uncover the loaves and bake for 35 to 40 minutes, or until dark brown.
18. Let the bread cool in the pans for 10 minutes.
19. Turn the loaves out onto a rack to finish cooling.

Yield: 2 loaves

Bread Machine Instructions
To make the bread in a bread machine:
1. Prepare the sweet potatoes as directed in steps 1 through 4 of the recipe.
2. Combine all the ingredients, except the sweet potatoes and pecans, in the bread pan in the order specified by the manufacturer's instructions.
3. Process on the sweet or raisin bread setting (#8).
4. Add the sweet potatoes and pecans at the beeps.

To prepare the dough in a bread machine:
1. Prepare the sweet potatoes as directed in steps 1 through 4 of the recipe.
2. Combine all the ingredients, except the sweet potatoes and pecans, in the bread pan in the order specified by the manufacturer's instructions.
3. Process on the dough setting (#9).
4. When the cycle is complete, turn the dough out onto a well-floured work surface.
5. Knead the sweet potatoes and pecans into the dough until evenly distributed.
6. Continue with step 10 of the recipe.

ABIQUIU SQUASH BLOSSOM BREAD

Abiquiu is a rural community about 50 miles north of Santa Fe, where my friend Elizabeth Berry grows squash blossoms for Coyote Cafe on her stunningly picturesque ranch. (If the name Abiquiu seems familiar, it may be because the famous southwestern artist Georgia O'Keeffe lived here.)

Squash blossoms are simply the plant's flowers, which develop into squash. They are a commonly used ingredient in Mexico, where they are considered a delicacy. With their intense yellow color, they make a great addition to this soft pan bread—they would not work well in a crusty, harder style of bread, for example, as their delicate and subtle flavor and texture would be lost. Squash blossoms are available from June through August. The rest of the year, you can substitute 18 to 20 edible nasturtium flowers, which will give the bread a peppery flavor. In either case, it's best to buy the blossoms from an organic source. This bread is ideal with summer salads, corn and mushroom dishes, and chilled soups such as gazpacho.

1 cup lukewarm water
¼ cup lukewarm milk
2 tablespoons olive oil
2 teaspoons active dry yeast

Dry Ingredients
3 cups bread flour
1 cup cornmeal
1 teaspoon sugar
2 teaspoons salt

12 to 14 squash blossoms, rinsed
1 tablespoon minced fresh parsley or cilantro

1. Place the water, milk, and olive oil in the bowl of a heavy-duty electric mixer or in a large mixing bowl.
2. Sprinkle the yeast over the mixture, stir in, and let sit for 2 minutes.
3. Add the dry ingredients.
4. Mix with the dough hook (or knead by hand) for 4 to 6 minutes, or until the dough is silky and elastic.
5. Transfer the dough to a lightly oiled bowl and cover with plastic wrap.
6. Let rise in a warm place for 1 hour, or until approximately doubled in volume.
7. Carefully fold the squash blossoms and parsley into the risen dough until evenly distributed.
8. Turn out onto a lightly floured work surface.
9. Cut the dough into 2 equal pieces and form into oblong loaves. (See photos and additional instructions on pages 206–207.)
10. Place in two oiled 8 x 4-inch loaf pans and cover with plastic wrap.

11. Let rise in a warm place for 30 minutes, or until approximately doubled in volume.

12. Preheat the oven to 400°.

13. Uncover the loaves and bake for 35 to 40 minutes, or until dark brown.

14. Let the bread cool in the pans for 10 minutes.

15. Turn the loaves out onto a rack to finish cooling.

Yield: 2 loaves

Bread Machine Instructions
To prepare the dough in a bread machine:
1. Combine all the ingredients, except the squash blossoms and parsley, in the bread pan in the order specified by the manufacturer's instructions.
2. Process on the dough setting (#9).
3. When the cycle is complete, turn the dough out onto a well-floured work surface.
4. Continue with step 5 of the recipe.

HAZELNUT BREAD

Not long ago, Andrew was driving down Route 1, the Pacific Coast Highway that runs from Seattle to San Diego, traveling through Washington and Oregon. He passed huge orchards of hazelnuts (also known as filberts) on the way—most hazelnuts in the United States are grown in the Pacific Northwest—and stopped to buy some of the delicious fresh nuts from a local farm.

When cooking with hazelnuts, it is important to remove the slightly bitter, papery brown skin that covers them (see page 209). Hazelnuts are revered in Europe, where they are a popular baking ingredient—especially in Viennese pastries. When toasted, their aroma permeates every crumb of this bread, which is a wonderful breakfast toast. Try it with the honeys or spreads in the next chapter or plain with coffee. (Hazelnut Bread is pictured on page 170.)

2 tablespoons butter

¼ cup lukewarm milk

2 teaspoons active dry yeast

2 eggs

1 tablespoon firmly packed brown sugar

Dry Ingredients

1½ cups bread flour

¼ cup whole-wheat flour

½ teaspoon salt

1 cup chopped hazelnuts, toasted (page 209)

1 egg, beaten

¼ cup crushed hazelnuts

1. Preheat the oven to 375°.
2. Place the butter in a saucepan and bring to a simmer. Cook over medium heat until the butter begins to smoke and has a nutty aroma. Set aside to cool.
3. Place the milk in the bowl of a heavy-duty electric mixer or in a large mixing bowl.
4. Sprinkle the yeast over the milk, stir in, and let sit for 2 minutes.
5. Whisk in the eggs, sugar, and cooled butter.
6. Add the dry ingredients.
7. Mix with the dough hook (or knead by hand) for 7 to 8 minutes, or until the dough is silky and elastic.
8. Add the toasted hazelnuts and continue mixing or kneading until evenly distributed.
9. Transfer the dough to a lightly oiled bowl and cover with plastic wrap.
10. Let rise in a warm place for 1 hour, or until approximately doubled in volume.
11. Turn out onto a lightly floured work surface.
12. Form into an oblong loaf and place in an oiled 8 x 4-inch loaf pan. (See photos and additional instructions on pages 206–207.)

13. Cover with plastic wrap and let rise in a warm place for 40 minutes, or until approximately doubled in volume.
14. Preheat the oven to 400°.
15. Uncover the loaf, and using a pastry brush, brush it with the beaten egg.
16. Sprinkle the ¼ cup crushed hazelnuts on top of the loaf and press gently with your hands to adhere the nuts to the loaf.
17. Bake for 40 to 45 minutes, or until dark brown.
18. Let the bread cool in the pan for 10 minutes.
19. Turn the loaf out onto a rack to finish cooling.

Yield: 1 loaf

Bread Machine Instructions
To make the bread in a bread machine:
1. Combine all the ingredients, except the toasted hazelnuts, beaten egg, and ¼ cup crushed raw hazelnuts, in the bread pan in the order specified by the manufacturer's instructions. You will not use the beaten egg or the ¼ cup of raw hazelnuts
2. Process on the sweet or raisin bread setting (#8).
3. Add the toasted hazelnuts at the beeps.

To prepare the dough in a bread machine:
1. Combine all the ingredients, except the toasted hazelnuts, beaten egg, and ¼ cup crushed raw hazelnuts, in the bread pan in the order specified by the manufacturer's instructions.
2. Process on the dough setting (#9).
3. When the cycle is complete, turn the dough out onto a well-floured work surface.
4. Knead the toasted hazelnuts into the dough until evenly distributed.
5. Continue with step 12 of the recipe.

POPPY SEED ROLLS

This bread was created in the American tradition of Parker House rolls, which are known for their puffy center. The rolls became famous in the mid-nineteenth century at a Boston hotel—The Parker House—opened by Harvey D. Parker. Mr. Parker was quite an innovator. In addition to the hotel, he ran a restaurant that served food 'round the clock, a practice that was unheard of at the time. The Parker House is still there, so stop by the next time you're in Boston and taste the authentic rolls. Poppy seeds, from the poppy flower, are native to the Middle East. There are close to a million seeds in a pound. They give these rolls a savory, nutty-seedy taste and a crunchy texture. Ideal for soups, stews, chili, and pot roasts, these rolls are plain enough to go with most foods that have distinct flavors. (Poppy Seed Rolls are pictured with Hazelnut Bread [page 168] and Red and GreenChile Brioche [page 174].)

1 cup lukewarm water
¼ cup lukewarm milk
2 tablespoons olive oil
2 teaspoons active dry yeast

Dry Ingredients

3½ cups bread flour
¼ cup semolina flour
1 teaspoon sugar
2 teaspoons salt

½ cup poppy seeds

1. Place the water, milk, and olive oil in the bowl of a heavy-duty electric mixer or in a large mixing bowl.
2. Sprinkle the yeast over the mixture, stir in, and let sit for 2 minutes.
3. Add the dry ingredients.
4. Mix with the dough hook (or knead by hand) for 4 to 6 minutes, or until the dough is silky and elastic.
5. Transfer the dough to a lightly oiled bowl and cover with plastic wrap.
6. Let rise in a warm place for 1 hour, or until approximately doubled in volume.
7. Turn out onto a lightly floured work surface.
8. Cut the dough into 2 equal pieces, cut each in half, and repeat until you have 16 pieces of dough that are roughly the same size.
9. Shape the pieces of dough into rolls. (See photos and additional instructions on pages 206–207.) Alternatively, leave the pieces in irregular, rustic shapes and sizes.
10. Preheat the oven to 400°.
11. Place the poppy seeds in a bowl.
12. Dip the tops of the rolls in a bowl of water,

(continued)

then dip the wet area in the poppy seeds so they adhere to the rolls.

13. Lightly butter or oil a 10-inch square baking pan or cake pan with sides at least 2 inches high, and dust with bread flour.

14. Place the rolls in the pan, leaving ½ inch between them.

15. Cover lightly with plastic wrap and let rise in a warm place for 40 minutes, or until approximately doubled in volume and risen together into one connected mass.

16. Remove the plastic wrap and bake the rolls for 20 to 25 minutes, or until dark brown.

17. Serve the rolls warm, separating them at the table.

Yield: 16 rolls

> *Bread Machine Instructions*
> ***To prepare the dough in a bread machine:***
> *1. Combine all the ingredients, except the poppy seeds, in the bread pan in the order specified by the manufacturer's instructions.*
> *2. Process on the dough setting (#9).*
> *3. When the cycle is complete, turn the dough out onto a well-floured work surface.*
> *4. Continue with step 5 of the recipe.*

BLUEBERRY AND CREAM CHEESE BREAD

This marbled bread makes terrific French toast. You can substitute raspberries, strawberries, or blackberries for the blueberries.

8 ounces cream cheese

2 tablespoons sugar

2 tablespoons butter, softened

2 eggs

1 cup lukewarm water

2 teaspoons active dry yeast

Dry Ingredients

4 cups bread flour

1½ teaspoons salt

2 cups blueberries

1. In the bowl of a heavy-duty electric mixer fitted with the flat beater, cream together the cream cheese, sugar, and butter.
2. Add the eggs, and cream for 1 minute longer.
3. Place the water in a separate bowl. Sprinkle the yeast over the water, stir in, and let sit for 2 minutes.
4. Add the yeast to the cream cheese mixture.
5. Add the dry ingredients and mix with the dough hook (or knead by hand) for 4 to 6 minutes, or until the dough is smooth and elastic.
6. Transfer the dough to a lightly oiled bowl and cover with plastic wrap.
7. Let rise in a warm place for 1 hour, or until approximately doubled in volume.
8. Carefully fold the blueberries into the risen dough until evenly incorporated.
9. Turn out onto a lightly floured work surface.
10. Form into a round loaf. (See photos and additional instructions on pages 206–207.)
11. Lightly butter or oil a 10-inch square baking pan or cake pan with sides at least 2 inches high and dust with bread flour.
12. Place the loaf seam side down in the pan.
13. Cover with plastic wrap and let rise in a warm place for 20 minutes, or until approximately doubled in volume.
14. Preheat the oven to 400°.
15. Uncover the loaf and bake for 35 to 40 minutes, or until dark brown.
16. Let the bread cool in the pan for 10 minutes.
17. Turn the loaf out onto a rack to finish cooling.

Yield: 1 loaf

Bread Machine Instructions
To make the bread in a bread machine:

1. Combine all the ingredients, except the blueberries, in the bread pan in the order specified by the manufacturer's instructions.

2. Process on the sweet or raisin bread setting (#8).

3. Add the blueberries at the beeps.

To prepare the dough in a bread machine:

1. Combine all the ingredients, except the blueberries, in the bread pan in the order specified by the manufacturer's instructions.

2. Process on the dough setting (#9).

3. When the cycle is complete, turn the dough out onto a well-floured work surface.

4. Continue with step 6 of the recipe.

RED AND GREEN CHILE BRIOCHE

Brioche is the rich but light French bread made with eggs, butter, and flour. It is tradition-ally baked in round, fluted molds that flare outward at the rim, and it usually sports a dis-tinctive topknot. This southwestern brioche, made with red chile powder and roasted green chiles, has come a long way from the neighborhood bakeries of France. It's adapted from a recipe in Andrew's acclaimed cookbook of modern American recipes, New Classic Desserts, *and it's the richest and most delicious brioche we've tried. It makes great toast, especially when topped with smoked salmon or caviar. (Red and Green Chile Brioche rolls are pictured on page 170.)*

1 tablespoon lukewarm water
1 tablespoon honey
2 teaspoons active dry yeast

Dry Ingredients
3½ cups all-purpose flour
1 tablespoon sugar
2 teaspoons salt

5 eggs
¾ cup butter, softened
2 teaspoons chile molido (freshly ground pure
    chile powder)
½ cup coarsely chopped red bell pepper
2 New Mexico green chiles, roasted, peeled, and
    coarsely chopped (page 209)

Egg Wash
1 egg
2 tablespoons milk

1. Place the water and honey in the bowl of a heavy-duty electric mixer or in a large mix-ing bowl.

2. Sprinkle the yeast over the mixture, stir in, and let sit for 2 minutes.

3. Add the dry ingredients and begin mixing with the dough hook (or knead by hand).

4. Add 3 of the eggs and mix for 2 minutes.

5. Add the remaining 2 eggs and mix for 5 min-utes; the dough should be sticky and loose.

6. Add the butter and mix (or knead by hand) for another 5 minutes, occasionally scraping down the sides of the bowl to ensure the but-ter is well incorporated.

7. Add the chile molido, bell pepper, and chiles and mix for 2 minutes, or until evenly dis-tributed.

8. Transfer the dough to a lightly oiled bowl and cover with plastic wrap.

9. Let rise in a warm place for 45 minutes, or until approximately doubled in volume.

10. Turn out onto a lightly floured work surface.

11. Cut the dough into 2 equal pieces and form into loaves. (See photos and additional in-structions on pages 206–207.)

12. Place the dough in two oiled brioche tins or round 8- or 10-inch pans.

13. Cover with plastic wrap and let rise in a warm place for 20 minutes, or until approximately doubled in volume.
14. Preheat the oven to 400°.
15. Whisk together the egg and milk to make the egg wash.
16. Uncover the dough and, using a pastry brush, gently brush the loaves with the egg wash.
17. Bake for 35 to 40 minutes, or until dark brown.
18. Let the bread cool in the pans for 10 minutes.
19. Turn the loaves out onto a rack to finish cooling.

Yield: 2 loaves

Bread Machine Instructions
To make the bread in a bread machine:

1. Combine all the ingredients, except the butter, bell pepper, green chiles, and egg wash, in the bread pan in the order specified by the manufacturer's instructions. You will not use the egg wash.

2. Process on the sweet or raisin bread setting (#8).

3. After the first 6-minute kneading, add the softened butter.

4. Add the bell pepper and green chiles at the beeps.

To prepare the dough in a bread machine:

1. Combine all the ingredients, except the butter, bell pepper, green chiles, and egg wash, in the bread pan in the order specified by the manufacturer's instructions.

2. Process on the dough setting (#9).

3. After the first 6-minute kneading, add the softened butter.

4. When the cycle is complete, turn the dough out onto a well-floured work surface.

5. Knead the bell pepper and green chiles into the dough until evenly distributed.

6. Continue with step 8 of the recipe.

GORGONZOLA BLUE-VEIN BREAD

Gorgonzola is the name of a town near Milan in Lombardy, where this sharp-flavored creamy blue cheese originated over 1,000 years ago. Legend has it that migrating herdsmen stopped in the village and paid for their room and board with cheese. The innkeepers stored the cheese in their cool, damp cellars, which provided the ideal conditions for the natural blue mold to form. The cheese proved highly popular, and the rest is history. Most of the best Gorgonzola is still produced in Lombardy. You can use an aged Stilton instead or domestic Maytag blue cheese (named after Fritz Maytag, the home-appliance magnate). This pleasantly soft bread is ideal for picnics or with fruit such as apples and pears. Enjoy it, too, with a glass of port or a robust red wine such as Merlot or Cabernet Sauvignon.

1 cup lukewarm water

2 tablespoons sugar

2 teaspoons active dry yeast

2 eggs

1 tablespoon butter, softened

Dry Ingredients

3¾ cups bread flour

½ tablespoon salt

2 tablespoons chopped fresh parsley (optional)

2 cups crumbled Gorgonzola cheese

Egg Wash

1 egg

2 tablespoons milk

1. Place the water and sugar in the bowl of a heavy-duty electric mixer or in a large mixing bowl.
2. Sprinkle the yeast over the mixture, stir in, and let sit for 2 minutes.
3. Add the eggs, butter, and dry ingredients.
4. Mix with the dough hook (or knead by hand) for 4 to 6 minutes, or until the dough is smooth and elastic.
5. Add the parsley and cheese and continue mixing or kneading for 2 minutes, or until evenly distributed.
6. Transfer the dough to a lightly oiled bowl and cover with plastic wrap.
7. Let rise in a warm place for 1 hour, or until approximately doubled in volume.
8. Turn out onto a lightly floured work surface.
9. Form into a round loaf. (See photos and additional instructions on pages 206–207.)
10. Lightly butter or oil a 10-inch square baking pan or cake pan with sides at least 2 inches high and dust with bread flour.
11. Place the loaf seam side down on the prepared pan.

12. Cover with plastic wrap and let rise in a warm place for 20 minutes, or until approximately doubled in volume.
13. Preheat the oven to 400°.
14. Whisk together the egg and milk to make the egg wash.
15. Uncover the dough and, using a pastry brush, gently brush the loaf with the egg wash.
16. Bake for about 35 to 40 minutes, or until dark brown.
17. Let the bread cool in the pan for 10 minutes.
18. Turn the loaf out onto a rack to finish cooling.

Yield: 1 loaf

Bread Machine Instructions
To make the bread in a bread machine:
1. Combine all the ingredients, except the parsley, Gorgonzola, and egg wash, in the bread pan in the order specified by the manufacturer's instructions. You will not use the egg wash.
2. Process on the sweet or raisin bread setting (#8).
3. Add the parsley and Gorgonzola at the beeps.

To prepare the dough in a bread machine:
1. Combine all the ingredients, except the parsley, Gorgonzola, and egg wash, in the bread pan in the order specified by the manufacturer's instructions.
2. Process on the dough setting (#9).
3. When the cycle is complete, turn the dough out onto a well-floured work surface.
4. Knead the parsley and Gorgonzola into the dough until evenly distributed.
5. Continue with step 6 of the recipe.

HERBED GOAT CHEESE BREAD

One happy outcome of the food revolution in the United States, which began in California in the early 1970s, is that there are now many excellent local goat cheese suppliers. One of our favorites is Laura Chenel's Chèvre in California, which was one of the first large-scale producers in the United States. It takes about five days, on average, to turn fresh goat milk into chèvre cheese. First, the milk is pasteurized and set with a culture and rennet. The next day, the curds are separated from the whey and then transferred to molds that allow the excess moisture to drain off. Later, salt is added to draw out more of the whey, then the goat cheese is unmolded and allowed to firm up. Herbed goat cheese is a classic combination of flavors that's perfect in this bread, which is great warm with a drizzle of olive oil or toasted. If you wish, you can make the same recipe using a ripe Brie or Camembert instead of the goat cheese.

4 ounces (½ cup) log goat cheese (chèvre)

1 tablespoon sugar

2 tablespoons butter, softened

2 eggs

¾ cup lukewarm water

2 teaspoons active dry yeast

Dry Ingredients

4 cups bread flour

1½ teaspoons salt

½ teaspoon freshly ground black pepper

Herbs

2 teaspoons chopped fresh parsley, or
1 teaspoon dried

2 teaspoons chopped fresh oregano, or
1 teaspoon dried

2 teaspoons chopped fresh rosemary, or
1 teaspoon dried

2 teaspoons chopped fresh basil, or
1 teaspoon dried

1. In the bowl of a heavy-duty electric mixer fitted with the flat beater, cream together the goat cheese, sugar, and butter.

2. Add the eggs, and cream for 1 minute longer.

3. Place the water in a separate bowl. Sprinkle the yeast over the water, stir in, and let sit for 2 minutes.

4. Add the yeast mixture to the cheese mixture.

5. Add the dry ingredients.

6. Mix with the dough hook (or knead by hand) for 4 to 6 minutes, or until the dough is smooth and elastic.

7. Add the herbs and continue mixing or kneading for 1 or 2 minutes, or until evenly distributed.

8. Transfer the dough to a lightly oiled bowl and cover with plastic wrap.

9. Let rise in a warm place for 1 hour, or until approximately doubled in volume.

10. Turn out onto a lightly floured work surface.

11. Form into a round loaf. (See photos and additional instructions on pages 206–207.)

12. Lightly butter or oil a 10-inch square baking pan or cake pan with sides at least 2 inches high and dust with bread flour.

13. Place seam side down on the prepared pan.

14. Cover with plastic wrap and let rise in a warm place for 20 minutes, or until approximately doubled in volume.

15. Preheat the oven to 400°.

16. Uncover the dough and bake for about 35 to 40 minutes, or until dark brown.

17. Let the bread cool for 10 minutes in the pan.

18. Turn the loaf out onto a rack to finish cooling.

Yield: 1 loaf

Bread Machine Instructions
To make the bread in a bread machine:
1. Combine all the ingredients, except the herbs, in the bread pan in the order specified by the manufacturer's instructions.
2. Process on the sweet or raisin bread setting (#8).
3. Add the herbs at the beeps.

To prepare the dough in a bread machine:
1. Combine all the ingredients, except the herbs, in the bread pan in the order specified by the manufacturer's instructions.
2. Process on the dough setting (#9).
3. When the cycle is complete, turn the dough out onto a well-floured work surface.
4. Knead the herbs into the dough until evenly distributed.
5. Continue with step 8 of the recipe.

RHUBARB-GINGER-LEMON BREAD

Rhubarb always reminds me of my grandmother. When I was a small child, I enjoyed the sweet rhubarb compote she made and, best of all, her delicious, comforting rhubarb pies. I also remember biting on a raw rhubarb stalk and squinting because it tasted so bitter, and then daring my friends to do the same without squinting (no one could!). This bread features a trio of bright, strong, and distinct flavors. The result is a zingy, exotic, and deliciously fruity bread, with the slightly tart tang of rhubarb, the spiciness of ginger, and the aromatic qualities of lemon. Enjoy this bread for breakfast with spiced tea and apricot or strawberry jam. It also makes awesome toast.

1½ cups sliced rhubarb
2 tablespoons sugar

1 cup lukewarm water
¼ cup lukewarm milk
2 tablespoons butter, melted
2 teaspoons active dry yeast

Dry Ingredients

4 cups bread flour
1 tablespoon firmly packed brown sugar
1½ teaspoons salt

1 tablespoon grated lemon zest
1 tablespoon grated ginger

Egg Wash

1 egg
2 tablespoons milk

1. Toss the rhubarb in a bowl with the sugar.
2. Transfer to a dry sauté pan and cook over medium heat for 7 to 8 minutes, or until just tender. Set aside to cool.
3. Place the water, milk, and butter in the bowl of a heavy-duty electric mixer or in a large mixing bowl.
4. Sprinkle the yeast over the mixture, stir in, and let sit for 2 minutes.
5. Add the dry ingredients, lemon zest, and ginger.
6. Mix with the dough hook (or knead by hand) for 4 to 6 minutes, or until the dough is smooth and elastic.
7. Transfer the dough to a lightly oiled bowl and cover with plastic wrap.
8. Let rise in a warm place for 1 hour, or until approximately doubled in volume.
9. Carefully fold the cooked rhubarb into the dough until evenly distributed.
10. Turn out onto a lightly floured work surface.
11. Cut the dough into 2 equal pieces.
12. Roll each piece out into a cylinder 12 to 14 inches long.
13. Gather the 2 pieces at one end, pinch together, and twist together. (Alternatively,

form the dough into 1 round loaf. See photos and additional instructions on pages 206–207.)

14. Lightly butter or oil a baking sheet, and dust with bread flour.

15. Place the loaf on the prepared baking sheet.

16. Cover with plastic wrap and let rise in a warm place for 40 minutes, or until approximately doubled in volume.

17. Preheat the oven to 400°.

18. Whisk together the egg and milk to make the egg wash.

19. Uncover the loaf and, using a pastry brush, gently brush the dough with the egg wash.

20. Bake for 35 to 40 minutes, or until dark brown.

21. Let the bread cool in the pan for 10 minutes.

22. Turn the loaf out onto a rack to finish cooling.

Yield: 1 loaf

Bread Machine Instructions
To make the bread in a bread machine:

1. Prepare the rhubarb as directed in steps 1 and 2 of the recipe.

2. Combine all the ingredients, except the rhubarb, lemon zest, ginger, and egg wash, in the bread pan in the order specified by the manufacturer's instructions. You will not use the egg wash.

3. Process on the sweet or raisin bread setting (#8).

4. Add the rhubarb, lemon zest, and ginger at the beeps.

To prepare the dough in a bread machine:

1. Prepare the rhubarb as directed in steps 1 and 2 of the recipe.

2. Combine all the ingredients, except the rhubarb, lemon zest, ginger, and egg wash, in the bread pan in the order specified by the manufacturer's instructions.

3. Process on the dough setting (#9).

4. When the cycle is complete, turn the dough out onto a well-floured work surface.

5. Continue with step 7 of the recipe, adding the zest and ginger along with the rhubarb.

STICKY ORANGE-CINNAMON ROLLS

Andrew's first professional position as a baker was at a cafe in Burlington, Vermont. He made these rolls for brunch every Sunday, and he soon discovered he never made enough. Not only were they popular with the clientele, but the staff would ambush the rolls as soon as they were out of the oven. In fact, the ambush became a cafe tradition. If you're in Santa Fe on the weekend, you're likely to find the same rolls at Coyote Cafe's General Store. They're perfect with morning coffee. If you're adventurous and love chiles, you can try our "Xubi" version, named after one of our bakers: add some chopped rehydrated black pasilla chiles to the orange spread—it gives these rolls a jolt that kick-starts your morning in the nicest way.

½ cup lukewarm milk

2 tablespoons sugar

2 teaspoons active dry yeast

2 eggs

½ cup butter, softened

Dry Ingredients

2 cups all-purpose flour

¼ teaspoon salt

Orange Spread

¾ cup butter, softened

1 cup firmly packed brown sugar

2 tablespoons honey

2 tablespoons freshly squeezed orange juice

1 tablespoon grated orange zest

1 tablespoon ground cinnamon

½ cup almonds or pecans, toasted (optional, page 209)

1. In the bowl of a heavy-duty electric mixer or in a large mixing bowl, whisk together the milk and sugar.
2. Sprinkle the yeast over the mixture, stir in, and let sit for 2 minutes.
3. Mix in the eggs, butter, and the dry ingredients.
4. Mix with the dough hook (or knead by hand) for 3 to 4 minutes; the dough should be slightly sticky.
5. Transfer the dough to a lightly buttered bowl and cover with plastic wrap.
6. Let rise in a warm place for 40 minutes, or until approximately doubled in volume.
7. Meanwhile, to prepare the orange spread, place the butter in the bowl of a heavy-duty electric mixer fitted with the flat beater.
8. Add the sugar, honey, orange juice, orange zest, and cinnamon.
9. Cream together for 3 to 4 minutes, or until completely incorporated, and set aside.
10. Turn the dough out onto a well-floured work surface.
11. With a rolling pin, roll the dough out into a rectangle about ¼ inch thick.

12. Using a spatula, spread half of the orange spread evenly over the dough.

13. Sprinkle the nuts over the spread.

14. Line a 10-inch square baking pan with foil and spread the remaining orange spread over the foil.

15. Beginning with the long bottom edge, roll up the dough jelly-roll style and pinch the seam together firmly to seal.

16. Using a serrated knife, cut the dough into 6 rolls.

17. Evenly space the rolls in the foil-lined pan and cover with plastic wrap.

18. Let the rolls rise in a warm place for 40 minutes, or until approximately doubled in volume.

19. Place a baking stone on the middle rack in the oven and preheat to 375°.

20. Bake the rolls for 30 to 35 minutes, or until the spread in the pan is bubbling and dark and the tops of the rolls are dark brown.

21. Let the rolls cool in the pan for 5 minutes.

22. Place another pan over the rolls and invert the baking pan, so the rolls are resting in the second pan and the orange spread on the foil is on top of them. Remove the foil.

23. Serve the rolls warm from the pan.

Yield: 6 rolls

Bread Machine Instructions
To prepare the dough in a bread machine:
1. Combine all the ingredients, except the orange spread ingredients and the nuts, in the bread pan in the order specified by the manufacturer's instructions.
2. Process on the dough setting (#9).
3. Prepare the orange spread as directed in steps 7 through 9 of the recipe.
4. When the cycle is complete, turn the dough out onto a well-floured work surface.
5. Continue with step 11 of the recipe.

SWEET
& SAVORY
ACCOMPANIMENTS

Fresh, crusty, aromatic bread warm from the oven demands a little creamy sweet butter and a comforting layer of honey or jam. Fresh or toasted, a slice of bread judiciously covered with a delicious flavored spread and enjoyed with a steaming cup of coffee or tea is the perfect breakfast, snack, or pick-up. The recipes in this chapter feature different and unusual flavors (or combinations of flavors) in traditional forms. For example, some of the flavor pairings, like some of the breads, were inspired by dessert or pastry combinations. All have been created to enhance and highlight Coyote's flavored breads, and you will find that they also enliven plain loaves.

Making your own honeys, jams, and spreads has several advantages. In addition to the satisfaction yielded by the creative process and the money you will save, you can ensure that these homemade products contain only high-quality ingredients—you get to choose each one, which should be organic whenever possible. The integrity of each ingredient is maintained because no preservatives, food color, or additives are used, resulting in a much more natural, flavorful, and healthful product. These items also make great gifts, especially when colorfully wrapped.

One of my most cherished memories involves honey and bread. I was with the renowned Italian writer, chef, and gourmet, Giuliano Bugialli, on a trip to Sardinia. One crisp fall morning, up in the mountains, we rose at 6 o'clock to see "music paper bread," a paper-thin flatbread, being made by the village women in a wood-burning oven. We took it hot from the oven and met up with some local shepherds who spread the bread with *miel amaro* (a bitter-edged honey) and some aged sheep cheese that was melted over a wood fire. We rolled up the bread to eat it, and washed it down with some robust red wine while overlooking the valleys below. The flavors were incredible, and the combination of the earthy bread, the intense cheese, and the slightly bitter, viscous honey were out of this world.

Honey has been gathered around the world since the Stone Age, and bees have been domesticated since ancient Egyptian times. Many biblical references reveal that honey was the main sweetening agent in those times in the Middle East, but we know it was the Romans who refined the art of honey making. The ancient peoples of Mesoamerica also raised bees for honey; when the Spanish arrived in Mexico and the pilgrims docked on the eastern seaboard of North America, both found the indigenous population using honey as a sweetener. The Aztecs and other pre-Columbian cultures also raised certain types of ants that produce honey in a similar way.

The color and flavor of honey is directly related to the flowers and plants from which the bees gather nectar. The nectar is then converted into honey in the storage cells of the honeycomb by the bees in a hive. Beekeepers often place the hives in locations where plants such as heather, clover, wild herbs, and citrus or soft fruit trees are abundant, so the flavor of the honey can be controlled. We highly recommend these scented honeys—preferably unheated and unfiltered, available from beekeepers or natural food stores—which can have subtle flavor nuances. In our recipes, we accentuate the natural flavorings and attempt to improve on Mother Nature; after all, dried chile powder, star anise, and roasted shallots are unlikely ingredients for even the strongest and most resourceful bees to bring back to the hive!

Long before refrigeration and modern transportation made fresh fruit a year-round luxury, fruit butters, preserves, and spreads were originally prepared or "put up" for the winter months. Just a few decades ago, fresh fruit in winter was a rarity at best; oranges, for example, were so scarce that they made an exotic and welcome present at Christmas just two or three generations ago. The early European settlers in North America realized the need to store preserved fruit, grains, meats, and vegetables for the harsh winters, and they learned many drying and preserving techniques from the Native Americans they encountered. Their pantries were often caves or primitive cellars in the ground, covered by branches or hides. As a child, I was entranced by my grandmother's magical pantry, with rows and rows of tightly sealed glass jars of cooked fruit, preserves, honey, and fruit butters. Even then, I remember feeling reassured that our family supply of goodies was secure.

Making spreads, preserves, jams, marmalades, and flavored honeys is surprisingly easy (most of the following recipes take no longer than an hour to make, and many can be prepared in 15 to 30 minutes). The recipes yield amounts that can be easily consumed in a few days or weeks, but if you feel so inclined, you can increase the quantities called for and put up larger batches.

If you plan to do your own canning, we recommend reading a comprehensive guide to the process, such as *Putting Food By* by Janet Greene, Ruth Hertzberg, and Beatrice Vaughn.

RED CHILE HONEY

New Mexican "chileheads" can't imagine any meal, even breakfast, without chile in some form. The heat of the chile is tempered here by the sweetness of the honey—this classic combination of sweet and hot is used in many cuisines. It will certainly spice up your morning toast! Try this honey on whole-wheat bread, one of the country or sourdough breads (pages 117–157), or a breakfast bread (pages 159–183). Or, warm it for slathering on sopaipillas or for pouring over waffles, pancakes, or vanilla ice cream. It also makes a great glaze for grilled meats or salmon. Use a wild, dark-colored honey if you can. Coyote howled at the moon when he tasted this combination!

2 teaspoons chile molido (freshly ground pure
   chile powder)
1 teaspoon chile caribe (red pepper flakes)
1 cup honey
Pinch of salt

1. Place the chile molido and chile caribe in a dry pan or skillet.
2. Toast over medium heat, shaking the pan occasionally, until the powder and flakes are fragrant, about 4 or 5 minutes. Do not let the chile burn, and beware of the strong fumes, which may make your eyes water.
3. Transfer to a saucepan and add the honey and salt.
4. Bring to a simmer over medium heat, stirring with a wooden spoon.
5. Turn off the heat and let cool for 10 minutes.
6. Pour into a clean glass jar and refrigerate.

Yield: About 1 cup

CINNAMON-CLOVE HONEY

In medieval Europe, spices such as cinnamon and cloves, products of the Arab spice trade, were a sign of affluence. Before the days of refrigeration, these spices were used to season meat and help disguise any displeasing rancidity. This honey is a marked improvement on the cinnamon sugar we used to put on toast as kids, and provides an instant pick-up when spread on morning toast, especially when accompanied by a perfumed cup of Earl Grey tea. Try it, too, as a delicious flavoring in tea, coffee, or hot chocolate.

1 cup wildflower, orange-blossom, or Tupelo
  honey
2 teaspoons ground cinnamon
½ teaspoon ground cloves

1. Place the honey, cinnamon, and cloves in a saucepan.
2. Bring to a simmer over medium heat, stirring with a wooden spoon.
3. Turn off the heat and let cool for 10 minutes.
4. Pour into a clean glass jar and refrigerate.

Yield: About 1 cup

> *Note:*
> *The pungent, sweet flavor of cardamom also perfumes honey delightfully. The combination is perfect with Indian flatbreads, wheat breads, pancakes, waffles, and sopaipillas. To make cardamom honey, simply follow the directions above, but use orange-blossom honey and substitute 2½ teaspoons ground cardamom for the cinnamon and cloves.*

MUSTARD-ROASTED SHALLOT HONEY

Roasted shallots have a sugary, caramel-like flavor that blends perfectly with sweet honey and sharp, hot mustard. Shallots are related to onions and garlic, and in terms of flavor characteristics, they fit neatly between the two. A herbed honey, made from rosemary or thyme nectar, is preferable for this recipe; look for one in gourmet or specialty stores. This condiment goes with ham, smoked meat, or turkey sandwiches, and is a great glaze for grilled chicken and salmon. These flavors are particularly well suited to the Pastrami Rye (page 58).

1 teaspoon canola or vegetable oil

2 tablespoons thinly sliced shallots

1 cup honey

2 tablespoons stone-ground mustard or whole-grain mustard

1. Heat the oil in a sauté pan or skillet.
2. Add the shallots and sauté over medium heat, stirring occasionally, for 10 to 12 minutes, or until they become crispy and dark caramel brown colored.
3. Transfer the shallots to a saucepan and add the honey and mustard.
4. Bring to a simmer over medium heat, stirring with a wooden spoon.
5. Turn off the heat and let cool for 10 minutes.
6. Pour into a clean glass jar and refrigerate.

Yield: About 1¼ cups

STAR ANISE HONEY

Star anise is the star-shaped pod of an evergreen tree that is related to the magnolia and native to China. It has a slightly bitter, licoricelike flavor similar to, but more pronounced than, regular anise. Star anise is most commonly used as a flavoring in Chinese cuisine (it is one of the ingredients in five-spice powder). This honey is an aromatic way to dress up breakfast toast or a special flavoring for after-dinner coffee and sambuca. Or, use it instead of plain honey in the bread recipes in this book. It also works well as a glaze or dipping sauce for Chinese-style duck.

1 cup honey
2½ teaspoons ground star anise, toasted
   (page 210)

1. Place the honey and star anise in a saucepan.
2. Bring to a simmer over medium heat, stirring with a wooden spoon.
3. Turn off the heat and let cool for 10 minutes.
4. Pour into a clean glass jar and refrigerate.

Yield: About 1 cup

PERSIMMON SPREAD

Bright orange shiny persimmons are underutilized in the United States. Uniquely rich, delicious, and versatile, they are wonderful additions to breads, cookies, sorbets, and compotes, and I like to stuff pork loins with them. Cooked down, they are also delicious swirled into vanilla ice cream. Persimmons are native to China and enthusiastically cultivated in Japan, where they are a classic temple offering. They are also grown commercially in California as well as in Mediterranean countries. There are many varieties, most of which taste very astringent unless fully ripe and soft, but the rounded, tomato-sized Fuyu type contains no tannins, making it sweet even when crisp and not fully mature. Persimmons are available from October through February, and this reduced fruit purée makes a welcome addition to the winter breakfast table.

4 ripe persimmons, stemmed and seeded
2 tablespoons firmly packed brown sugar
Pinch of freshly ground black pepper
Pinch of salt

1. Place all the ingredients in a saucepan.
2. Bring to a simmer over medium heat, stirring with a wooden spoon.
3. Decrease the heat to low and cook, stirring occasionally, for 25 to 30 minutes, or until reduced and thickened.
4. Let cool slightly.
5. Pour into a clean glass jar or container, cover, and refrigerate.

Yield: About 1½ cups

PUMPKIN SPREAD

Few people go to the trouble of cooking fresh pumpkin, but it has a more delicate and elegant flavor than canned pumpkin purée. This spread contains the traditional fall flavors that make it the perfect spread for holiday breakfasts and brunches. Use it with plain breads, or with the Pepita-Sage Harvest Sourdough (page 142). It's another sweet spread that can also be poured over ice cream or heated and used as a sauce for roasted duck or pork.

1 small pumpkin, or ½ medium pumpkin
   (about 1 pound)
½ cup sugar
2 tablespoons dark molasses
¼ teaspoon ground nutmeg
¼ teaspoon ground cinnamon
Pinch of salt

1. Preheat the oven to 375°.
2. Cut the pumpkin into several pieces, remove the seeds, and place on a baking sheet.
3. Roast for 20 minutes and let cool.
4. Remove the pumpkin flesh from the rind, discarding the rind, and transfer to a food processor.
5. Add the sugar, molasses, nutmeg, cinnamon, and salt and purée for 30 seconds.
6. Transfer the purée to a nonreactive saucepan and bring to a simmer over medium heat.
7. Reduce the heat to low, stirring occasionally, and cook for 25 to 30 minutes, until reduced and thickened.
8. Let cool slightly.
9. Pour into a clean glass jar or container, cover, and refrigerate.

Yield: About 1½ cups

PEAR BUTTER

Unlike other fruit, the flavor and texture of pears improves once they are picked. In fact, they will not fully ripen until they are picked or fall to the ground. There are many varieties of pears, but the most common (and delicious)—Bartlett, Comice, and Anjou—work equally well in this recipe, provided they are soft and ripe. However, our favorite for this recipe is the slender-necked winter Bosc pear, which has the most intense flavor. This spread complements cheese breads particularly well, perhaps accompanied by a glass of port.

3 large pears, peeled, cored, seeded, and
    coarsely chopped
2 teaspoons freshly squeezed lemon juice
¼ cup firmly packed brown sugar
1 tablespoon brandy

1. Place all the ingredients in a nonreactive saucepan.
2. Bring to a simmer over medium heat, stirring with a wooden spoon.
3. Decrease the heat to low, stirring occasionally, and cook for 25 to 30 minutes, or until reduced and thickened.
4. Let cool slightly.
5. Pour into a clean glass jar or container, cover, and refrigerate.

Yield: About 1 cup

TOMATO-SUNDRIED TOMATO JAM

The intense flavors of sundried tomatoes combined with sugar enhance the natural sweetness of the fresh tomatoes in this jam, yet it is savory and not too sweet. In addition, the chile sauce gives it a delicious kick. Buy sundried tomatoes that are slightly supple and not too dry or brittle (a sign that they lack freshness), and try to find a supplier that carries unsulphured sundried tomatoes. This is a great spread for any bread that contains Mediterranean flavors, such as the Fennel–Black Olive Bread (page 96), any of the focacce (pages 102–108), or the Spanish Manchego, Caper, and Anchovy Bread (page 136). This jam will keep, covered, for up to 10 days in the refrigerator.

8 dry-packed sundried tomato halves

½ cup water

2 large tomatoes, coarsely chopped

¼ teaspoon salt

1 tablespoon sugar

1 tablespoon Coyote Cocina Prankster's Red Chile Sauce or another red chile sauce

1. Place the sundried tomatoes and water in a saucepan.
2. Bring the water to a simmer, reduce the heat to low, and cook gently for 15 minutes.
3. Drain and chop the rehydrated tomatoes.
4. Transfer to a clean saucepan and add the fresh tomatoes, salt, sugar, and chile sauce.
5. Bring to a simmer over medium heat, stirring with a wooden spoon.
6. Decrease the heat to low, stirring occasionally, and cook for 25 to 30 minutes, or until reduced and thickened.
7. Let cool slightly.
8. Pour into a clean glass jar or container, cover, and refrigerate.

Yield: About 1 cup

TANGERINE·CAMPARI MARMALADE

The bright red Campari, an Italian bitters apéritif, makes this a visually striking marmalade, while its bittersweet flavor highlights the citric tangerines. A lot of bitters recipes, like some herbal liqueurs (such as Chartreuse and Benedictine), were originally made in monasteries for medicinal purposes. To reduce the bitterness in this marmalade, use the more herbal-toned French Dubonnet. Alternatively, if you'd like to increase the bitterness, try the Italian Punt e Mes. This is an excellent marmalade for breakfast bread, toast, or muffins, and it makes a tangy glaze for grilled chicken, duck, and pork.

4 tangerines

4 cups water

1 cup sugar

½ cup Campari

4 teaspoons cornstarch

1. Remove the peel of 3 of the oranges in strips with a peeler or citrus zester. Be sure to leave the bitter white pith behind. Julienne the strips of peel. (Discard the peel of the remaining tangerine.)
2. Pour 2 cups of the water into a nonreactive saucepan and bring to a boil.
3. Add the julienned peel and blanch for 15 minutes.
4. Drain the blanched peel and set aside.
5. Remove the white pith from the tangerines, slice in half, and remove the seeds.
6. Coarsely chop the tangerines and place in a large nonreactive saucepan.
7. Add the blanched peel, 1¾ cups of the water, the sugar, and Campari.
8. In a bowl, whisk the cornstarch with the remaining ¼ cup water until thoroughly combined and then whisk into the saucepan.
9. Bring to a boil, lower the heat, and simmer, stirring occasionally, for 35 to 40 minutes.
10. Let cool.
11. Pour into a clean glass jar or container, cover, and refrigerate.

Yield: About 1½ cups

QUINCE-CARDAMOM MARMALADE

The word "marmalade" is derived from the Portuguese word marmelada, *which means quince jam. I think of the quince as a distinctively medieval Old World fruit and, indeed, it has been cultivated in Asia and Europe for centuries. The quince looks like a cross between a yellow-skinned apple and a pear, and its crisp, starchy flesh has a tart flavor that is far more pleasant when cooked. During the Roman Empire, quinces were revered, and they remain a prized ingredient in France, where their texture and flavor are considered superior to the apple, which supplanted it in popularity. The fruit is less well known in the United States, although at Coyote Cafe we are fortunate to have a wonderful supply from Alamogordo, which is in the southern part of New Mexico. Quince is high in pectin, a natural thickening agent, which makes it an ideal ingredient for preserves, jellies, and marmalades. The aromatic cardamom lifts the flavors of the quince, making it a delicious addition to bread, toast, or muffins.*

4 teaspoons cornstarch

5 cups water

2½ cups sugar

2 teaspoons ground cardamom

3 quinces, cut in half, stemmed, seeded, and
    coarsely chopped

1. In a bowl, whisk together the cornstarch with ¼ cup of the water until thoroughly combined.
2. Pour into a saucepan, add the remaining 4¾ cups water and the sugar, and whisk together.
3. Add the cardamom and quince.
4. Bring the mixture to a boil, lower the heat, and simmer for about 1 hour, stirring occasionally.
5. Let cool.
6. Pour into a clean glass jar or container, cover, and refrigerate.

Yield: About 1½ cups

GINGER-RHUBARB PRESERVES

Rhubarb, which is native to northern central Asia and related to buckwheat, first came to Europe in the late Middle Ages when its roots were used for medicinal purposes. Seventeenth-century reference books claim that the leaves could be eaten as a vegetable, but in fact they contain oxalic acid, which can be toxic and should be avoided. It was considerably later, in the nineteenth century, that the stalks of the rhubarb plant were recognized as edible. Rhubarb is usually eaten as a fruit, typically in desserts, but botanically it's classified as a vegetable. As the Rhubarb-Ginger-Lemon Bread recipe on page 180 proves, the flavors of ginger and rhubarb mix very well. This preserve goes particularly well with any bread containing chiles, with breakfast waffles, or over ice cream.

1 cup water

1 teaspoon cornstarch

¼ cup minced ginger

2 cups sugar

3 cups sliced rhubarb (½ -inch pieces)

1. Pour the water into a saucepan, and whisk in the cornstarch. Set aside.
2. Place the ginger and ¼ cup of the sugar in a separate saucepan.
3. Cook over medium heat, stirring, until the ginger is translucent, about 5 or 6 minutes.
4. Transfer to the cornstarch mixture and add the remaining 1¾ cups sugar and the rhubarb.
5. Bring to a boil, decrease the heat, and simmer for 45 minutes, stirring occasionally.
6. Let cool.
7. Pour into a clean glass jar or container, cover, and refrigerate.

Yield: 1½ to 2 cups

BLACK CHERRY-ANCHO SPREAD

The carmine-colored, fragrant ancho chiles are the dried form of poblanos and one of the most commonly used dried chiles in Mexican cuisine. Anchos are the sweetest of all chiles and have a mild flavor, with complex tones of raisin, dried plum, licorice, tobacco, and coffee. When buying anchos, make sure they are supple, which indicates freshness. They should also have a dark reddish tint when you hold them up to the light; if they look black, they are probably mislabeled negro or mulato chiles. Black cherries complement these flavors well, and the two ingredients are sometimes used to make savory sauces in southwestern cuisine. Try this spread with meat sandwiches, as a stuffing for pork, or as a breakfast preserve, especially with the Hearty Five-Grain Bread (page 72) or the Cinnamon Buckwheat Bread (page 62).

2 or 3 small dried ancho chiles, stemmed and seeded
4 cups pitted fresh black cherries
1 cup sugar
2 teaspoons freshly squeezed lemon juice

1. Break up the anchos and pulverize them in a food processor, or chop with a sharp knife into very small pieces.
2. Transfer to a nonreactive saucepan and add the cherries, sugar, and lemon juice.
3. Bring to a simmer and keep at a constant low boil, stirring occasionally, for 35 to 40 minutes, or until thickened.
4. Let cool.
5. Pour into a clean glass jar or container, cover, and refrigerate.

Yield: 1½ to 2 cup

INGREDIENTS, TECHNIQUES, & SOURCES

INGREDIENTS

The most basic bread consists of simple ingredients: flour, water, salt, and, often, a leavening agent such as yeast. Yet from these humble ingredients, you can make the most satisfying loaves and have the foundation for straightforward but innovative, flavorful breads. Once you understand the fundamental principles, you can adapt the method for mixing, fermenting, and rising the dough, as well as the selection and combination of ingredients, to produce the widest range of flavored breads imaginable. Remember—breads are only as good as the ingredients from which they are made.

Flour

The product of milled grain, flour is the primary ingredient in bread. The most commonly used flours, at least in western cuisines, are derived from wheat, which is the most important cereal crop worldwide. Other grains commonly used in bread making include rye and corn. In this book, we also use oats, buckwheat, quinoa, amaranth, millet, and rice, as well as ground seeds.

There are three major types of wheat: hard, soft, and durum.

• **Hard wheat** is high in proteins, two of which, when activated by water, combine to form gluten. This is a strong yet elastic, weblike substance that holds the carbon dioxide gas bubbles re-leased by the yeast or leavening agent, causing the bread to rise and giving it a framework and structure. The gluten content makes hard-wheat flour the preferred type for making leavened bread; when ground, it is referred to as bread flour. Hard wheat is the main type grown in the colder climates of the northern United States and in Canada.

• **Soft wheat** (the main type of wheat crop in the southern United States and in Europe) is high in starch and low in gluten. It is called cake flour when ground; as the name suggests, it is typically used for cakes, cookies, and pastries that should be dense and have a soft texture. Some authorities assert that soft wheat has more flavor than hard wheat.

• **Durum wheat** is high in gluten (it is the hardest wheat variety of all) but less suitable for baking because when ground it absorbs less water than other flours, creating a bread dough that is difficult to work with. Instead, durum wheat is usually ground into semolina, which is also used to make pasta and couscous.

All-purpose flour is a white, finely textured mixture of hard and soft wheat flours (usually in a 80:20 ratio), combining the high gluten content of the former and the soft texture of the latter. It is usually presifted and enriched with minerals such as iron, niacin, riboflavin, and thiamine (and sometimes other vitamins), to compensate for the lack of wheat germ and bran, which are removed in the milling and refining process. All-purpose flour is available bleached or unbleached; we strongly recommend unbleached, stone-ground all-purpose flour, which has not been treated chemically and which contains naturally occurring yeasts that have not been destroyed by the heat of the commercial milling process or by bleaching. Unbleached flour is aged naturally to allow the organic oxidation process to turn the pale tan-colored flour to white. It has a superior wheat flavor compared to bleached flour.

Whole-wheat flour is milled from the entire wheat grain or berry, including the bran (the brown outer layer of the wheat grain or berry, which contains fiber, minerals, and vitamins) and the wheat germ or embryo (which contains nutrients, proteins, and flavorful oil), as well as the endosperm, from which white flours are made (which contains the gluten and is rich in carbohydrates). These elements make whole-wheat flour more healthful than white flour as well as tastier. However, they also make it more perishable, so it needs to be stored carefully. Seal the flour in an airtight bag and freeze if keeping more than a few weeks. Whole-wheat flour contributes body and substance as well as flavor to breads, but because it is relatively lower in gluten, whole-wheat loaves tend to require more yeast and a longer rising time. Finely ground whole-wheat flour works best for the recipes in this book, although a medium grind can also be used.

Rye flour contains little gluten, so breads made solely with it would be dense and heavy in texture. For this reason, we mix it with wheat flour to give the bread structure and texture. Most rye flour (also called light rye) is made from the endosperm of the grain only (like white wheat flours), whereas dark rye flour (also called pumpernickel) is processed from the whole grain (like whole-wheat flour). Medium-ground rye flour works best for these recipes.

Cornmeal is finely ground flour derived from dried sweet corn kernels. Medium and coarsely ground cornmeal is also available (polenta is a type of the latter). In these recipes, finely or medium-ground cornmeal is preferable. Because cornmeal con

tains no gluten, it is usually necessary to combine it with wheat flour. Yellow cornmeal is the most common type, but white, blue, and even red cornmeals, ground from corn kernels of these colors, are available. We often use cornmeal in the recipes in this book to dust baking sheets and the baking stone so the breads will not stick to the baking surfaces. Sprinkling loaves with a little cornmeal also gives them added texture.

Regardless of the flour or meal type, we recommend buying stone-ground flour, preferably organic, which has no additives and nothing removed. Some of the best-quality flours for bread baking can be found in the bulk foods section of natural foods groceries or health food stores. All flours should be stored in an airtight container in a cool, dry place. In the summer, it's a good idea to keep them in the refrigerator or freezer.

Liquid

Water is usually the liquid ingredient added to flour to activate the gluten, as well as to activate the action of the leavening agent. Bottled spring water or distilled water is best for bread making because tap water often contains chlorine, fluoride, and minerals that can affect the yeast's rising action and the flavor of the bread; it can also be too acid or alkaline, which will affect the yeast and the development of gluten. In some of the recipes, we use the cooled water in which potatoes or beans were cooked, which provides a little extra flavor and enhances the fermentation process. Milk (whether whole, lowfat, or skim) is used to give a richer, softer texture and flavor, and other liquids, such as buttermilk, cream, beer, and vegetable or fruit juices can likewise be substituted to provide different textures or flavors. Regardless of the liquid used to activate the yeast, it is important that it be lukewarm (around 80° to 90°). If it is too cold, the yeast will be inhibited, and if it is too warm, the yeast will be killed.

Leaveners

Commercial and wild yeast, baking soda, and baking powder are the leavening (or rising) agents most commonly used in bread making. However, beaten eggs and internal moisture in the dough that is converted into steam in the oven are other factors that cause bread to rise.

Baker's yeast is a live single-cell organism that converts flour and water—its food—into carbon dioxide, the gas that stretches the gluten fibers, making the dough rise and expand. Yeast is available as fine brown granules—active dry yeast—and in fresh form. The recipes in this book call for the readily available active dry yeast, which is sold at supermarkets and other stores in jars and .25-ounce packages. Fresh yeast, sold in compressed cake form that can be easily crumbled, has a limited life span (about 2 weeks, refrigerated), which makes it less practical for the casual home baker. However, if you prefer, use ½ ounce fresh yeast for each 2¼ teaspoons to 1 tablespoon of active dry yeast called for in these recipes. Fresh yeast activates more quickly than dried, but the two are otherwise interchangeable. The very finely ground, active dry bread machine yeast can also be used; it is marketed to dissolve faster than the standard-sized granules in doughs. Yeast should be stored in a cool place—the refrigerator is ideal. If, in proofing the yeast in lukewarm liquid, it does not become foamy after a few minutes, it is no longer active and should not be used. High-quality baker's yeast is available in bulk by mail order (see page 210).

Baking powder and **baking soda** are chemical rising agents that produce carbon dioxide (like yeast) when mixed with liquid, heat or both (see page 24). Avoid baking powder that contains aluminum sulfate; if necessary, substitute a mixture of 1 part baking soda to 2 parts cream of tartar.

Salt

Salt is the original bread flavoring, and it helps enhance the natural flavor of grains. Almost all breads contain salt; otherwise they would taste too sweet or bland. Even sweet breads and pastries have a small amount of salt. Salt also works with the gluten to strengthen the structure of the bread, yet inhibits it enough to prevent the dough from becoming sticky and rising too quickly or too much. It also helps to make the crust crispy. We have used table salt in these recipes, but if you prefer kosher salt, increase the amount used by about 25 percent. If you use sea salt, grind it to the same consistency as table salt.

Sweeteners

Granulated white sugar is the most common type of sweetener used in the kitchen as well as in these recipes, but we also use brown sugar, confectioners' sugar, honey, molasses, fruit juices, and maple syrup to provide nuances of flavor, texture, and color when appropriate (the latter three ingredients also yield valuable nutrients). Yeast consumes sweeteners and thrives on them. While sweeteners speed the action of yeast, they are not essential to activate the yeast or for rising, and wild yeast does not need them at all. Bread can usually be made successfully without sugar, if you prefer. Sweeteners help give the bread a tender crumb and contribute to a crispy, dark crust. If you wish to substitute a type of liquid sweetener, such as honey or molasses, for sugar in a recipe, reduce the other liquids by 2 tablespoons to compensate.

Other Basic Ingredients

Oils and fats, such as unsalted butter, olive oil, canola oil, and corn oil, lubricate the gluten fibers, allowing dough to be worked more easily, and making it softer and more velvety. This is desirable in most breads, but not in rustic country breads (pages 117–139), which contain no oil or fat for this reason. Oils and fats tend to inhibit the rising action of yeast, so they are generally used sparingly. They contribute enriching flavors to breads, prolonging the shelf life. Make sure that any butter or oil you use does not smell rancid, as this will adversely affect the flavor of the bread.

Eggs add richness and softness to breads. They are an essential ingredient in brioche, and they are added to many of the other breakfast breads (pages 159–183) to provide a delicate texture.

FERMENTATION PROCESS

Fermentation occurs when yeast consumes the naturally occurring sugars in the flour (and any added sweetener) to produce alcohol (which evaporates during baking) and carbon dioxide. This gas is then trapped by the gluten in thousands of tiny pockets in the dough to create the airy, cellular structure characteristic of leavened bread. The fermentation process softens and smoothens the gluten in the flour and makes it more elastic. Controlling the life of yeast is one of the most important factors in producing a light, high-quality loaf.

The rising, or proofing, of the dough is a simple and fascinating process that is affected by a number of factors. The most important of these are the temperature of the ingredients and the environment in which the dough is placed. Yeast activity is more rapid at warmer temperatures and slower at lower temperatures. Liquids should be lukewarm, and other ingredients such as flour, butter, oil, or eggs should be at room temperature. Some sources suggest that yeast activity is optimized by using liquids at higher temperatures (90° to 95°, for example), but the slower fermentation process at a lower temperature (80° to 90°) accentuates the flavor. In any event, liq-

uids hotter than 115° will kill the yeast. Once the dough is activated, regulating the fermentation process becomes a key factor in making flavorful, well-risen breads; fermentation temperature is perhaps a baker's greatest tool and ally in producing great breads. The dough should be allowed to sit at a constant, draft-free room temperature of 75° to 80°.

There are several methods for fermenting yeast:

The straight yeast method is the simplest technique and the one used most often in this book. Yeast is added to lukewarm liquid and, once it begins to activate—producing a foamy, bubbly "bloom"—is added to the dry ingredients and flavorings and mixed into a dough.

The sponge method is an alternative for creating flavorful breads. Yeast is mixed with liquid and a little flour, and this batterlike mixture is allowed to sit and ferment for several hours or overnight to develop a tangy flavor before other ingredients are added. Because the flour in the sponge absorbs the liquid for longer, this method tends to produce moist loaves.

The starter method is an ancient, natural method of fermentation that existed before commercial yeasts were available. In the starter method, naturally occurring (wild) yeasts, instead of commerical yeasts, are used. Yeast spores are present in flour itself, in dairy products, in the air, and on the surface of fruits (such as grapes), potatoes, and leaves. A starter is created over several days by mixing equal parts of flour and water and letting the mixture ferment at room temperature to capture wild yeasts and to develop flavor and sourness. (Of course, the starter can be initiated with commercial yeast, which makes the process much easier, although expert bakers will tell you the flavor is different.) Once a starter is established, it can be replenished and kept going indefinitely as a base for making doughs. To make bread, a little of the starter is removed and ingredients are added to it to make the dough. Meanwhile, flour and water are added to the starter to keep the fermentation process going. This cycle can be repeated indefinitely, and many bakers (especially in Europe) maintain starters that originated several generations ago. Starters can be refrigerated for weeks between feedings and can even be frozen, but they must then be rejuvenated with a few feedings before they are used to make bread. Starters will die if they are not fed every few weeks (usually 2 to 4 weeks).

This simplified explanation of starters does not attempt to explore the complexities of preparing dough with wild yeasts. The sourdough breads in this book are intended to be an introduction to the natural fermentation process. They are outstanding yet simple recipes that feature the distinctive tang of sourdough and a crisp, rustic crust. For a more comprehensive understanding of this fascinating topic, we recommend that you consult some of the sources listed on page 211, especially the books by Daniel Leader, Joe Ortiz, and Nancy Silverton.

WORKING WITH BREAD DOUGHS

The consistency of bread doughs depends, of course, on the ratio of wet to dry ingredients.

However, there are factors, such as the humidity or dryness of your location or the particular climatic conditions on the day you are baking, the altitude, and even the proximity to high-voltage power lines, that make preparing doughs an inexact undertaking.

A NOTE ABOUT ALTITUDE

All of the recipes in this book have been tested in Santa Fe, New Mexico, at an altitude of 7,000 feet. Dough rises faster at higher altitudes because the carbon dioxide released by the yeast expands more easily in the thinner air and there is less atmospheric pressure on the dough. Conversely, dough rises more slowly at sea level, so take this into account.

There is not a significant difference in the amount of ingredients needed to successfully bake the same loaf at sea level and altitude. However, dough is drier at higher altitudes and wetter at sea level, so reduce the amount of liquid slightly when baking at sea level and add flour in small increments when baking at altitude. Slightly more yeast is also needed at sea level. The table below gives recommended adjustments. Use it as a guideline only, remembering that weather conditions will also affect the dough.

Altitude Adjustments per Recipe

Ingredients	7,000 Feet	3,500 Feet	Sea Level
Liquid	—	up to 2 tablespoons less	up to ¼ cup less
Yeast	—	up to ¼ teaspoon more	up to ½ teaspoon more
Sugar	—	up to ½ teaspoon more	up to 1 teaspoon more
Salt	—	—	up to ¼ teaspoon less

KNEADING

In general, the dough should be kneaded—mixed with a heavy-duty electric mixer fitted with a dough hook or by hand—until it is smooth, elastic, no longer sticky, and just beginning to pull away from the side of the mixing bowl. Flatbread and rustic bread doughs should be wetter. Although this makes them more difficult to handle, the resulting well-developed interior texture of the loaves is worth it. Kneading the dough develops the gluten, resulting in light, airy loaves. Most people tend to err on the side of under-kneading dough, which will adversely affect the texture. Dough loves physical treatment—it's difficult to overknead it—so don't scrimp on kneading! Many of our recipes call for the flavoring ingredients to be added after most of the kneading has occurred; this is to prevent them from becoming squished or broken up, both for appearance and to retain as much of their flavor as possible. The main objective is to knead the dough until the flavoring ingredients are evenly distributed throughout.

RISING

Usually, the kneaded dough is transferred to an oiled bowl (ceramic, glass, or earthenware are all fine), turned to coat lightly with oil, and left to rise until approximately doubled in volume. Oiling or buttering the bowl prevents the dough from sticking when you turn it out and keeps the moisture inside the dough. The bowl should be covered with plastic wrap or a damp towel so that a crust does not form on the top of the dough and to keep the moisture in, thus helping it rise. Keep the bowl in a warm (75° to 90°), draft-free place while the dough is rising. If you can't tell whether the dough has doubled in volume, poke it with your finger: if an indentation is left and the dough feels spongy, it is ready.

PUNCHING DOWN

Most bread doughs require punching down after the first and second risings. The purpose of this is to expel large gas bubbles, restimulate the gluten, and refine the texture of the dough. Uncover the risen dough in the bowl, and punch down with your fist—not too violently, or you may damage the gluten. You may knead the dough briefly before re-covering it and letting it rise again or shaping it into a loaf.

SHAPING

To shape the dough, turn it out onto a well-floured work surface and liberally flour your hands; the flour prevents the dough from sticking to either the work surface or your hands. The recipes in this book usually call for shaping the dough into free-form rounds, ovals, or rolls, or placing it in standard loaf pans, but these are only suggestions; there are many shapes and forms to choose from. It takes practice to learn how to shape loaves, so be patient and refer to the photos (see pages 206–207). If a loaf doesn't turn out quite the way you want, you can always explain that it's shaped in a rustic style! Besides, the shape doesn't affect the flavor.

Here are some basic dough-shaping instructions:

• **Short Loaf:** With the heel of your hand, flatten and pull the dough horizontally into an oblong shape (step 1, below). Fold the dough up from the long bottom edge, three-quarters of the way to the top edge (step 2, below), then fold the two ends inward to meet in the middle (step 3, below). Beginning with the long bottom edge, roll up the dough jelly-roll style (step 4, below) and pinch the seam firmly to seal (step 5, below). Tuck in the ends and even out the loaf by gently rolling it with the palms of both hands (step 6, below). If you wish, place the dough in an oblong loaf pan (especially for sandwich bread).

• **Baguette:** Follow the short loaf shaping instructions, but roll into a longer loaf.

• **Round Loaf:** Dust the dough with flour and, with both hands, push the middle upward as though you are turning it inside out (see step 1, opposite

page). Gather the dough at the bottom and pinch it together to seal (see step 2, opposite page). Place the loaf seam side down on the work surface and, with your hands cupped on each side, press down gently while moving the dough around in a circular motion, shaping it into a round loaf of even thickness (see step 3, opposite page).

• **Round Rolls (Boules):** Shape into small rounds by gathering each piece of dough in the center and pinching together to seal (see step 1, opposite page). Cup your hand over a piece of dough and press down gently while rolling the dough around in a circular motion (see step 2, opposite page) shaping the dough into a tight, round ball. Repeat until all pieces of the dough are shaped. The dough should stick a little to the work surface. If the surface seems too dry and the dough slips around on it, sprinkle a little water on it. If the surface is too wet and sticky, sprinkle a little flour on it.

Shaping a Short Loaf

step 1

step 2

step 3

step 4

step 5

step 6

• **Oblong (or Oval) Rolls:** With the heel of your hand, flatten and pull a small piece of dough horizontally into an oblong shape, as you would for a short loaf. Beginning with the long bottom edge, roll up the dough jelly-roll style (see step 4, opposite page) and pinch the seam firmly to seal (see step 5, opposite page). Tuck in the ends and even out the loaf by gently rolling it with the palms of both hands (see step 6, opposite page).

More adventurous bakers might want to create elongated "bloomer" loaves, topknotted cottage loaves, or circular ring loaves (baked in a ring mold). All loaves should be baked seam side down on the baking sheet or in a loaf pan.

PROOFING

After the dough has been shaped and placed in a pan or on a baking sheet, it is covered again and allowed to rise, or proof, a final time. Proofing times can vary, and covering the loaf and placing it in the refrigerator overnight or leaving it at room temperature for several extra hours extends the dough's fermentation, giving it more flavor. To tell when the dough has finished proofing, press it gently; it should feel spongy. Avoid poking it with your finger, as you would for the rising stage, because you don't want to leave an indentation in the dough.

DUSTING, SLASHING, AND SNIPPING

There are many ways to finish the dough to enhance its appearance or flavor. Misting it with water and sprinkling it with flour or cornmeal gives the baked loaf a dark rustic look and adds texture. Brushing loaves with an egg wash gives them an attractive glaze, and seeds or nuts gently pressed into

Shaping a Round Loaf

step 1

step 2

step 3

Shaping Round Rolls

step 1

step 2

the top of the loaves after they're spritzed with water contribute flavor as well as crunchiness. Slashing the loaf carefully with a razor blade cutter (available from art supply stores), standard razor blade, or sharp serrated knife not only provides an attractive design but allows the loaf to expand more, giving a greater amount of crisp crust (it can also prevent the loaf from expanding in an uneven shape or splitting). Make slashes at a 45-degree angle with swift, deep strokes on the diagonal, in a crisscross or checkerboard pattern, or lengthwise in the style of the French *pain brie*— or in any pattern you choose.

An alternative form of decoration is to snip the top of the dough in an upward motion with sharp kitchen scissors. This technique creates peaks and points.

BAKING TECHNIQUES

Preheat the oven at least 20 to 30 minutes before you are ready to bake the bread, so it will be evenly heated. Oven temperature is critical, especially in the first 8 to 10 minutes of baking, and for this reason, we recommend using an independent thermometer (use a good-quality mercury type and avoid the inexpensive, unreliable spring-operated models) in the oven to double-check the accuracy of the oven thermostat. Oven thermostats can sometimes be off as much as 50°. Make sure you conserve the oven's heat by opening and closing the door quickly. Resist the urge to open the oven just to peek at the bread. Trust us—it's doing just fine.

USING A BAKING STONE

Baking stones imitate a professional baker's stone-lined oven. It creates an even distribution or heat and contributes to a nice, crispy crust. The stone should be preheated along with the oven for at least 20 to 30 minutes. For breads that are slid directly onto the stone to bake, dust the baking stone beforehand with a little cornmeal so the dough does not stick. When baking rolls and other forms on baking sheets or in pans, place the sheets or pans directly on the stone. Place the stone on a rack that's positioned low enough in the oven so the bread doesn't touch the oven ceiling once it expands. A middle or lower middle rack should work fine. Porous quarry tiles can be used instead of a baking stone, and a black carbon-steel baking sheet also makes a satisfactory substitute.

SPRITZING OR STEAMING THE OVEN

Many of the recipes call for spritzing the preheated oven with water in a spray bottle. This creates humidity, which allows the yeast to develop a bit longer, resulting in "oven pop" or "oven spring"—an extra rise that helps a crisp crust form. Spritzing also imitates professional baking ovens that release steam into the oven at the touch of a button. This effect can be achieved in several ways:

• *Spray bottle misting* should be done before and, for a crisper crust, after placing the bread in the oven. Use a plastic spray bottle, crack the door open slightly, and spritz with several squirts. Repeat this several times during the first few minutes of baking, but don't squirt the water directly over the bread.

• *Hot brick misting* involves heating a clean clay brick in the bottom of the oven while it is preheats. Prepare a pan of cold water at least 1½ inches deep. Using oven mitts, remove the brick and very carefully drop it into the pan of water. Working quickly, slide the loaf onto the baking stone, place the pan below the bread, and close the oven door. The hot brick will cause the water to steam, creating the necessary humidity in the first few minutes of baking.

DETERMINING DONENESS

Assuming you have double-checked the oven temperature, the bread should be ready at the end of the baking time specified in the recipes. Many of the breads will have a dark, crisp crust. Others, like the flatbreads and quick breads, will be a golden brown but not crusty. Remove the bread from the oven and, while holding it in one hand with a kitchen towel, tap the bottom of the loaf. If it sounds hollow, enough moisture has evaporated and the bread is done. If not, the center is probably moist and soggy, and the bread should be returned to the oven to bake for 5 to 10 minutes longer, or until it sounds hollow when tapped.

COOLING

It is important to let the bread cool in the pan or on the baking sheet for at least 10 minutes. You can then turn it out onto a wire rack to cool further. Unless the recipe states otherwise, you should cut bread only after it has cooled, allowing at least 30 minutes for its internal structure and starches to solidify. When cutting, use a sharp serrated knife.

STORING BREAD

The breads in this book should remain fresh for several days. Keep bread in a cool, dry place, preferably unrefrigerated (except when specified by the recipe). Bread can be frozen once it is cooled; for best results, wrap securely and freeze for up to 2 weeks. Defrost bread, uncovered, for 2 to 3 hours, then place it in a preheated 400° oven for 10 to 12 minutes to recrisp the crust.

DEFINITIONS AND METHODS

Certain ingredients require roasting or toasting before being added to the recipes in this book. The methods involved are described below.

Roasting Corn Kernels

Cut corn kernels from the cob with a sharp knife. Heat a large, dry, heavy-bottomed skillet, add the corn in no more than two layers, and roast over high heat for 4 to 5 minutes, tossing continuously, just until the kernels begin to smoke.

Roasting Chiles and Bell Peppers

Roasting fresh chiles and bell peppers develops their naturally complex flavors and makes them easier to peel. To roast, place the peppers on a wire rack over a grill, over a gas flame, or under a broiler. Blister and blacken the skins evenly, without burning the flesh. Transfer to a bowl, cover with plastic wrap, and let steam for 15 to 20 minutes. Then remove the skin with your fingers or with the tip of a sharp knife. Remove and discard the seeds (unless the recipe instructs otherwise) and internal ribs, and prepare as directed. *Warning: Do not touch your face or eyes after handling chiles until you have thoroughly washed your hands. If you have sensitive skin, wear rubber gloves when handling chiles.*

Toasting Almonds, Brazil Nuts, Walnuts, Pecans, Pistachios, Hazelnuts, and Piñons (Pine Nuts)

Place the nuts in a dry, heavy-bottomed skillet and toast over medium heat for 3 to 5 minutes, stirring occasionally, until lightly browned. Alternatively, toast on a baking sheet in a 250° oven for 5 to 7 minutes, or until fragrant.

Toasting Peppercorns

Place the peppercorns in a heated dry, heavy-bottomed skillet. Toast over medium-high heat for 3 or 4 minutes, or until they begin to crackle and become aromatic. Alternatively, toast on a baking sheet in a 375° oven for about 5 minutes.

Peeling and Seeding Tomatoes

Bring a stockpot of water to a boil. Drop in the whole tomatoes and blanch for 1 minute. Remove with a strainer and let cool. When cool, peel the skins and cut in half. Gently squeeze the tomato halves to remove the seeds.

Toasting Spices and Seeds

Place the spices or seeds in a dry skillet over low heat. Toast, stirring frequently, for about 1 minute, or until fragrant. Alternatively, place on a baking sheet and toast in a 350° oven for 5 to 7 minutes, or until fragrant.

SOURCES

Cheese

Dallas Mozzarella Co.
2944 Elm St.
Dallas, TX 75266
(214) 741-4072

Cabot Cheese
Mail-Order Department
P.O. Box 128
Cabot, VT 05647
(802) 639-3198

Sonoma Cheese Factory
2 W. Spain St.
Sonoma, CA 95476
(800) 535-2855
(707) 996-1912 (fax)

Chiles, oils, vinegars, spices, and polenta entero

Dean & Deluca
560 Broadway
New York, NY 10012
(212) 431-1691

Dried fruits and nuts

American Spoon Foods
411 E. Lake St.
Petoskey, MI 49770
(800) 327-7984

Flour, yeast, and baking equipment

King Arthur Flour
PO Box 876
Norwich, VT 05055
(800) 827-6836

Southwestern ingredients

Coyote Cafe General Store
132 W. Water St.
Santa Fe, NM 87501
(800) 866-HOWL

Monterrey Foods
3939 Caesar Chavez Ave.
Los Angeles, CA 90063
(213) 263-2143

Specialty ingredients and baking supplies (including Lora Brody's dough enhancers)

Williams-Sonoma
P.O. Box 7456
San Francisco, CA 94120-7456
(800) 541-2233

BIBLIOGRAPHY

For further reading and additional recipes, we highly recommend the following books. This is by no means a comprehensive listing, but it covers a lot of interesting and informative ground.

Acton, Eliza. *The English Bread Book*. Lewes, Sussex, England, state: Southover Press, 1990.

Alford, Jeffrey, and Naomi Duguid. *Flatbreads: A Baker's Atlas*. New York: William Morrow, 1995.

Baylis, Maggie, and Coralie Castle. *Real Bread: A Fearless Guide to Making I.*, 2nd ed. San Rafael, CA: Cole, 1980.

Beard, James. *Beard on Bread*. New York: Ballantine, 1973.

Black, Maggie. *The Medieval Cookbook*. London: British Museum Press, 1992.

Brody, Lora, and Millie Apter. *Bread Machine Baking: Perfect Every Time*. New York: Morrow, 1993.

Cheney, Susan Jane. *Breadtime Stories*. Berkeley, CA: Ten Speed Press, 1990.

Clayton, Bernard, Jr. *The Complete Book of Breads*. New York: Simon and Schuster, 1973.

David, Elizabeth. *English Bread & Yeast Cookery*. London: Penguin, 1979.

Duff, Gail. *Bread: 150 Traditional Recipes from Around the World*. New York: Macmillan, 1993.

Eckhardt, Linda W., and Diana C. Butts. *Rustic European Breads from Your Bread Machine*. New York: Doubleday, 1995.

Eckhardt, Linda W., and Diana C. Butts. *Bread in Half the Time: Use Your Microwave & Food Processor to Make Real Yeast Bread in 90 Minute.*, New York: Crown, 1991.

Galli, Franco. *The Il Fornaio Baking Book*. San Francisco: Chronicle, 1993.

Gisslen, Wayne. *Professional Baking*. New York: Wiley, 1985.

Gubser, Mary. *America's Bread Book*. New York: Quill, 1985.

Gubser, Mary. *Mary's Bread Basket & Soup Kettle*, New York: William Morrow, 1974.

Gubser, Mary. *Quick Breads, Soups, & Stews*. Tulsa, OK: Council Oak, 1991.

Haedrich, Ken. *Country Baking: Simple Home Baking with Wholesome Grains & the Pick of the Harves.*, New York: Bantam, 1990.

Hensperger, Beth. *Bread*. San Francisco: Chronicle Books, 1988.

Jones, Judith B., and Evan. *Book of Bread*. New York: Harper and Row, 1982.

Leader, Daniel, and Judith Blahnik. *Bread Alone: Fresh Loaves from Your Own Hands*. New York: William Morrow, 1993.

Moore, Marilyn. *The Wooden Spoon Bread Book*. New York: Atlantic Monthly Press, 1987.

Ortiz, Joe. *The Village Baker*. Berkeley, CA: Ten Speed Press, 1993.

Robertson, Laurel. *The Laurel's Kitchen Bread Book*. New York: Random House, 1984.

Shulman, Martha Rose. *The Bread Book*. New York: Macmillan, 1990.

Silverton, Nancy. *Nancy Silverton's Breads from the La Brea Bakery*. New York: Artisan, 1996.

Time-Life Books. *Breads*. New York: Time-Life Books, 1981.

Toussaint-Samat, Maguelonne. *The History of Food*. Oxford, England: Blackwell, 1987.

INDEX

For a free catalog and/or to order Mark Miller's chile (dried and fresh), corn, chile heat scale, and squash posters and other cookbooks, write
Ten Speed Press/Celestial Arts, P.O. Box 7123, Berkeley, California 94707
or call 1-800-841-BOOK